12/25/01

Dear David,

With best wishes,

Ariel

TORT LIABILITY UNDER UNCERTAINTY

Tort Liability under Uncertainty

ARIEL PORAT
AND
ALEX STEIN

OXFORD
UNIVERSITY PRESS

OXFORD
UNIVERSITY PRESS

Great Clarendon Street, Oxford OX2 6DP

Oxford University Press is a department of the University of Oxford.
It furthers the University's objective of excellence in research, scholarship,
and education by publishing worldwide in

Oxford New York

Athens Auckland Bangkok Bogotá Buenos Aires Cape Town
Chennai Dar es Salaam Delhi Florence Hong Kong Istanbul Karachi
Kolkata Kuala Lumpur Madrid Melbourne Mexico City Mumbai Nairobi
Paris São Paulo Shanghai Singapore Taipei Tokyo Toronto Warsaw

with associated companies in Berlin Ibadan

Oxford is a registered trade mark of Oxford University Press
in the UK and in certain other countries

Published in the United States
by Oxford University Press Inc., New York

First published 2001

British Library Cataloguing in Publication Data
Data available

Library of Congress Cataloging in Publication Data
Data available

ISBN 0–19–826797–5

1 3 5 7 9 10 8 6 4 2

Typeset by Hope Services (Abingdon) Ltd.
Printed in Great Britain
on acid-free paper by
Biddles Ltd, Guildford and King's Lynn

Acknowledgements

We would like to thank Ron Allen, Omri Ben-Shahar, Eyal Benvenisti, Robert Cooter, Hanoch Dagan, Richard Friedman, Israel Gilead, Zohar Goshen, Alon Harel, Tal Shani, Assaf Jacob, Peter Tillers, and Omri Yadlin for their comments, suggestions, and critique.

Parts of this book were presented at faculty workshops and seminars held by the John M. Olin Center of Law and Economics, University of California at Berkeley School of Law, by the Benjamin N. Cardozo School of Law, Yeshiva University, by the Faculty of Law, the Hebrew University of Jerusalem, by the Northwestern University School of Law, and by the Tel-Aviv University Faculty of Law. We would like to express our gratitude to all those who participated in these workshops and seminars.

Special thanks go to Ophir Nave for his superb research assistance and to Dana Rothman for her excellent editorial work.

Ariel Porat and Alex Stein

Contents

List of Cases

Canada:

Israel (Hebrew):

United Kingdom:

United States:

Introduction

THIS book conducts an inquiry into the allocation of tort liability in cases involving uncertain facts. This inquiry is both positive and normative in nature. The book analyses and criticizes the doctrinal arrangements that control the allocation of liability in torts in factually uncertain cases and offers its own approach to such cases. Labelled the 'evidential damage doctrine', this approach identifies the wrongdoer responsible for the factual indeterminacy of the case and holds him or her liable for that indeterminacy. The resulting liability principles aim at rectifying the plaintiff's evidential incapacitation. The proposed approach thus supplements the doctrinal arrangements that impose liability *under* uncertainty with a new doctrinal mechanism that imposes liability *for* uncertainty.

This discussion takes place within the confines of the English and American tort doctrines. We provide an updated depiction of those doctrines to the extent that they govern the allocation of tort liability in conditions of uncertainty. Reference is occasionally made to doctrinal arrangements that apply in other jurisdictions, such as in Canada and Israel. This book is designated for legal academics and practitioners, for law students, and for policy-makers in the areas of torts, risk, and insurance. In this Introduction, we lay out the general context of our discussions throughout the book. We set this context by depicting three developmental stages that shaped the contours of the Anglo-American doctrine of torts. Subsequently, we provide our readers with a roadmap to the book by outlining the issues examined in each of its chapters.

The tort doctrine as evolved in Anglo-American jurisdictions has always maintained an implicit, but yet solid, connection with the ability of judges and jurors to determine the facts necessary for imposing liability for damage. This connection has transformed into a single principle that combines the moral with the epistemological. This principle holds that the factual base of a case must be sufficiently determinable, so that judges and jurors can adequately reconstruct the relevant past events in order to impose tort liability in conformity with its underlying moral grounds. Under this principle, 'the relevant past events' are the action taken by the alleged wrongdoer, the damage that the alleged victim sustained, and the causal process that connects the action with that damage. The qualification 'adequately' in this principle refers to the existing epistemological background and fact-finding methods, that is, the tools that judges and jurors can employ in their capacity as fact-finders.

There is more than one way of describing the development of this connection. While not claiming that we give a uniquely accurate depiction of this development from a historical point of view, we distinguish between its three different stages. In the distant past, liability in torts was encapsulated by the doctrine of trespass. Under the trespass doctrine, physical interference with another person's body or property generally amounted to an actionable tort. When any such interference inflicted damage, the damaged party could recover compensation from the wrongdoer.[1]

The trespass doctrine premised liability for damage on direct contact between the wrongdoer and his victim. Under this doctrine, a person's rights in property and to bodily integrity delineated the boundaries of his or her individual domain that uninvited strangers could not legally cross. A crossing of those borders thus amounted to a forcible interference with that person's rights, which activated the remedial mechanism set by the doctrine. This requirement of direct contact was definitional: it was anchored in the types of conduct that constitute trespass. In this way, the doctrine conditioned the victim's entitlement to a remedy on the existence of a sequence of events that directly connected his or her damage to the wrongdoer's forcible action. Under this doctrine, a forcible action that the wrongdoer directed against the victim was straightforwardly perceptible. Therefore, complaints about trespass were relatively easy to verify or refute at trial.

The trespass doctrine was therefore the 'direct contact' paradigm of tort liability. Under that formulation, the term 'direct' is synonymous with 'straightforward'. This term is holistic rather than atomistic: it refers to a synthetic rather than analytic mode of fact-finding, and its underlying epistemological standard is common sense rather than scientific induction. This term therefore does not refer to a decomposition of the damage's occurrence into its underlying causes and to a subsequent determination of the proximate cause through a meticulous analysis of complex data. The definition of trespass left no room for such complexities. Furthermore, the living conditions at the time when this doctrine prevailed made fact-finding relatively easy (albeit not necessarily accurate). People living in rural and not densely populated areas knew a good deal about their neighbours. Therefore, a person could easily summon witnesses to testify to his or her neighbour's whereabouts and reputation. More often than not, witnesses residing in the same community could also testify to the alleged trespass. Thus, when Mrs Smith complained that a bull belonging to Mr Jones had destroyed her fence, she could produce several neighbours as witnesses to the event. Under such a scenario, Mr Jones would do best to admit his liability and compensate Mrs Smith. Typically, the simple facts of *Smith v Jones* could be

[1] M. Brazier and J. Murphy (eds.), *Street on Torts* (10th edn., London, Edinburgh and Dublin, 1999) 11–12; W. V. H. Rogers (ed.), *Winfield and Jolowicz on Tort* (15th edn., London, 1998) 47–8; W. P. Keeton *et al.* (eds.), *Prosser and Keeton on Torts* (5th edn., St. Paul, Minn, 1984) 29–30.

verified by the local sheriff, who also would lock up Mr Jones in jail if he failed to compensate Mrs Smith.[2]

The direct contact paradigm of tort liability had lasting prevalence both in England and in the United States,[3] and we can still find its remnants in the contemporary doctrine of torts. The nineteenth century's urban, technological, and industrial developments were the beginning of the end for this paradigm. These developments were both for the better and worse of society. They improved the living conditions of many by providing better transportation, more food, better health care, and more education. But they also worsened the living conditions of many by exacerbating alienation, exploitation, and poverty; by damaging the environment; by generating new diseases; and by proliferating weapons for mass destruction. In the realm of torts, the good and the bad also appeared in pairs. The growing industrial power magnified the potential for large-scale accidents and massive exposure to toxic, environmental, and other hazards. This risk materialized in physical injuries and property damage unprecedented both in scale and severity. The new urban conditions and the capitalist enterprise segregated populations according to relative wealth and divided residential areas into wealthy, middle-class, and poor. As a direct outcome of the uneven distribution of wealth and labourers' need to live close to the factories in which they worked, poor neighbourhoods and industrial areas developed in the same vicinity. Together with the rest of the poor, the working class consequently became exposed to toxic and other hazardous substances emitted from the neighbouring factories. The wealthier segments of the population were protected from those hazards incomparably better than the poor. Consequently, they did not face the same level of risk in terms of both the gravity and probability of ensuing injuries,[4] nor did they have a substantial incentive to minimize

[2] *Prosser* (n. 1 above). The early common law developed a supplement to the trespass doctrine, labelled 'trespass on the case' (or simply 'case'). This supplement was the precursor to modern negligence law. The 'trespass on the case' writ was designed to allow plaintiffs to recover compensation for indirect injuries and some consequential losses. To succeed in a 'trespass on the case' action, the plaintiff had to show fault on the defendant's part (which was not required under the trespass writ). For example, a defendant who negligently left a barrel on the road could be held liable for losses resulting from that obstruction. If a carriage carrying another person and her belongings overturned due to that obstruction, the defendant would have to compensate that person for her injuries and proprietary damage. Technically, that damage may have resulted from the physical contact of the victim and her belongings with the carriage and the ground. Yet, the defendant would assume responsibility for that damage because this consequential contact resulted from the initial contact between the barrel and the carriage (or one of the horses). See C. O. Gregory, 'Trespass to Negligence to Absolute Liability' (1951) 37 *Virginia L Rev* 359, 361–70. Note that this initial contact is still covered by the direct-contact paradigm of liability.

[3] See Gregory (n. 2 above); *Prosser* (n. 1 above); *Street* (n. 1 above).

[4] R. L. Abel, 'Torts' in D. Kairys (ed.), *The Politics of Law: A Progressive Critique* (1982) 185, 186–93.

that risk. Numerous workplace accidents at factories and railroads further aggravated this inequity in the distribution of the risk of injury.[5]

The doctrine of torts failed to provide adequate remedies for the damage that industry inflicted on its victims. Under the direct contact paradigm of tort liability and the 'case' extension, it was impossible to obtain redress for damage resulting from exposure to a hazardous substance. Arguably, this impossibility was predicated on the latent character of the damage, the virtual invisibility of its infliction and the absence of a tangible contact between the wrongdoer and his or her victim. At the time of the industrial revolution, causal affiliation of such damage to the victims' exposure to toxic or other potentially harmful substances was generally impossible. To impose liability on the alleged wrongdoer, the law of torts still required its old epistemological guarantee for correctness: a straightforwardly ascertainable trespass-like invasion into the victim's domain. The tort doctrine declined to impose liability when this epistemological guarantee was lacking, which allowed many wrongdoers to externalize both hazards and full-blown damage.

Another offspring of the industrial revolution was the massive production of consumption goods, both safe and unsafe. Consumption of unsafe products often results in personal injuries and other damage. Premised in the direct contact paradigm of liability and in the trespass-on-the-case, the existing tort doctrine generally failed to protect consumers who sustained such damage. This failure was the product of two factors. One factor was the doctrinal requirement of direct interference with another person's rights, which still served as a precondition for imposing liability in torts. In the absence of such interference, the manufacturer of an unsafe product and the product's victim were diagnosed with a lack of 'privity': the existing doctrine regarded them as lacking a legal relationship with one another. Under this doctrine, liability for an unsafe product could derive only from a contract, that is, from a legal relationship formed directly by the product's seller and purchaser.[6] The other factor responsible for the doctrine's failure to protect consumers was the problem of causation. This problem manifested itself in the absence of the manufacturer's 'final touch' in the actual infliction of the consumer's damage. This 'final touch' was an essential component of the direct contact paradigm of tort liability. Manufacturers and consumers were separated by an increasingly growing chain of intermediaries responsible for marketing, storage, and retail distribution of manufactured products. These products did not reach their ultimate consumers directly from their manufacturers. A defect in a product that caused damage to the product's consumer could, consequently, be attributed to a number of possible wrongdoers. In some cases, the occurrence of the damage could also result from the consumer's improper use of the

[5] Ibid. See also R. L. Abel, 'A Socialist Approach to Risk' (1982) 41 *Maryland L Rev* 695.
[6] See *Prosser* (n. 1 above) 681–5.

product. The resulting causal indeterminacy erected yet another barrier for liability in torts.

As already mentioned, the industrial revolution also brought with it substantial benefits for society. One of those benefits was the incremental improvement of the legal treatment of accidents and risks of damage. Several factors were responsible for this improvement. The most important of these factors was the rapid augmentation of scientific and technical knowledge that occurred chiefly in the twentieth century. This advancement allowed the development of technological devices that improved the safety of products, services, and workplaces. Furthermore, it substantially improved people's understanding of damage-related causes and effects, which meant that they were able to tighten their control over risks of accidents by raising the level of precautions they took. It correspondingly heightened people's awareness of their ability to estimate risks by applying probability calculus. The taming of chance that commenced in the nineteenth century[7] thus continued in the twentieth century at an accelerated pace. This development manifested itself in numerous studies of probability and decision theory. Many of those studies were remarkable in their innovation, breadth, mathematical sophistication, and applicability to practical affairs.[8] Together with the expanded body of scientific and technical knowledge, these advancements enabled people to control risks far better than had previously been possible. With the help of these advancements, people capable of controlling risks were subsequently identified as accountable for those risks.

The ever-growing understanding of different risks of damage and people's ability to estimate the materialization rate for such risks also explain the prevalence of insurance. The insurance industry is a relatively old business, but its function as a mechanism for spreading damage across the insured population is relatively new.[9] Throughout the twentieth century, both potential victims of damage and prospective wrongdoers purchased at an increasing rate insurance policies that secure their indemnification for losses and compensation duties. Their insurance contracts utilized two basic phenomena, identified and analysed by the probability and decision-making theories. One of these phenomena is the 'law of large numbers' and the other, 'risk-aversion'.[10] The law of large numbers verifies the materialization of both accident rates and damage rates in the long run of cases. Risk-aversion is a person's general tendency to prefer certainty over uncertainty when all else is equal. A person is averse to risk if he or she prefers an immediate loss of £100

[7] See I. Hacking, *The Taming of Chance* (1990).

[8] See J. Von Plato, *Creating Modern Probability* (1994) 1–9.

[9] See generally G. T. Schwartz, 'The Ethics and the Economics of Tort Liability Insurance' (1990) 75 *Cornell L Rev* 313. See also J. Stapleton, 'Tort, Insurance and Ideology' (1995) 58 *MLR* 820.

[10] See G. T. Schwartz, 'Insurance, Deterrence and Liability' in P. Newman (ed.), *The New Palgrave Dictionary of Economics and the Law*, Vol. II (1998) 335–6.

to a 10 per cent chance of sustaining damage of £1,000. Because the marginal utility of the average person's income steadily diminishes, most people are in fact risk-averse. They value their bottom pound more than the top pound and consequently are willing to purchase insurance against risks. Insurance companies have utilized the 'law of large numbers' as a vehicle for pooling the insured in a way that eliminates those risks. Consequently, the insurance companies are risk-neutral: for them, receiving £100 is a perfect substitute for future indemnification liability in the amount of £1,000, if the probability of bearing that liability is 10 per cent or less. Insurance companies therefore charge premiums for risks from their risk-averse clients to an extent that covers the companies' expenses and yields profits. In this way, the insurance mechanism spreads the costs of damage amongst the insured individuals. This cost-spreading mechanism is a variation on the 'one for all, and all for one' principle coined by Dumas in *Les Trois Mousquetaires*. Its formula reads 'One for all *ex ante*, and all for one *ex post*', when *ex ante* and *ex post* indicate the points in time before the occurrence of the damage and after its occurrence, respectively. In many countries, including Great Britain, this formula has also been utilized to promote social welfare. This mechanism is at work in compulsory large-scale insurance facilities, such as social insurance and pension, health insurance, workers' compensation funds, and personal injury insurance for traffic accidents. Many such apparatuses provide compensation for damage regardless of fault. This mechanism is also at work in self-insurance. Large industrial enterprises and state agencies are increasingly dispensing with liability insurance and setting aside financial reserves to cover future liability for damage they inflict. They are able to do so, and thereby save on insurance premiums, because they can utilize the 'law of large numbers' as do insurance companies.

Along with the advances outlined in this Introduction, the insurance industry has elevated the management of risks to the level of applied science. As demonstrated by decision theorists, risk of damage is open to a precise monetary assessment. This risk equals the cost of rectifying the damage multiplied by the probability of the damage's occurrence.[11] This pivotal formula is known as the 'expected damage', and it is applied in many of the discussions throughout the book. Expected damage is not a merely abstract concept. By applying the 'law of large numbers', one can calculate the losses that will be incurred in the long run of cases when one knows the cost of the relevant damage and the probability of its occurrence. The competitive market for applied risk-management, and the insurance market in particular, has indeed generated an impressive warehouse of data with regard to a variety of risks and types of damage.

[11] See R. A. Posner, *Economic Analysis of Law* (5th edn., 1998) 12–17.

These developments can explain the gradual shift in the tort liability paradigm that occurred during the twentieth century. This shift led to the replacement of the direct contact paradigm with liability for damage based upon externalization of risk. Under the new paradigm of tort liability, a person is liable for a damage when he or she wrongfully exposes another person to a risk of sustaining that damage and when the damage results from materialization of that risk. This paradigm has discarded the old perception of direct contact as a necessary condition for treating a person's action as the cause of the ensuing damage. Direct contact is no longer required as an epistemological guarantee for imposing liability in torts. The new paradigm of tort liability has identified its own epistemological guarantee in the expanded knowledge on various risks of damage and in the human ability to exercise control over those risks.

The replacement of the direct contact requirement substantially expanded the scope of liability in torts. If no limits were to be set to this expansion of tort liability, courts would face a multitude of lawsuits and severe indeterminacy in the attribution of responsibility for damage. Moreover, if any imposition of any risk of damage by an individual were to constitute a ground for holding him or her liable in torts, excessive deterrence would ensue. This deterrence would chill many activities that are socially beneficial. Manufacturing of goods, transportation, and medical services are just a few such activities. For these reasons, the new tort liability doctrine set the wrongfulness requirement as a condition for holding a person liable for damage. To be liable in torts, a defendant must be shown to have wrongfully inflicted the plaintiff's damage. The plaintiff must thus demonstrate that his or her damage resulted from a risk to which he or she was wrongfully exposed by the defendant. In the absence of that requirement, perceiving the allegedly 'active' wrongdoer as 'acting upon' the allegedly 'passive' victim would be profoundly problematic for at least two reasons. First, this role description could easily be reversed without distorting the narrative: the alleged victim could easily be depicted as wilfully failing to prevent or even as coming upon his or her damage. Second, as a matter of empirically universal fact, any damage that occurs between individuals results from at least two distinct activities—not just one—and such activities are accompanied by a myriad of other factors causally connected to the occurrence of the damage.[12]

Wrongful imposition of a risk of damage is a thoroughly normative notion. This notion has no ascertainable referent in empirical reality. Not surprisingly, many courts that applied and developed this notion have translated it into the concept of 'negligence'. The negligence concept, in turn, is based on the existence of a 'duty of care' and on its violation by the defendant. The

[12] See O. W. Holmes, Jr, *The Common Law* (1881) 84ff; R. H. Coase, 'The Problem of Social Cost' (1960) 3 *J Law & Economics* 1, 13; S. R. Perry, 'The Impossibility of General Strict Liability' (1988) 1 *Canadian J L & Jurisprudence* 147, 154–9.

concept of 'duty of care' is, of course, equally normative. As such, it has been held to depend on the 'foreseeability' of the damage, another normative concept that refers to a reasonable person's ability to perceive the relevant risk and the ensuing damage. All these concepts obviously required meaning that could only be supplied from the outer normative domain. Indeed, several competing theories of tort liability offer a number of meanings as stuffing for 'negligence' (and for strict liability). The most influential of those theories are that of deterrence and that of corrective justice. We apply these theories throughout the book and outline their basic tenets in this Introduction.

In England, the landmark House of Lords' decision *Donoghue v Stevenson*[13] inaugurated the foundational shift from the 'direct contact' to the 'externalized risk' paradigm of tort liability. This decision exerted a remarkable influence on the Anglo-American legal systems. The refined 'duty of care' concept laid out in the decision was a major doctrinal advancement. After *Donoghue v Stevenson*, the concept of 'privity' expanded far beyond direct-contact cases. Under the expanded liability framework, distant wrongdoers could owe compensation duties to their distant victims if the risk externalized by any such wrongdoer had materialized into his victim's damage. As already explained, the reasons underlying this expansion were partly moral and partly epistemological. In its epistemological aspect, the expansion was predicated on the courts' ability to determine the factual transformation of risks into underlying damages.

This book focuses on the third and current developmental stage of the tort doctrine. This stage features an altogether different combination of moral and epistemological problems. The most important of these problems is that of untraceable and indivisible damage. Untraceable damage is damage that the fact-finder cannot causally attribute to any particular wrongdoer even when she can identify the wrongdoers who externalized the risks that might have materialized into that damage. The difference between risks that did (or did not) materialize, on the one hand, and risks that might have materialized, on the other, is evidential in nature. If the fact-finder were to have enough evidence, he or she could identify the origin/s of the damage; however, evidence that could facilitate this identification is unavailable. Indivisible damage is damage that the fact-finder cannot apportion between the relevant parties by causally attributing its fractions to their respective causes. In an indivisible-damage case, the causes of the aggregate damage are known, but its fractions are without any identifiable causal traces. The indivisible-damage problem is, therefore, a variant of the more general problem of untraceable damage. Throughout the book, we refer to this general problem as the problem of indeterminate causation.

[13] *Donoghue v Stevenson* [1932] AC 562 (HL).

This problem arises due to three factors. One factor is the multiplicity of risks to which people are exposed in their daily affairs and complex interactions. Another factor is the scarcity of information that could identify the relevant risks, their origins, and the causal processes that transform risks into damage. Finally, there is a marked inequity between people in the distribution of control over multifarious risks of damage and of the power to externalize those risks. Corporations and professionals, such as car producers, drug and food manufacturers, physicians, and many others, have appropriated the power of externalizing risks that produce untraceable damage. The ordinary person's ability to defend himself or herself against this power is manifestly limited, and hence the inequity.

Under the traditional legal doctrine, a plaintiff who sustained untraceable damage would usually be denied remedy. Such a plaintiff would be unable to establish her or his case against any chosen defendant on a balance of probabilities. Because the plaintiff's damage is untraceable, her or his allegation that the damage was inflicted by a particular defendant would not be more probable than not. Her or his action would, consequently, fail. Chapter I of the book justifies this outcome in regular cases. However, cases in which the defendant externalizes risks that recurrently transform into untraceable damage are not regular. Such cases deserve special treatment because they involve large and recurrent losses, both private and social. Leaving the producers of such losses undeterred is patently inefficient. Leaving the tort victims, who sustained these losses, uncompensated is patently unjust.

The famous *Agent Orange* litigation provided a striking illustration of this problem. This litigation involved a hazardous chemical substance known as Agent Orange, which the United States Army used during the Vietnam War to destroy dense flora. Numerous American soldiers were exposed to this substance and contracted different illnesses. After the War, many of these veterans and their families sued the US government and the producers of Agent Orange for the damage allegedly inflicted. The damage, however, was untraceable because the veterans' illnesses could equally have resulted from causes unrelated to Agent Orange. In a typical case, the chance that the plaintiff's illness had resulted from his exposure to Agent Orange was below 50 per cent. Consequently, the plaintiff's evidence would fail to satisfy the preponderance-of-the-evidence requirement, so that the defendant would prevail in the lawsuit. Assume, for example, that the probability of each veteran's case equals 40 per cent and that the total number of Agent Orange lawsuits is 100,000. Under that scenario, if all veterans were to be denied remedy under the regular preponderance-of-the-evidence standard, 40,000 deserving plaintiffs would be denied compensation. Furthermore, the wrongdoers responsible for that damage would be left undeterred. This impunity would enable both them and similarly situated wrongdoers to externalize large-scale risks. Such outcomes frustrate the objectives of the law of torts and are obviously disturbing.[14]

The famous DES litigation is yet another type of case in which the application of the regular burden-of-proof doctrine would frustrate the objectives of the law of torts. DES was a drug designed to prevent miscarriage. Manufactured by hundreds of companies, this drug turned out to be latently carcinogenic to female foetuses. Twenty-five years later, many women whose mothers took the drug during their pregnancies became afflicted with uterine cancer. These women sued the manufacturers of DES for the damage associated with their illness. None of the plaintiffs could evidentially link the specific pills that her mother used to a specific manufacturer. However, it was established by a preponderance of the evidence that the drug was not tested properly prior to its marketing and that the manufacturers ignored certain findings indicating a risk of cancer. Furthermore, the plaintiffs' mothers were not cautioned about those risks. Finally, the drug was marketed under its generic rather than brand name, which foiled any attempt to trace each drug back to its actual manufacturer.

Once again, under the preponderance-of-the-evidence standard, the plaintiffs' action would fail. In any individual case, the plaintiff could furnish a scenario under which the particular DES pill that her mother had taken during her pregnancy was produced by the defendant. The probability of such a scenario would, however, be extremely low. At the same time, dismissing the actions against the DES manufacturers would leave those manufacturers undeterred and their victims uncompensated. This outcome would thus constitute a large-scale defeat of the objectives of tort law. For this reason, a number of American courts held DES manufacturers proportionately liable. Under these rulings, each defendant had to compensate each plaintiff in accordance with the defendant's share in the DES market.[15]

During the past decade, actions for large-scale damage—which have become known as 'mass torts'—have increasingly grown in number. Cigarette smokers have sued tobacco companies for different diseases associated with smoking. Firearm victims have sued weapon manufacturers for encouraging the illegal sale and possession of firearms and for correspondingly increasing the victims' risk of sustaining injury. Former users of the allegedly carcinogenic cellular phones are now suing for their injuries. These and similar lawsuits involve externalization of risks, untraceable large-scale damage, and indeterminate causation. In any such lawsuit, application of the regular burden-of-proof requirement would absolve defendants from liability in torts. The traditional objectives of the law of torts—corrective justice and deterrence—would thus be systematically frustrated. To promote

[14] The actual Agent Orange litigation ended in a global settlement. See *In re 'Agent Orange' Product Liability Litigation* 597 F Supp 740 (EDNY 1984), *aff'd* 818 F 2d 145 (2d Cir 1987).

[15] *Sindell v Abbott* 607 P 2d 924 (Cal 1980).

these objectives properly, the law therefore needs to reshape its proof requirements and properly to adjust its tort liability principles.

The uncertainty problem is prevalent in cases that involve large-scale damage, but it does not arise in such cases alone. This problem appears in several other categories of cases in which it equally threatens to frustrate the objectives of the law of torts. The uncertainty problem therefore requires a general solution, which this book seeks to provide. The law of torts has already developed a number of particularized solutions to the uncertainty problem. Throughout the book, we subject these solutions to critical examination. The aim of this book is to place these solutions on a principled footing and to supplement them with a comprehensive treatment of the uncertainty problem. Our discussion and proposals rest upon two principal theories of tort liability: that of deterrence and that of corrective justice. Occasionally, we allude to retributive concerns as well. These three theories of liability in torts merit a brief introduction.

Deterrence is usually identified with economic efficiency. At its foundation lies the idea that tort law needs to provide both the potential wrongdoer and the potential victim (and, at times, third parties as well) with an incentive to behave in a way that will minimize, to the extent possible, the aggregate cost of accidents and of their prevention. This behaviour will augment social welfare. Accordingly, a legal rule that reduces both the cost of accidents and the cost of their prevention is an economically efficient rule. This rule will be justified by the deterrence objective of the law of torts.[16]

Justice is an irreducibly complex concept with a variety of different connotations. The type of justice commonly alluded to by tort law theorists is corrective justice. Under the principles of corrective justice, any state of affairs that was created due to one person's wrongful injury to another person must be rectified, so that the latter is restored to her *status quo ante*. Aristotle premised this principle on the postulation that a wrongful injury violates the equality between people in their dealings with one another.[17] Theorists emphasizing the centrality of corrective justice to the area of torts are yet to reach common ground in identifying the characteristics of the wrongful injury that merits (or demands) rectification.[18] What these theorists do agree on and

[16] G. Calabresi, *The Cost of Accidents* (1970); R. A. Posner, 'A Theory of Negligence' (1972) 1 *J Legal Studies* 29; G. Calabresi and T. Hirschoff, 'Toward a Test for Strict Liability in Torts' (1972) 81 *Yale LJ* 1055. For a sceptical view with regard to the deterrence capacity of the law of torts see S. Sugarman, *Doing Away With Personal Injury Law* (1989).

[17] Aristotle, *Nichomachean Ethics*, Vol. V (Martin Ostwald, trans., 1962) 4 .

[18] R. Epstein, 'A Theory of Strict Liability' (1973) 2 *J Legal Studies* 151; G. Fletcher, 'Fairness and Utility in Tort Theory' (1972) 85 *Harvard L Rev* 537; J. L. Coleman, 'Corrective Justice and Wrongful Gain', in *Markets, Morals and the Law* (Cambridge, 1987) 184; J. L. Coleman, *Risks and Wrongs* (Cambridge, 1992) 329–85; E. J. Weinrib, 'Understanding Tort Law' (1989) 23 *Valpariso U L Rev* 485; E. J. Weinrib, *The Idea of Private Law* (1995) 145–70; E. J. Weinrib, 'Correlativity, Personality, and the Emerging Consensus on Corrective Justice' (2001) 2 *Theoretical Inquiries in Law* 107; S. R. Perry, 'The Moral Foundation of Tort Law' (1992) 77 *Iowa L Rev* 449.

what makes their approach unique is that they examine the different internal characteristics of damaging occurrences and attempt to discern *from those characteristics alone* whether the injury was wrongful. Under corrective justice, nothing is relevant but the actions of the wrongdoer and the victim. Factors extraneous to the wrongdoer–victim relationship, such as augmentation of general social welfare and just distribution of wealth in a given society, are excluded from consideration. For corrective justice, the body of doctrine identified as 'torts' has a single objective: 'to be tort law'.[19]

Another type of justice relevant to the area of torts is retribution. This type of justice alludes to the morality of 'just deserts'. Corrective justice focuses upon doing justice to the victim, whereas retributive justice focuses upon doing justice to the wrongdoer. Doing justice to the wrongdoer entails imposition of tort liability in the light of the moral traits of the wrongdoer's behaviour. Corrective justice theorists perceive the principles of corrective justice as doing justice to the victim and to the wrongdoer simultaneously. Under corrective justice, this outcome is achieved by eradicating wrongful losses created by the wrongdoer. The victim is compensated for the damage that he or she wrongfully sustained, and the wrongdoer is forced to make good the damage by compensating the victim. However, moral factors determining justice to the wrongdoer are often autonomous in nature. The wrongdoer's fault will not always be proportionate to the victim's damage. Forcing such a wrongdoer to compensate the victim for his entire damage—as prescribed by the prevalent doctrine of tort liability—may therefore be seen as problematic. Indeed, this matter has presented a challenge to different scholars in their efforts to justify the prevalent doctrine.[20] Some of these scholars have criticized the doctrine and proposed appropriate changes in the law.[21]

This book adopts a pluralistic, rather than monistic, approach to tort liability. In our opinion, one type of consideration pertaining to the imposition of liability in torts need not exclude other types.[22] Indeed, while the law of

[19] Weinrib, *Understanding Tort Law*, ibid. at 526. For critical comments on Weinrib's theory, see K. W. Simons, 'Justification in Private Law' (1996) 81 *Cornell L Rev* 698; H. Dagan, 'The Distributive Foundations of Corrective Justice' (1999) 98 *Michigan L Rev* 138; A. Porat, 'Questioning the Idea of Correlativity in Weinrib's Theory of Corrective Justice' (2001) 2 *Theoretical Inquiries in Law* 161; J. Gordley, 'The Purpose of Awarding Restitutionary Damages: A Reply to Professor Weinrib' (2000) 1 *Theoretical Inquiries in Law* 39.

[20] T. Honoré, 'Responsibility and Luck: The Moral Basis of Strict Liability' (1988) 104 *LQR* 530; J. Waldron, 'Moments of Carelessness and Massive Loss', in D. G. Owen (ed.), *Philosophical Foundations of Tort Law* (1995) 387.

[21] See, for example, C. H. Schroeder, 'Corrective Justice and Liability for Increasing Risks' (1990) 37 *University of California Los Angeles L Rev* 439; C. H. Schroeder, 'Corrective Justice, Liability for Risks, and Tort Law' (1990) 38 *University of California Los Angeles L Rev* 143.

[22] Ernest Weinrib is the most ardent proponent of the pure corrective justice approach to liability in torts. See Weinrib, *The Idea of Private Law* (n. 18 above). Other supporters of corrective justice do not altogether deny the importance of deterrence. See Coleman, *Risks and Wrongs* (n. 18 above) 197–211; G. P. Fletcher, 'The Search for Synthesis in Tort Theory' (1983) 2 *Law & Philosophy* 63. For pluralistic approaches to tort liability that allow deterrence and corrective

torts should care about victims being compensated by wrongdoers, it should also care about placing potential wrongdoers under the economically optimal level of deterrence. The tort doctrine should, therefore, be responsive to both deterrence and corrective justice concerns. At times, it should also promote retribution. Therefore, the theoretical lens through which we examine the different doctrinal arrangements is rotated. The law reform proposals that we make throughout the book and, in particular, our proposal to impose liability *for* uncertainty, are also based on the principles of both deterrence and corrective justice and occasionally allude to retribution.

As far as positive law is concerned, this book provides a comprehensive and updated doctrinal picture that captures the existing solutions to the uncertainty problem in torts. We focus predominantly on the solutions developed in England and the United States. Reference is also occasionally made to other jurisdictions, such as Canada and Israel, but our depiction of their doctrinal approaches is selective and fragmentary. This book's primary objective is normative rather than expository. The existing doctrinal approaches to the problem at hand are still incomplete and thus open to further developments. We hope to contribute to these developments by offering a systematic analysis of the problem and by identifying the ways in which it can be resolved. For that reason, we have chosen to organize our discussion around issues rather than jurisdictions.

Our discussion proceeds in the following order. Chapter I examines the general doctrine that determines the level of proof in civil trials and allocates the burdens of proof. This discussion delineates the advantages and limitations of that doctrine and identifies special cases that should be governed by special proof requirements. Chapter II identifies the paradigmatic tort cases featuring the uncertainty problem, that is, the problem of untraceable damage and indeterminate causation. We divide those cases into discrete categories and demonstrate that none of these categories of cases should be governed by the general burden-of-proof doctrine. Unqualified application of that doctrine to cases falling under these categories would systematically deny remedy to plaintiffs, thus frustrating the objectives of the law of torts. As demonstrated in Chapter II, positive law has devised for some of those cases a number of special rules that deviate from the general burden-of-proof requirement. The most important members of this family of rules are discussed individually in Chapters III to V. The solution that these special rules provide to the problem at hand is, however, only partial.

In Chapter III, we analyse the *res ipsa loquitur* presumption. This presumption has three different variants: the weak variant, which merely allows the fact-finder to infer the defendant's negligence from the presumption's

justice to work side by side, see I. Englard, *The Philosophy of Tort Law* (1993) 85–92; G. T. Schwartz, 'Mixed Theories of Tort Law: Affirming Both Deterrence and Corrective Justice' (1997) 75 *Texas L Rev* 1801.

basic facts; the intermediate-strength variant, which requires the fact-finder to draw such an inference if the defendant fails to produce exonerating evidence; and the strong variant, which requires the fact-finder to hold the defendant negligent if the defendant fails preponderantly to establish his faultlessness. We examine the rationales underlying each of these variants of *res ipsa* and offer a new rationale that stems from our general proposal to impose liability for uncertainty (the evidential damage doctrine developed in Chapter VI).

Chapter IV investigates the risk-of-damage notion together with the forms of tort liability for externalized risks of damage. These forms include the 'lost-chance' doctrine, under which wrongful conduct that reduces the victim's chances not to sustain the relevant damage constitutes an actionable tort. We demonstrate that liability for bare risk is unjustified and that liability for lost chances ought to be treated as actionable only in special cases, which we identify. Generally, liability for lost chances is justified in cases in which the damage has yet to materialize and in specific cases involving recurrent transgressions. We analyse the existing forms of liability for bare risk, as adopted by the positive law of torts, and criticize each of them. As demonstrated in this chapter, liability for lost chances often functions as an implicit and underdeveloped form of liability for uncertainty (or for evidential damage, as we prefer to conceive it). In such cases, liability for lost chances needs to be accommodated within the comprehensive evidential damage doctrine, which we develop in Chapter VI.

Chapter V deals with collective liability. This form of liability is suitable for cases known as 'indeterminate defendant'. In such cases, several wrongdoers separately engage in a similar activity, but only one of them—who cannot be identified—actually causes damage to the plaintiff. Here, collective liability can be, and often is, used as a vehicle for preventing wrongdoers from causing damage and seeking refuge in the shadows of uncertainty. This form of liability also aims at providing tort victims with appropriate compensatory remedies. Collective liability is recognized by American law under three legal doctrines: the market-share liability doctrine; the doctrine of enterprise liability; and the doctrine of alternative liability. We provide an exposition of these doctrines and analyse their advantages and shortcomings. We also expose the ways in which these doctrines relate to the doctrine of evidential damage (liability for uncertainty). In addition, we suggest extending collective liability into new domains where the existing legal doctrines have yet to reach. Specifically, we show that collective liability is especially attractive in cases of recurrent transgressions.

In Chapter VI, we propose a new form of liability in torts: liability for uncertainty or the 'evidential damage' doctrine. This doctrine distinguishes between two types of case: cases in which accuracy in fact-finding is undermined by circumstances for which no person can be blamed and cases in which the existing uncertainty and the consequent inability of the court to determine the facts accurately result from a person's wrongful conduct. The evidential damage doctrine should apply to the latter category of cases. Under that doctrine, a person responsible for the factual uncertainty of a case will assume liability in torts for that evidential damage. Chapter VI outlines the criteria for assigning this liability and develops a remedial mechanism for compensating evidentially damaged plaintiffs. From the deterrence perspective, this form of liability would serve a dual purpose: it would help the law to maintain optimal deterrence with respect to both primary and evidential damage. From the corrective justice viewpoint, this form of liability would enable plaintiffs to recover the appropriate compensation for wrongfully sustained losses. We demonstrate that evidential damage is a distinct type of loss—namely, a damage to a person's autonomy—which ought to be made actionable in torts in accordance with corrective justice. Chapter VI thus demonstrates that the evidential damage doctrine is justified on grounds of both deterrence and corrective justice.

Chapter VII concludes the book by returning to the paradigmatic categories of cases identified in Chapter II. In Chapter VII, we compare the solutions offered for these categories of cases by the positive law, on the one hand, and by the evidential damage doctrine, on the other hand. This comparative discussion further delineates the advantages of the evidential damage doctrine. However, we refrain from making a far-reaching proposal to replace the existing doctrinal solutions to the uncertainty problem with the evidential damage doctrine. This book's normative agenda is supplementational rather than exclusionary. We therefore propose to co-ordinate the application of the existing legal doctrines with application of the evidential damage doctrine. Indeed, the law ought to combine the evidential damage doctrine and the particularized doctrinal solutions to the problem at hand into one coherent body. Such a combined approach would promote the fundamental objectives of the law of torts better than any of its alternatives would.

I

Liability under Uncertainty: Allocating the Risk of Error

A. THE NATURE OF THE PROBLEM

LAW, experience, and philosophy of induction tell us that fact-finding in adjudication is a matter of probability rather than certainty.[1] In tort litigation, upon which this book focuses, a fact will generally be held established when it is 'more probable than not'. This standard applies in all civil trials and is known as 'proof on a balance of probabilities' or 'proof by a preponderance of the evidence'.[2] By applying this standard, the law acknowledges that a quest for absolute certainty is not one of its objectives. By virtue of this standard, judges are called upon to apply the controlling substantive law on the factual scenario that is comparatively the strongest, but not a certainty.

Why is this so? And what makes one factual scenario comparatively better than another? These questions are crucial to understanding fact-finding under the uncertainty that takes place in adjudication in general and in tort cases in particular. This chapter attempts to answer these questions.

Unavailability of certainty is a partial answer to these questions. Any 'fact' upon which people act in their daily affairs is clouded by doubts, and fact-finding in adjudication is no exception. Adjudicative fact-finding is a

[1] Causes of this uncertainty are examined in A. Stein, 'The Refoundation of Evidence Law' (1996) 9 *Canadian J L & Jurisprudence* 279, 296–321.

[2] See, e.g., I. H. Dennis, *The Law of Evidence* (1999) 362–7. This chapter focuses only on the burden of persuasion, also known as the 'legal burden'. This burden must be distinguished from that of production (or the burden of adducing evidence). The persuasion burden allocates risk of error in evidentially balanced cases, that is, in cases in which the allegations advanced by both the plaintiff and the defendant fail to satisfy the controlling standard of proof (in civil trials, the balance of probabilities). This burden's function is to single out the bearer of the risk of error. The production burden is a duty to adduce evidence that needs to be brought before judges or jurors in order to raise an issue. This burden's function is to identify the party who will be exposed to an adverse ruling if an issue pertaining to the case is left evidentially unsubstantiated. See Dennis, ibid. 341–6. This fundamental distinction was pioneered by James Bradley Thayer, 'The Burdens of Proof' (1890) 4 *Harvard L Rev* 45. The same later appeared in Thayer's book *A Preliminary Treatise on Evidence at Common Law* (1898) ch. 9. For a modern Thayerate approach, see A. Stein, 'Allocating the Burden of Proof in Sales Litigation: The Law, Its Rationale, A New Theory, And Its Failure' (1996) 50 *U Miami L Rev* 335. As widely acknowledged, the importance of the production burden in civil litigation has substantially diminished since the advent of modern discovery law. See, e.g., R. J. Allen, 'Presumptions in Civil Actions Reconsidered' (1981) 66 *Iowa L Rev* 843, 860: 'It is difficult to imagine a case today in which the sanction of possible dismissal would generate more evidence than discovery schemes.'

branch of practical reasoning in which facts must be determined one way or another in order to allow the relevant action to be taken. Practical reasoning, to which adjudicative fact-finding belongs, would, indeed, be thoroughly impoverished—and, indeed, stalled in indecision—if fact-determination were prevented by philosophical (or other) doubts that disqualify every uncertain fact for being a 'non-truth'. There is, therefore, a clear social necessity to rely in practical matters upon imperfect facts. This necessity is also reflected in language. In day-to-day language, 'fact' is a concept that admits different degrees of certainty and, thus, entails the assumption of the risk of error. Theoretically, the notion of fact entails immutability, but in the ordinary, as opposed to technical-philosophical, discourse, facts lacking that quality are nevertheless taken as 'facts', as long as there are good probabilistic reasons for treating them as such. These reasons are usually grounded on evidence that points to the existence of the relevant facts. Some facts are consequently conceptualized as stronger, and some as weaker. Facts thus become conditioned on their evidential base even when the base is known to be deficient. This contingency and the corresponding assumption of the risk of error do not automatically expel people's findings from the category of facts.

This familiar answer to the 'Why is it so?' question is still partial, for it does not account for the particular degree of certainty chosen by the civil proof doctrine. This answer does not explain the supremacy of the preponderance-of-the-evidence standard over other probabilistic alternatives. Nor does it justify the specific ingredients of the civil proof doctrine that control the application of the preponderance-of-the-evidence standard. Unavailability of certainty is still not a justification for the doctrinal allocation of the risk of error. Allocation of the risk of error in proceedings that determine people's rights is a moral and political decision. Materialization of that risk results in a non-vindication of an underlying substantive right: it entails denial of remedy to a deserving plaintiff or imposition of liability on a non-liable defendant. Reasons for allocating the risk of error in adjudication are, therefore, situated in the moral and political domain. Those reasons can, therefore, be justified only on moral and political grounds. These grounds differ sharply from the relevant epistemological and pragmatic factors that point merely to the non-existence of immutable facts, to the prevalence of the risk of error, and to the consequent fallibility of fact-finders.

Our inquiry into the functions of the civil proof doctrine therefore becomes an exegesis of that doctrine's political morality. As such, it takes place within two distinct frameworks: that of fairness and that of utility. Both frameworks are employed here as explanatory and justificatory tools. The fairness framework attempts to explain and justify the workings of the civil proof doctrine from the point of view of corrective justice. The utility framework does the same from the deterrence perspective. Because these frameworks pursue different objectives that often clash with one another, they are examined separately. We focus initially on the utility framework and then discuss the relevant fairness principles.

This discussion presents and compares three different rules by which factually uncertain cases can be adjudicated. One of those rules, the preponderance-of-the-evidence standard, awards the plaintiff full recovery if her case is more probable than not. This rule is generally adopted by the positive law. Under another rule, the plaintiff recovers only the probabilistic fraction of the litigated amount. This fraction equals the litigated amount multiplied by the probability of the plaintiff's case, as determined by the judges at trial (*ex post*). Finally, under the third rule, the plaintiff may be awarded the expected value of his damage, calculated on the basis of the information that was reasonably available to the defendant *ex ante*, that is, at the time the defendant took the litigated action. This amount would, thus, equal the probability of the defendant's transgression multiplied by the plaintiff's damage, when both factors are determined from the defendant's *ex ante* perspective. This third approach has an important derivation: arguably, expected damages could be collected from wrongdoers regardless of whether they actually damaged their plaintiffs. This derivation is discussed in greater detail in Chapter IV.

B. BURDEN OF PROOF AND UTILITY

1. Maximizing the Number of Correct Decisions

Under the preponderance-of-the-evidence standard, the party whose evidence preponderates that of her opponent must prevail. In probabilistic terms, this precept is identified as 'the P>0.5 rule', and we will use this term throughout the discussion. The P>0.5 rule is commonly credited for its capacity to minimize the number of adjudicative errors. Any other rule of decision would produce more errors and less correct decisions than this rule does. Proof of this creditworthy capacity is straightforward. By focusing on the total amount, rather than on the individual consequences, of adjudicative errors, the error-minimizing objective treats every error as a fixed disutility unit (u). Consequently, there is no difference between errors that harm defendants (false positives) and errors that harm plaintiffs (false negatives). The utility principle therefore ordains that a party whose case has probability P should win the case whenever $Pu>(1-P)u$, that is, whenever P>0.5. In short, judges will maximize the total number of correct decisions by treating their best chances of arriving at the factually correct result as decisive.

This maximization of correct decisions indeed appears to serve an important utilitarian objective, promulgated ever since Bentham: greater accuracy in fact-finding ('rectitude of decision', in Bentham's words[3]) gives more space to the controlling substantive law. It implies that liability would be allocated more accurately, so there would be less underdeterrence (because more wrongdoers would be found liable) and less overdeterrence (because fewer faultless defendants would be found liable).[4]

The P>0.5 rule can be supported from yet another economic angle. This rule does not merely maximize the number of correct decisions; it promotes an additional utilitarian objective by minimizing the total amount of wrongful transfers.[5] This justification of the rule plausibly assumes that substantive law allocates entitlements by using efficiency criteria. Under that assumption, any deviation from the controlling substantive law would violate the chosen efficiency criterion and, consequently, amount to a wrongful transfer. Let D denote the value of the litigated good; and let p_1 and p_2 denote, respectively, the probabilities of the plaintiff's and the defendant's conflicting allegations. As always is the case:

$0 < p_1 < 1$; $0 < p_2 < 1$; when 1 stands for certainty and 0 for impossibility.

At least one of the parties is, therefore, bound to bear the risk of error, that is, the risk of sustaining damage up to D (trial expenses of the parties are ignored, for the sake of simplicity). Decisions that judges can make under these conditions are as follows:

d_1 = the plaintiff loses (risk of error imposed on the plaintiff);
d_2 = the defendant loses (risk of error imposed on the defendant);
d_3 = compromise reflecting the expected value of each allegation: the plaintiff recovers from the defendant p_1D; p_2D goes to the defendant (by not allowing the plaintiff to recover that amount).

By allowing S_1 and S_2, respectively, to denote the actual states of affairs—that can favour either the plaintiff or the defendant—we can assess the average damage (and thus the long-run damage in terms of wrongful transfers) that each of the above decisions would produce:

Decision	Damage in S_1 Cases	Damage in S_2 Cases	Total Damage
d_1	p_1D	0	p_1D
d_2	0	p_2D	p_2D
d_3	p_1p_2D	p_2p_1D	$2p_1p_2D$

[3] See Jeremy Bentham, *Rationale of Judicial Evidence*, Vol. 5 (ed. J. S. Mill, 1827) 1–8.

[4] See J. Kaplan, 'Decision Theory and the Factfinding Process' (1968) 20 *Stanford L Rev* 1065, 1071–2; D. Kaye, 'Naked Statistical Evidence' (1980) 89 *Yale LJ* 601, 605 n. 19.

[5] See D. Kaye, 'The Limits of the Preponderance of the Evidence Standard: Justifiably Naked Statistical Evidence and Multiple Causation' (1982) *American Bar Foundation Research J* 487.

Hence, in order to minimize the overall damage, a litigant should be allowed to recover the full amount of her claim when the probability of her allegations exceeds 0.5 and thus is greater than the probability of her opponent's case. This factor determines the general standard-of-proof requirement. This requirement, however, does not yield an accomplished rule of decision, for it says nothing about balanced cases where the probabilities of competing factual accounts are equal. For such cases, the law should provide a residual decision rule that would designate the bearer of the persuasion burden and of the consequent risk of non-persuasion. As will now be explained, the bearer of that burden and the corresponding risk of error should generally be the plaintiff (subject to the 'affirmative defence doctrine' that we discuss below in this chapter).

In balanced cases—that is, whenever $p_1=p_2=0.5$—the overall damage that each of the available decisions would incur would be the same. Yet, in such cases, defendants should generally prevail. This decision rule would eliminate the enforcement costs that would be incurred if the plaintiff were to be awarded recovery.[6] Apart from that, allowing the plaintiff to recover when $p_1=0.5$ would induce filing of a greater number of unmeritorious lawsuits, which would increase litigation expenditures.[7] When $p_1=p_2=0.5$, decision d_1 would also be optimal because 'taking' is generally more harmful than 'not giving'. This perception can be justified by the diminishing utility of wealth.[8]

The above utilitarian analysis is, however, still incomplete. By assuming that the utility of wealth steadily diminishes, we could arrive at an entirely different conclusion that favours d_3. This conclusion would be reached if, driven by the diminishing-utility-of-wealth assumption, we were to decide to minimize the amount of *large* errors.[9] By employing the conventional (but still imprecise) estimation of the average large error as amounting to D^2, we would arrive at the following:

Decision	Damage in S_1 Cases	Damage in S_2 Cases	Total Damage
d_1	p_1D^2	0	p_1D^2
d_2	0	p_2D^2	p_2D^2
d_3	$p_1(p_2D)^2$	$p_2(p_1D)^2$	$p_1p_2D^2$

[6] See Stein (n. 2 above) 343.

[7] See R. K. Winter, 'The Jury and the Risk of Non-Persuasion' (1971) 5 *Law & Society Rev* 335, 337.

[8] See R. A. Posner, *Economic Analysis of Law* (5th edn., 1998) 604. But perhaps it has to do more with the 'endowment effect' that causes people to put greater value on psychologically vested, as opposed to psychologically unvested, rights. See A. Tversky and D. Kahneman, 'Rational Choice and the Framing of Decisions' (1986) 59 *J of Business* S251, S260. See also Stein (n. 2 above) 343 n. 38.

[9] See N. Orloff and J. Stedinger, 'A Framework for Evaluating the Preponderance-of-the-Evidence Standard' (1983) 131 *University of Pennsylvania L Rev* 1159.

Under these conditions, decision d_3, which allows each party to recover the expected value of her or his claim, becomes optimal: $p_1p_2D^2$ is less than both p_1D^2 and p_2D^2.

This conclusion, however, holds true only when our comparison between the available decision rules is confined to their corresponding *immediate* losses. For obvious reasons, this confinement is unjustified: our analysis needs to continue by accounting for other losses to the extent that they may be incurred. As already indicated, in addition to minimizing the total amount of wrongful transfers, the $P>0.5$ rule maximizes the sheer number of correct decisions. As such, it minimizes the incidence of both false positives and false negatives. Under the expected-value rule (d_3), the number of correctly decided cases would always be zero. The expected-value rule would, consequently, weaken the behavioural incentives set by the substantive law: it would do so both in reducing the penalty for non-compliance and in eroding the difference between complying and not complying with the relevant legal standard. This would clearly amount to a social loss.[10]

This broader perspective is captured by the following formal model,[11] in which

- g = the expected gain from a potentially harmful action contemplated by a person;
- p = the probability that the person will be detected as a possible violator of the relevant legal standard;
- f = a pecuniary sanction (say—a fine that derives from the amount of harm associated with the contemplated action) that would be imposed on the person by the court if it finds him or her liable;
- ϵ_1 = the probability of the type-I error (false positive), that is, the probability that a non-liable defendant will be mistakenly found liable;
- ϵ_2 = the probability of the type-II error (false negative), that is, the probability that a liable defendant will be mistakenly found not liable.

For the sake of simplicity, this model assumes that the person is neutral towards risk (a standard assumption that this book makes in various contexts). The model further assumes that the probability of the person's detection as a possible violator (p) is constant. The latter assumption is made for the sake of simplicity as well: detection errors are bound to occur, and their actual rate has no impact on the lesson to be learnt from the model. If detection errors could be reduced, the incidence of adjudication errors would obviously decline.

[10] See Stein (n. 1 above) 335–6.

[11] This model was recently developed by A. M. Polinsky and S. Shavell, 'The Economic Theory of Public Enforcement of Law', (2000) 38 *J of Economic Literature* 45, 60–2, and it draws on I. P. L. Png, 'Optimal Subsidies and Damages in the Presence of Judicial Error' (1986) 6 *International Review of Law and Economics* 101.

Based on the above assumptions, the person would take the contemplated action when

$$g - p(1 - \epsilon_2)f > - p\epsilon_1 f.$$

The left side of this inequality represents the difference between the person's gain and expected loss that arise from the harmful action. The person's expected loss equals the fine, multiplied by the person's probability of being detected and subsequently found liable. The right side of the inequality is a negative sum that represents the person's initial position: even if the person does not take the contemplated action, he may be erroneously detected as a violator and subsequently found liable. This initial loss is predicated on the existence of errors in the legal system, and its magnitude would depend on the size of the fine and on the incidence of both detection and judgmental false positives. The person, therefore, would rationally take the contemplated action if its outcome improves his initial position. Consequently, the action would be taken even if the left side of the inequality yields a negative sum, as long as that sum is less than $p\epsilon_1 f$. This implies that deterrence will be reduced not only by false negatives, but also—albeit less trivially—by false positives.

Formally, the potentially harmful action will be taken if

$$g > p(1 - \epsilon_2)f - p\epsilon_1 f,$$

that is, if

$$g > pf(1 - \epsilon_2 - \epsilon_1).$$

This formula demonstrates that both types of error ought to be reduced in order to optimize deterrence and thereby augment social welfare. False negatives dilute deterrence and thus reduce social welfare by lowering the expected fine for potential violators. False positives dilute deterrence less trivially: they do so by eroding the difference between the fine expected from violating the law and from not violating it. For obvious reasons, false positives also chill socially desirable activities. For example, if courts too often fail to distinguish between the negligent and the careful truck-drivers, some of the drivers who are both rational and careful might decide not to drive their trucks.[12] The lesson to be learnt from this analysis is straightforward: the optimal proof requirement is one that maximizes the total number of correct decisions, an outcome that the P>0.5 rule attains.

[12] See generally L. Kaplow and S. Shavell, 'Accuracy in the Determination of Liability' (1994) 37 *J Law & Economics* 1.

2. The 'Winner Takes All' Principle and Probabilistic Recoveries

(a) The P>0.5 Rule and the Ex Ante *Probability of Transgression*

The P>0.5 rule is supported by an additional economic reason that arises from the clash between this rule and another competing theory.[13] This theory criticizes the rule for choosing a wrong object for maximization. Facts pertaining to a litigated event are reconstructed by judges on the basis of evidence that becomes available at trial, that is, after the event (*ex post*). Based on this evidence, judges must determine the probability of the plaintiff's allegation that the defendant violated the litigated entitlement. This evidence, however, need not be the same evidence that the defendant could reasonably consider before the event (*ex ante*). Two sets of information, not one, thus appear to be at work, and they also differ from one another: information available to judges *ex post* is not the same information that was available *ex ante* to prospective transgressors. The two sets of information could, of course, be aligned (to the extent feasible) if individuals were to have enough incentives for improving their earlier decisions by acquiring more information (for example, through experts or legal advice). This would make the individuals better informed about their actions' consequences in terms of both harm and liability. Accuracy *ex post* promotes this objective by inducing individuals to acquire information *ex ante*: failure to do so increases the risk of the individual's liability. However, as noted by Louis Kaplow, 'individuals will be induced to learn information ex ante only if their benefits from adjusting behaviour exceed the cost of the information'.[14]

This condition is unlikely to be satisfied when the two sets of information are substantially misaligned. In numerous cases, the required alignment would be exorbitantly expensive, if not altogether unattainable.[15] Moreover, normative postulation that individuals ought to be induced to acquire more information *ex ante* does not establish that accuracy *ex post* is the best inducement. A direct requirement that individuals obtain the best information that can practicably be obtained prior to acting in a potentially harmful way might provide a better inducement. This direct inducement is already embedded in the negligence doctrine and in many other liability rules that are based on objective, rather than subjective, standards of conduct.[16]

[13] See A. Stein, 'Of Two Wrongs that Make a Right: Two Paradoxes of the Evidence Law and Their Combined Economic Justification' (2001) 79 *Texas L Rev* 1199.

[14] L. Kaplow, 'The Value of Accuracy in Adjudication: An Economic Analysis' (1994) 23 *J Legal Studies* 307, 317.

[15] See ibid. 316–25.

[16] See, e.g., W. P. Keeton, *Prosser and Keeton On Torts* (5th edn., 1984) 185 (negligence standards require individuals to seek information prior to acting in a potentially hazardous way).

Therefore, if the law is determined to use its civil liability mechanisms, such as torts, for setting optimal deterrence for economic actors, then it should focus on the *ex ante* probability of transgression as determined by a reasonable economic actor in deciding whether to take the (subsequently) litigated action. The *ex post* probability of litigated events is a poor proxy for the actor-centred probability. In such circumstances, efforts directed at attaining accuracy *ex post* therefore amount to a waste of resources. Moreover, by inducing excessive investments in the acquisition of information accuracy *ex post* produces various effects that are detrimental to deterrence and to efficiency in general.[17]

Take, for example, contractor C who builds a fence for houseowner H and undertakes that the fence will withstand bad weather. At the time of making this undertaking C properly estimated the risk that the fence will not withstand bad weather and collapse as amounting to 5 per cent. This estimation turned out to be wrong *ex post* because there was something that C did not know and could not plausibly ascertain. A year later, the fence collapsed after being exposed to severe winds and floods. H sues C for damages, claiming that the fence did not withstand the weather. C contends that the fence collapsed because someone must have damaged its foundations during that year. At the ensuing trial, an expert witness testifies that the damage-through-bad-weather scenario, advanced by H, is more likely than C's competing scenario because the weather was particularly bad during the past year. The expert further clarifies that H's scenario has a 60 per cent likelihood. The court finds this testimony credible. By applying the preponderance-of-the-evidence standard, it holds that the damage was caused by bad weather.

From the deterrence perspective, the *ex post* probability of the damage-through-bad-weather scenario could not be rationally accounted for by C at the time that he built the fence. The court and the parties therefore wasted resources in their combined efforts to determine that probability. The court's holding in favour of H's scenario is doubtless more accurate than the alternative. Such decisions would also produce more correct than incorrect verdicts in the long run of cases. Thus, out of a hundred similar cases, sixty would be decided correctly and only forty incorrectly. Yet, the court's holding would induce no changes in behaviour, since any rational contractor situated similarly to C would estimate the relevant risk as amounting to only 5 per cent. In accordance with this estimate, the rational contractor would not make an increased investment in the construction to further prevent it from falling down. He would not make such an investment even when he is aware of the P>0.5 rule and its accuracy-enhancing effect. This awareness will have no impact on the contractor's behaviour when he is unaware of the information

[17] See Kaplow (n. 14 above) 365–6. For an earlier analysis of this issue, which points to similar and several other problems, see G. P. Fletcher, 'Paradoxes in Legal Thought' (1985) 85 *Columbia L Rev* 1263, 1284–92.

that might become available at his trial. Under these conditions, the contractor will rationally assume that any *ex post* information will be distributed randomly across cases. He will, of course, speculate that he may be underestimating the risk that the fence will collapse due to bad weather. He will also speculate that the court might make a finding to that effect, based on the information that might become available at his trial. These speculations, however, will be treated by him as equally plausible as conjectures that point in the opposite direction. Being indifferent to the conflicting speculations, the contractor will cancel them out. Accordingly, he will base his decision on the information available at the time of his decision.[18]

In the long run, this decision should also prove to be perfectly rational. Contractor C must account for the possibility that the *ex ante* and the *ex post* information might not be similar. Yet, under the given facts, there is no reason to believe that the discrepancy between the two types of information is systematically slanted in a particular way. C's assessment of the risk may turn out to have been too optimistic in some cases and too pessimistic in others, but there is no reason to believe that the former cases—to which the present example belongs—will outnumber the latter. Therefore, amongst the fences constructed by C, only 5 per cent will actually collapse due to bad weather, so he will not be held responsible for more than 5 per cent of the fences in the long run of cases.

Arguably, houseowner H should prevail in his lawsuit against C under the scenario that his fence belongs to the above 5 per cent. After all, this scenario is more likely than not. Holding C liable would, therefore, not expand his general liability for collapsed fences beyond 5 per cent. By contrast, holding C not liable in this and similar cases would bring his liability to below 5 per cent, in which case, the deterrence would be insufficient. This argument would be correct only if one assumes that future information will not be slanted in any

[18] Negligence regimes mitigate this problem by conditioning the defendant's liability for a damaging occurrence on the foreseeability of that occurrence. If the occurrence was not foreseeable, the defendant will not be liable for the damage. Judges must determine this issue on the basis of information that was reasonably available to the defendant prior to taking the litigated action. Information that surfaced after the event is largely irrelevant to this issue, so judges must not use it. See, e.g., Keeton (n. 16 above) 170 ('The actor's conduct must be judged in light of the possibilities apparent to him at the time'); Fletcher (n. 17 above) 1285 (same).

This mitigation of the problem is far from sufficient, because foreseeability is an indivisible legal standard that judges apply only *ex post*. Application of this standard is dichotomous: a damaging occurrence is either foreseeable or not. There is no such thing, for example, as a 5% foreseeability, so in the present case, C would have to consider whether a 5% risk to the fence makes the potential damage fully foreseeable. Application of this standard also depends on how judges will treat the relevant risk, an *ex post* factor of which C is informed only partially at the time of contemplating his action. See generally L. Kaplow, 'Rules versus Standards: An Economic Analysis' (1992) *Duke LJ* 557. Furthermore, the foreseeability standard applies only to the type, rather than size, of the relevant harm, so it does not affect the quantum-of-damage decisions. See Keeton (n. 16 above) 290–3. The size of the future damage and the corresponding extent of legal liability therefore remain unascertainable *ex ante*. These factors can only be approximated prior to the event. See nn. 24–9 below and accompanying text.

particular direction. However, this is too crude an assumption to proceed upon if one takes into account the creation and the operation of a secondary market for trial information—a factor that we consider in the next few paragraphs. But even if one takes this argument as essentially correct, one must still consider the actions of the other ninety-nine houseowners who commissioned fences from C. Any such person would sue C in the event that her fence were to collapse. Consequently, 100 lawsuits would be adjudicated; 200 experts would submit rival opinions, over which 200 lawyers would conduct adversarial warfare; and, finally, 100 judges (and possibly 1,200 jurors) would have to work hard on identifying the fences that collapsed due to bad weather. This massive investment in fact-finding could only be justified if it were economically necessary.

But is it really necessary from an economic point of view? Why not devise a cheaper mechanism that would allow every houseowner—damaged and undamaged alike—to recover from C a sum that equals, say, 5 per cent of the houseowner's payment for the fence plus 5 per cent of the external damage that a falling fence produces in the average case?[19] Under this framework, proof of each houseowner's payment to C would be cheap. Determination of the expected average damage figure might be costly, but since this knowledge needs to be acquired only once, its costs would be spread across many cases. This mechanism would, therefore, be much cheaper than conventional adjudication, while its effect on deterrence would be at least as good.[20]

In fact, this mechanism's impact on efficiency would be better than that of conventional adjudication. Accuracy *ex post* is expensive: it requires substantial investments in information and other litigation efforts on the part of both C and the houseowners. Both C and the houseowners may be *antecedently* unwilling to commit themselves to such investments. Instead of making that commitment, each party will consider his prospect of being defeated at trial due to erroneous fact-finding. Each party will consider it not only as a general prospect. He will also consider the possibility that he will be defeated at trial because his opponent invested in the litigation more than he did. Therefore, before entering into each fence-building transaction, C will have either to invest in the acquisition of information or to account for his prospects of paying more in liability damages. The houseowners, in turn, will have either to invest in the acquisition of information or to consider their prospect of obtaining less compensation. Aware of his increased transaction cost or, alternatively, of his increased liability risk, C will attempt to charge more for his fences. Aware of their increased transaction costs or, alternatively, of their risk of receiving less in money damages, the houseowners will only be willing to pay less for C's fences. Consequently, transactions that could otherwise be

[19] By removing liability from C, this mechanism would induce those houseowners who are averse towards risk to insure their fences appropriately immediately after their construction.

[20] See Kaplow (n. 14 above) 330–1.

efficient would not be made.[21] Adjudicative accuracy would thus produce anomalous effects that sharply contrast with its strong intuitive appeal.

To sum up, accuracy *ex post* is an investment-dependent opportunity rather than a static good. In a regime that favours accuracy *ex post*, an individual who obtains more evidence to credibly support her case has a greater chance of prevailing at trial. This regime therefore fosters a secondary market for competitive adversarial investments in information. To obtain accuracy *ex post*, litigants must appropriately invest in the determination of facts (both before and during trial), and the level of their investments will depend on competition. This creates the secondary market, market for evidence and for associated litigation efforts.[22] This market will affect the individuals' conduct in the primary market, that is, in the market for goods, services, risks, and precautions. The secondary market may, indeed, have an adverse effect on the primary market. Thus, when prospective litigants are rationally unwilling to commit themselves to the required investments, inefficiencies are bound to occur. In such cases, each party will account for the possibility that he will be wrongfully defeated in the future trial because his opponent's investment in information and other litigation efforts outscored his. This prospect will foil transactions that are otherwise efficient and will chill many other socially beneficial activities, including those that are regulated by the law of torts. Accuracy *ex post* is, therefore, socially beneficial only when its attainment is relatively inexpensive; but when its attainment is inexpensive, it does not substantially differ from accuracy *ex ante*.[23] Therefore, the law should focus on accuracy *ex ante* rather than on accuracy *ex post*.

(b) The 'Winner Takes All' Principle and the Expected Damage Standard

From the perspective that focuses on the information-cost problem, the law creates a distortion by allowing plaintiffs to recover the entire damage, instead of its expected average value as determined under the *ex ante* probability of transgression. In contemplating a potentially damaging action, an economic actor compares her damage-avoidance costs with the expected, rather than actual, damage, that is, with the prospective damage, as reduced by the probability of its (rationally hoped for) non-occurrence. In the average case, this estimation would correspond to the average level of harm associated with the type of actions to which the contemplated action belongs. Basing the trial award system on the expected average level of harm would

[21] Theoretically, C and his clients may enter into a contractual arrangement that will replace conventional adjudication with the mechanism we suggested. However, asymmetric information, co-ordination problems, and high transaction costs would usually frustrate such arrangements.

[22] See Stein (n. 13 above) 1212–3.

[23] As already mentioned, individuals should, indeed, be encouraged to expand the informational base upon which they decide to act, but only if the expansion is relatively inexpensive.

thus tax the wrongdoers for their externalities in an efficient Pigouvian way. Under that system, damages to be paid by a wrongdoer would be equal to a tax that would have been imposed on him by the state had he paid in advance for his harmful externalities.[24] In reality, some wrongdoers inflict harm that is greater than the average; some inflict harm that falls below its average amount (including zero harm); and others inflict the average harm. For example, wrongdoer A may inflict damage that amounts to 10, and wrongdoers B and C may inflict damages that equal 20 and 30, respectively. For the sake of simplicity, let us assume that the *ex ante* probability of inflicting each damage is 0.5 and that none of the (then) potential wrongdoers can estimate in advance the magnitude of the future damage. Under that set-up, the total amount of the expected average damage equals 30. An advance externality tax imposed on A, B, and C would divide this damage equally, so that each of them would pay 10 (the expected average damage in each case would equal $0.5 \cdot 20 = 10$). None of them, therefore, should be forced to pay more than 10 in money damages. This compensation amount would be efficient because in the absence of case-specific information that could be available *ex ante*, A, B, and C must not be forced into avoiding the damage in their individual cases if the cost of avoiding it exceeds this amount.[25] Forcing them to do so would be manifestly inefficient. Although their individual victims would sustain damages in the amounts of 10, 20, and 30, respectively, those victims should seek redress elsewhere, especially since the compensation case made out by each of the victims is merely probable rather than certain. Ideally, a Pigouvian tax should be collected from every potential wrongdoer, so that the total amount of the tax would allow the state to fully compensate the victims (or to promote other socially useful policies).[26]

The underlying motivation of the 'winner takes all' principle is transparently clear: the $P > 0.5$ rule allegedly maximizes the number of correct verdicts; by contrast, any probabilistic recovery rule would yield zero correct decisions, which would frustrate the law's accuracy-maximizing objective. This objective, however, is misguided. An efficiency-oriented legal system should value adjudicative accuracy only when it is instrumental to efficiency and not for its own sake.[27]

In short, accuracy in the adjudicative assessment of a plaintiff's damage is beneficial only when it aligns with the *ex ante* assessment of the damage by a

[24] See generally W. J. Baumol, 'On Taxation and the Control of Externalities' (1972) 62 *American Economic Rev* 307 (delineating Pigou's tax criteria and identifying their operational limitations).

[25] In pollution cases, things would be different because the aggregated pollution level is a pivotal factor. The last pollution unit that takes the pollution above its tolerable level may, consequently, be treated as more harmful than the previous pollution units. Pollution and similar cases therefore deserve special treatment. See Posner (n. 8 above) 412.

[26] The 'winner takes all' principle may also create distortions in deterrence. See Chapter IV below.

[27] See generally Kaplow (n. 14 above).

rational economic actor. If such an actor is unable to cost-efficiently assess the actual damage that would result from her contemplated action, then she will base her action on the average damage. In such cases, spending resources on determining the plaintiff's actual damage will be wasteful. Such cases are far from exceptional: the specifics of the plaintiff's damage are typically unknown *ex ante* to his (then) prospective injurer.[28] The present level of investment in the adjudicative determination of plaintiffs' damages is, therefore, socially wasteful.[29] Under this theory, the law's formula for optimal awards should be P*d*. In that formula,

> *d* is the average, rather than actual, damage; and
> P is the *ex ante* probability of transgression.

(c) The P>0.5 Rule and the 'Winner Takes All' Principle as Justified by Drawbacks in Law-Enforcement

The P*d* approach would, indeed, be unimpeachable if there were no drawbacks to law-enforcement.[30] Unfortunately, law-enforcement does suffer from serious drawbacks, a factor that must, therefore, be taken into account in devising the policy for litigation awards. Ideally, violations of deterrence-driven entitlements, including those that the law labels 'private', should be prosecuted by the state. The state-prosecution mechanism, however, is manifestly inefficient for remedying torts and similar violations: the costs involved in searching for and prosecuting such violations are enormous. Thus, when a person externalizes risk, the risk is often invisible until it materializes into a tangible damage. The state cannot, therefore, exercise efficient control over impositions of bare risks.[31] The state is also unable to police many, if not most, damaging occurrences that take place among private individuals. To understand the extent of this problem, one should consider the costs that such policing would incur, given that individuals have no private incentives to report transgressions. The state-prosecution mechanism is, consequently, applied only in special regulatory areas, such as criminal law, that involve particularly harmful (and, therefore, regulated) activities. As a result of this enforcement constraint, tort and similar violations are prosecuted by self-interested individuals, upon whom the state has conferred a licence to sue.

This phenomenon explains the fundamental law-enforcement drawback: *the state has to privatize the licence to sue and to subsidize adjudication*, which is bound to generate inefficiencies. These inefficiencies spawn from the divergence between the private and the social incentives to use the adjudication

[28] See L. Kaplow, 'Accuracy in Adjudication', in P. Newman (ed.), *The New Palgrave Dictionary of Economics and the Law*, Vol. 1 (1998) 1, 4.
[29] Ibid.
[30] See Stein (n. 13 above).
[31] See Chapter IV below.

facility.[32] Owners of the privatized licence to sue should be expected to use it opportunistically: they should be expected to turn that licence into an instrument for advancing their private goals, irrespective of social consequences. The privatized licence to sue can be misused in two ways: it can be utilized both insufficiently and excessively.[33] The licence might be underused—thus failing to produce the desired social benefits—if adjudication is costly and accrues insufficient income to private entrepreneurs. Adjudication must therefore be partially subsidized and promise attractive awards to successful plaintiffs. But the licence to sue might also be overused: a privately advantageous lawsuit might incur excessive social costs that outweigh the adjudication's social benefits. Corrective measures that minimize the amount of both overusers and underusers of the licence to sue are, therefore, in order. As will now be demonstrated, the combination of the P>0.5 rule and the 'winner takes all' principle is one such measure.

What would happen with the overusers and the underusers of the licence to sue, if the ideal-world formula for optimal awards (P*d*) were adopted in our non-ideal litigation milieu as a replacement for the P>0.5 rule and the 'winner takes all' principle? The answer is obvious: both overusers and underusers of the licence to sue would increase in number. There would be more underusers because the awards awaiting successful plaintiffs under the ideal formula would be considerably less attractive than under the 'winner takes all' principle. Apart from that, it would usually be easier for a plaintiff (in contrast to a state agency) to prove his or her personal damage than to establish the average damage figure. Under the ideal formula, plaintiffs would, thus, also have to spend more on litigation, which would inevitably reduce the number of deserving plaintiffs. The deterrence objective of the law would consequently be frustrated.

The overuser community would also grow in number: since any meaningful probability that attaches to a lawsuit would suffice for recovery, more unmeritorious lawsuits would be brought and expensively processed through adjudication. The overuse problem would be further exacerbated by externalized adjudication expenses: the P*d* rule invites too many plaintiffs to eat away the adjudication subsidy as an almost free lunch. Overusers of the licence to sue would also fail to produce the deterrence benefits that the P*d* rule strives to attain. Since their only interest is to secure for themselves a profitable outcome from the venture, such plaintiffs would settle for any profit that *they*—not the deterrence programme—would consider agreeable. They would thus largely accept cheap settlement offers made by defendants and would let their lawsuits be bought off at nuisance value. Consequently, cheap settlements that leave wrongdoers underdeterred could be expected to mushroom.

[32] See S. Shavell, 'The Fundamental Divergence Between the Private and the Social Motive to Use the Legal System' (1997) 26 *J Legal Studies* 575.

[33] See Stein (n. 13 above).

Lawsuits, largely frivolous, initiated by the overusers would also generate an adverse selection impact or, alternatively, an additional adjudication cost externality. Aware of their lawsuits' frivolous nature and cognizant of the ensuing judicial mistrust of *all* lawsuits, the overusers would attempt to pool with the owners of good lawsuits. The latter would, consequently, have to consider an additional investment in litigation in order to differentiate their lawsuits from the bad ones. Because a lawsuit's expected return would already be pared down (for reasons given above), this additional expenditure would turn some good lawsuits into non-profitable ones, so that their holders would resultantly prefer not to initiate them in the first place. The 'market-for-lemons' scenario[34] is, perhaps, too morbid for the present context: intuitively, the additional differentiating investment that would have to be made by owners of good lawsuits does not appear to be large enough so as to bring the (once profitable) basic investment in the lawsuit up to a level that wipes out completely the expected returns. Good lawsuits therefore seem unlikely to be driven away from the courts. But under this more optimistic scenario, the additional lawsuit-differentiating expenses would still actually be incurred. Those expenses would be socially wasteful and should therefore be counted as a harmful externality.

The 'winner takes all' principle (as deriving from the $P>0.5$ rule) tackles these problems by branching off into two rules:

(1) the full-recovery rule, activated when $P>0.5$;
(2) the zero-recovery rule that applies when $P\leq0.5$.

The full-recovery rule would make litigation decidedly more attractive for potential underusers of the licence to sue. Under this rule, successful plaintiffs would recover more damages than justified by deterrence. They also would have to prove only their personal damages, which would usually be less expensive than establishing an impersonal average damage figure. This would increase the underusers' expected income from litigation substantially. The zero-recovery rule would make litigation considerably less attractive for potential overusers of the licence to sue. Under this rule, low-probability lawsuits would be driven away from the courts. Since the rule requires plaintiffs to establish their personal damages, personally undamaged plaintiffs would be driven away. Finally, by raising the stakes of the average litigation (in comparison with the ideal Pd approach), this rule would increase the investment in litigation on the part of both plaintiffs and defendants. Rather than make this increased investment, at least some unmeritorious plaintiffs might prefer not to file their lawsuits.[35]

[34] As famously set up by G. Akerlof, 'The Market for Lemons: Quality Uncertainty and the Market Mechanism' (1970) 84 *Quarterly J of Economics* 488.

[35] See Stein (n. 13 above) 1228–9.

Before praising the 'winner takes all' principle, however, we must still look at the other side of the coin. Under this principle, some transgressors (which we can label 'high-probability transgressors') are overdeterred, while other transgressors (which we can label 'low-probability transgressors') are underdeterred. The amount of overdeterrence (caused by the full-recovery rule) equals D–P*d*, with D representing the plaintiff's award. This amount may be further increased or decreased in light of the difference between the *ex ante* probability of transgression and its adjudicative *ex post* surrogate. The amount of underdeterrence (caused by the zero-recovery rule) equals P*d*. This is the price that the 'winner takes all' principle exacts.

Intuitively, this price is worth paying in dealing with unsystematic transgressions. If incurred sporadically, this price would hardly exceed the costs that the application of the Pigouvian P*d* rule would incur. But if the price were incurred systematically, as would occur in recurrent-transgression cases, then the opposite would be true.[36] The 'winner takes all' principle would defeat the deterrence objective of the law if a low-probability transgressor could repeat his or her conduct time and time again (theoretically, *ad infinitum*) without being penalized. The deterrence objective would also be defeated if a high-probability transgressor were to gain nothing from taking precautions that reduce the transgression's probability, but still keep it above the level of 0.5. In such settings, prominently exemplified by market-share liability in torts, a strong case can be made for substituting the 'winner takes all' principle with the P*d* rule. These special settings are examined in Chapters IV–VII. However, in usual cases, the P>0.5 rule would be optimal.

Thus far, we have demonstrated that the P>0.5 rule and the 'winner takes all' principle have a solid utilitarian justification. The misalignment between the information upon which judges base their verdicts (information *ex post*) and the information upon which prospective transgressors base their actions (information *ex ante*) still requires explanation. We will now demonstrate that the existing drawbacks in law-enforcement, which justify the P>0.5 rule and the 'winner takes all' principle, also justify the law's approach to the misalignment problem.[37]

Because in the sequence of events, litigation always comes after the litigated occurrence, full alignment between the two sets of information is either impossible or unaffordable. For that reason, the burden of proof doctrine develops a system under which the *ex post* probability of transgression, as determined at trial, functions as an inexpensive surrogate for the *ex ante* probability of transgression. Under that system, the plaintiff's entitlement functions as a tool for aligning the two probabilities. Similarly to other elements of his lawsuit—such as the transgression that the plaintiff attributes to

[36] See S. Levmore, 'Probabilistic Recoveries, Restitution, and Recurring Wrongs' (1990) 19 *J Legal Studies* 691.

[37] See Stein (n. 13 above) 1221–6.

the defendant and the damage originating from that transgression—the plaintiff must establish his entitlement by a preponderance of the evidence.

The probability of the plaintiff's entitlement aligns the *ex post* probability of transgression with the probability of transgression that existed *ex ante* in the following way. Legal entitlements almost uniformly feature the *visibility element*: under the definition of virtually any entitlement, information about its existence is reasonably available to potential transgressors. This element permeates the entire body of private law. It is embedded in the publicity requirements that attach to property rights,[38] in the mutual disclosure requirements that attach to contractual entitlements,[39] and in the duty of care requirement that limits liability in torts.[40] Therefore, in establishing the probability of his or her entitlement as more probable than not, the plaintiff would also be establishing that the entitlement was reasonably ascertainable at the time and in the circumstances of its breach. When the probability of the defendant's transgression is similarly established, the plaintiff's combined proof would imply—on a balance of probabilities—that the entitlement was breached in circumstances that made it reasonably ascertainable *ex ante*. Specifically, the plaintiff's proof would entail that the defendant knew, or should have known, about the plaintiff's entitlement at the time that he violated it. Because the defendant's action falls into the violation category, the defendant—who knew (or should have known) about the violated entitlement—was also aware (or should have been aware) of the action's transgressing potential.

The key question, therefore, is whether the entitlement—as defined by the controlling substantive law—extends to cases in which the *ex ante* probability of transgression amounts to what it is in the case at hand. If the answer is negative, then the entitlement has not been established and the defendant prevails.[41] If the answer is positive, then the entitlement's probability acquires a pre-emptive status. Because the *ex ante* probability of transgression does not exonerate the transgressor under the entitlement's conditions, this

[38] See, e.g., J. S. Johnston, 'Legal Formalities' in *The New Palgrave Dictionary of Economics and the Law*, Vol. 2 (n. 28 above) 524–30.

[39] See, e.g., A. W. Katz, 'Contract Formation and Interpretation' in *The New Palgrave Dictionary of Economics and the Law*, Vol. 1 (n. 28 above) 425, 429–30.

[40] Strict liability is not really an exception to this observation, as there are virtually no cases where a reasonably unascertainable entitlement has received a strict liability protection. Strict liability is generally imposed in connection with unusual and abnormal dangers over which potential wrongdoers exercise control. See Keeton (n. 16 above) 537, 545–59. The resulting entitlements are accordingly ascertainable by potential wrongdoers. Duties of care that judges impose by applying the negligence standard are not unexceptionably visible *ex ante*. The evidence doctrine, however, should not be held responsible for such deviations.

[41] Under the negligence doctrine, for example, if the *ex ante* probability of transgression is low, the judges may hold the defendant not negligent. See Keeton (n. 16 above) 170, 185 (noting that negligence standards require individuals to seek information prior to acting in a potentially hazardous way; but 'the actor's conduct must be judged in light of the possibilities apparent to him at the time').

probability becomes immaterial. The entitlement's probability will thus override the *ex ante* probability of transgression as an incentive for potential transgressors. Aware of the entitlement's nature and probability, a potential transgressor must introduce an appropriate adjustment into the *ex ante* probability of transgression. This adjustment substitutes any initial level of the *ex ante* probability of transgression with the level of the entitlement's probability. This reasoning aligns the two sets of information—the one that judges use *ex post* and the one that existed *ex ante*—with the maximal feasibility that can be attained without incurring exorbitant adjudication costs.

Note that under the existing doctrine, in determining the ultimate probability of the plaintiff's case, judges must not multiply the probability of the alleged transgression by the probability of the entitlement.[42] This seems to violate one of the basic precepts of probability calculus: the multiplication rule for conjunctive probabilities. This, however, is only ostensibly so, because the only function of the entitlement's probability is to align the *ex post* probability of the alleged transgression with the probability of transgression that existed *ex ante*. Under this framework, the entitlement's probability functions as a misalignment-corrector for the *ex post* probability of transgression, not as its conjunctive companion. This special function separates the two probabilities and accordingly removes the probability of the litigated entitlement from the multiplication formula. Indeed, this removal is justified by the law's deterrence policy. In accordance with that policy, the law is primarily interested in the *ex ante* probability of transgression; and because this probability cannot be determined at trial at an affordable cost, the law substitutes it with a suitable surrogate.[43] The P>0.5 rule, as traditionally applied, thus becomes fully justified by utility.

3. The 'Winner Takes All' Principle and Punitive Damages

The 'winner takes all' principle has a significant policy implication for punitive damages in torts. From the deterrence perspective, punitive damages are an important policy instrument: they can be utilized as an award-correcting tool by a legal system that suffers from drawbacks in law-enforcement. Drawbacks in law-enforcement dilute deterrence. This dilution can be counteracted through imposition of punitive damages that enhance deterrence and, thus, raise its level back to the optimal. Law-enforcement drawbacks would, therefore, be offset by punitive damages. This possibility is economically attractive because elimination of law-enforcement drawbacks would

42 Nor should they multiply any of those probabilities by that of the plaintiff's damage. As already explained, plaintiffs' awards have a special function in law. This function separates the probability of the plaintiff's damage by making it non-conjunctive. Consequently, the damage element is excluded from the multiplication formula for conjunctive probabilities.

43 See Stein (n. 13 above) 1222–4.

usually be expensive. In contrast, fixing of punitive damages requires only an informed decision to change the law, so it would be relatively cheap.

In making such decisions, legislators and judges must account for the punitive trait of the 'winner takes all' principle. By forcing defendants to pay increased compensation in order to increase the number of socially beneficial lawsuits and thereby counteract the potential underenforcement of the law, the 'winner takes all' principle performs an essentially punitive function. Under this principle, the defendant's overpayment equals (1–P)D, when P, once again, is the probability of the plaintiff's case and D is the relevant damage. This overpayment must be treated as a punitive ingredient of trial awards because it intensifies general deterrence at the expense of the individual defendant. If so, then (1–P)D is the sum by which punitive damages must be reduced whenever they are explicitly imposed.

Punitive damages must therefore be calculated in the following way.[44] In a trial for damage D, let q denote the defendant's *ex ante* probability of being subjected to law-enforcement. The defendant's *ex ante* probability of escaping law-enforcement would thus equal 1–q. The odds of escape versus enforcement ('the enforcement odds') would, accordingly, be (1–q)/q. The total damage award, including both actual and punitive damages, would amount to 1/q·D=D/q (1/q functions here as an award multiplier that compensates for the liability-escaping chances, thus bringing the award to the optimal level of deterrence). The award's punitive component would consequently equal (D/q)–D, that is, [(1–q)/q]·D (the actual damage multiplied by the enforcement odds). As already noted, the punitive ingredient of the full-recovery rule is (1–P)·D, when P denotes the probability of the defendant's transgression. The optimal punitive award should, therefore, amount to D·[(1–q)/q)–(1–P)] (the actual damage multiplied by the difference between the enforcement odds and the probability of non-transgression).[45]

4. Burden of Proof and Affirmative Defences

Under the conventional proof doctrine, each party is required to prove her or his own case. Consequently, the burden of persuasion is systematically shifted from one party to her or his opponent. This burden is borne by the plaintiff only in regard to her primary allegations against the defendant, such as breach of contract or commission of a tort. Affirmative defences, such as mistake, misrepresentation, duress, and frustration in contracts, as

[44] As developed by A. M. Polinsky and S. Shavell, 'Punitive Damages: An Economic Analysis' (1998) 111 *Harvard L Rev* 870. See also A. M. Polinsky and S. Shavell, 'Punitive Damages', in *The New Palgrave Dictionary of Economics and the Law*, Vol. 3 (n. 28 above) 192, 193–4.

[45] See Stein (n. 13 above) 1230–1.

well as contributory fault and non-mitigation of the damage in torts, need to be established by the defendant on the balance of probabilities.[46] The plaintiff, in other words, is required to prove that the defendant failed to comply with the relevant legal standard. The defendant who expands the trial beyond this issue by bringing forth an excuse or by alleging that the plaintiff has not complied with some other pertinent legal standard must preponderantly prove any such defence.

The doctrinal distinction between a 'cause of action' and a 'defence' derives from the substantive law. At times, this distinction appears to be merely semantic. For example, in a lawsuit brought for a breach of contract, an allegation that the contract was frustrated is functionally similar to the defendant's denial of its breach. Yet, the defence of frustration needs to be established by the defendant, while a breach of contract is a cause of action that the plaintiff must prove. In a tort lawsuit, an allegation of contributory fault is functionally similar to the defendant's denial of causation between his negligence and the relevant fraction of the litigated damage. Yet, contributory fault attributed to the plaintiff needs to be preponderantly proved by the defendant, while the causation issue must be proved by the plaintiff because it belongs to the cause of action. Arguably, this problem undercuts the explanatory value of the economic rationale underlying the $P>0.5$ rule.[47] Under this rationale, the plaintiff ought to be denied recovery whenever the overall probability of his case does not exceed 0.5.

This obstacle is not insurmountable. The $P>0.5$ rule directs judges to accept the competing account of events whose probability exceeds 0.5. This is a general precept that extends to the determination of both the cause of action and any defensive issue. As indicated above, this precept is the essence of the standard of proof doctrine. This general doctrine must be distinguished from the rules allocating the burden of persuasion which apply only in balanced cases, where the competing accounts of events are equally probable. Due to their limited scope of application, the burden of persuasion rules must be understood and applied as residual. These rules encompass two basic precepts. Under one of them, when the competing factual accounts relate to the cause of action and are equally probable, the judge must hold the defendant not liable. Under the second precept, when the plaintiff's cause-of-action scenario is more probable than not, while the competing accounts of events that cover a defensive issue are equally probable, the defendant must be held liable. In American evidence law, this precept is known as the 'affirmative defence' doctrine,[48] and we will use this convenient label throughout our discussion.

[46] See I. H. Dennis, *The Law of Evidence* (1999) 358–60.

[47] As explained below, the fairness-based justification of the doctrine does not entail this problem.

[48] See J. W. Strong et al., *McCormick on Evidence* (5th edn., 1999) 509–11, 530–2. 'Affirmative defence' is a term that usually refers to defences recognized in criminal law. Ibid.

In torts, the economic logic of the affirmative defence doctrine can easily be understood. Affirmative defences that apply in torts, such as contributory fault, hold the plaintiff responsible for the litigated damage or for a fraction of that damage. In this way, they absolve the defendant from liability that would otherwise be imposed. An affirmative defence issue can arise only when the facts under which the defendant must be held liable in torts are more probable than not. There is therefore—*ex hypothesi*—an economically sufficient reason for holding the defendant liable for the litigated damage; and since the defendant failed to neutralize that reason, the court should, indeed, hold him or her liable. Let it be assumed, for example, that a person's cheapest cost-avoider position is the controlling reason for holding that person liable in torts. This principle holds that liability in torts, as determined by the controlling substantive law, must be imposed on the person (the defendant, the plaintiff, or both) who could have prevented the litigated damage at the lowest possible cost. Other economic criteria are, of course, also possible, but this would not change our analysis. Under any affirmative defence scenario, the defendant would, therefore, be the cheapest cost-avoider who seeks to avoid liability by arguing that there are special circumstances that shift the cheapest cost-avoider status to the plaintiff. If these special circumstances are merely as probable as not, while the facts identifying the defendant as the cheapest cost-avoider are more probable than not, the defendant must then be the cheapest cost-avoider. The case, therefore, must not be decided in the defendant's favour, as in a usual balanced case not involving an affirmative defence.[49] This outcome is dictated by the $P>0.5$ rule and its economic rationale.

C. BURDEN OF PROOF AND FAIRNESS

We now turn to explaining the burden of proof doctrine from the fairness perspective. This perspective has many facets, and equality and corrective justice are only two of them. Our discussion will nevertheless be confined to these two facets of fairness. This limitation is imposed not just for the sake of brevity. Equality and corrective justice both lie at the core of the notion of fairness. They also combine into an influential non-utilitarian theory of tort liability, which we apply throughout the book. Most importantly, these two facets of fairness provide the most coherent non-utilitarian justification for the burden of proof doctrine.

In the present context, the principle of equality requires that risk of error be allocated equally between the plaintiff and the defendant. This specific

[49] Furnishing the same economic justification for the affirmative defence doctrine as applied in contract litigation would be more difficult. This issue, however, falls outside of this book's agenda.

requirement derives from a more basic equality precept: when the state acts through its courts as an arbiter of civil disputes and thus forces its dispute-resolving decisions upon citizens, it must treat the plaintiff's and the defendant's interests with equal concern and respect.[50] Losses undeservedly sustained by the plaintiff and by the defendant must, therefore, be treated as equally regrettable. Consequently, risk of error in civil litigation should be allocated equally between the parties: it should be allocated in a way that does not favour one party over the other.[51]

The corrective justice principles lend support to a presumptive rule in favour of the status quo. Under that rule, the justice machinery forcibly intruding into individual affairs must be activated only as a means for reinstating the status quo; and this must be done only when there is sufficient evidence pointing to the fact that the status quo has been wrongfully interrupted. Underlying this rule is a self-explanatory precept: reasons for activating the justice machinery must be stronger than the reasons for keeping it dormant. When the relevant reasons are evidential, reasons for activating the justice machinery must be evidentially stronger than the reasons for not activating it.[52] The doctrinal requirement that the plaintiff must prove his case by a preponderance of the evidence can be explained as deriving from this precept.

The ideal implementation of the equality principle would require that each party be awarded the relative value of his or her case. A plaintiff, therefore, would recover from the defendant a sum of money equalling PD, when P represents the probability of the plaintiff's allegations and D represents the value of the litigated good. Accordingly, the sum amounting to (1–P)D would go to the defendant. Under this approach, pursuit of equality in the allocation of the risk of error would acquire independent significance. Equality would be pursued for its own sake, regardless of the demands set by the substantive law. This approach breaks away from the notion of adjectivity that lies at the heart of the burden of proof doctrine and subordinates the doctrine, together with other procedural and evidentiary arrangements, to the substantive law and its underlying objectives. This approach would thus frustrate the primary purpose of the law of evidence and procedure: the implementation of the substantive law.[53] In virtually every legal system, the substantive law structures

[50] See R. Dworkin, *Taking Rights Seriously* (1977) chs. 3, 4; R. Dworkin, *Law's Empire* (1986) chs. 6, 7.

[51] See Stein (n. 1 above) 333–42; J. Brook, 'Inevitable Errors: The Preponderance of the Evidence Standard in Civil Litigation' (1982) 18 *Tulsa LJ* 79, 85; R. J. Allen, 'Burdens of Proof, Uncertainty and Ambiguity in Modern Legal Discourse' (1994) 17 *Harvard J L & Public Policy* 627, 634; D. Hamer, 'The Civil Standard of Proof Uncertainty: Probability, Belief and Justice' (1994) 16 *Sydney L Rev* 506.

[52] See A. Porat and A. Stein, *Liability for Uncertainty: Making Evidential Damage Actionable* (1997) 18 Cardozo L. Rev 1891, 1918–25, and sources cited therein.

[53] This instrumentalist conception is, of course, closely associated with Bentham. See G. Postema, 'The Principle of Utility and the Law of Procedure: Bentham's Theory of

judicial decisions by prescribing a framework of strictly dichotomous legal categories, such as 'contract/no-contract', 'tort/no-tort', 'will/no-will'; and so forth.[54] Any such law requires judges to adjudicate cases in an all-or-nothing fashion. In a breach-of-contract lawsuit, for example, a judge ought to determine whether or not a contract was made; whether or not it was breached; whether or not it was frustrated; whether or not its conditions are illegal; and so forth. More nuanced doctrines—such as those that apportion liability for damage by accounting for the parties' comparative fault—operate in a similar way. For example, in applying the comparative fault doctrine, a judge has to determine whether or not the plaintiff was at fault, i.e., whether or not the plaintiff negligently contributed to the occurrence of the litigated damage or negligently failed to mitigate it. Although this and affiliated doctrines allow apportionment of liability for damage, the fault activating these doctrines always has to be determined in an all-or-nothing fashion. Judges, for instance, are not allowed to hold a plaintiff responsible for 40 per cent of the litigated damage upon finding a 0.4 probability that the damage was self-inflicted. If there is a 0.6 probability that the damage was caused by the defendant, the defendant should be held liable for the entire damage.

Indeed, corrective justice is indivisible in principle. This dogmatic principle cannot be upset by the mere presence of uncertainty in fact-finding. If there are preponderantly strong reasons for finding that the status quo was wrongfully disturbed by the defendant, the defendant must be forced to reinstate the status quo. If the defendant inflicted damage on the plaintiff, he or she must then be forced to make good the whole damage rather than its probabilistic fraction. If the reasons for holding that the status quo was wrongfully disturbed by the defendant are not preponderantly strong, the justice machinery must be left dormant. It should not be activated by forcing the defendant to rectify a fraction of the litigated damage that equals the probability of the allegations brought by the plaintiff. Because this probability is not higher than the probability favouring the defendant's case, the defendant must prevail. This general approach is justified by the need to maintain stability of legal entitlements. Corrective justice cannot be maintained without this stability. If legal entitlements were to become fractional, so that each entitlement would be contingent upon the probability of its underlying facts, the key components of the corrective justice mechanism—that of status quo and those of right and wrongfulness—would be eroded beyond repair. The status quo baseline, necessary for application of the corrective justice mechanism,

Adjudication' (1977) 11 *Georgia L Rev* 1393. But see R. Summers, 'Evaluating and Improving Legal Process—A Plea for "Process Values"' (1974) 60 *Cornell L Rev* 1; and M. D. Bayles, 'Principles for Legal Procedure' (1986) 5 *Law & Philosophy* 33 (ascribing intrinsic value to certain procedural arrangements).

[54] Dworkin termed such categories 'dispositive concepts', because the law requires judges to dispose cases only through these categories. R. Dworkin, *A Matter of Principle* (1986), ch. 5.

would lose its stability. The concept of wrongfulness, along with the very notion of right, would disappear altogether.[55] The resulting indeterminacy would create a chaotic legal world that would have no indisputably right objects for corrective decisions. In that world, corrective justice would simply make no sense.

Under the framework of equality and corrective justice, risk of error attendant upon the determination of factual issues that pertain to a single legal category cannot, therefore, be equitably divided between the parties. If the equality principle were unrelated to the substantive law, it could prescribe equitable sharing of this risk by allowing a plaintiff to recover from the defendant in proportion to the probability of the plaintiff's case. However, as part of the law of evidence and procedure, which combine into an inherently adjective mechanism aimed at implementing the substantive law, the equality principle cannot acquire such autonomy. It therefore must be applied differently. Unauthorized to divide the risk of error with regard to an indivisible legal category, it is bound to place the entire risk upon one of the parties. Under this constraint, the plaintiff and the defendant will be treated as equals in the sense that neither will be accorded preference over the other in factual findings unless his (or her) case is supported by better reasons. A party whose factual allegations are supported by weaker reasons will, consequently, bear the risk of error. Hence, a party will prevail in the entire case when his (or her) allegations are more probable than not.

This allocation of the risk of error still does not provide a tie-breaking rule for balanced cases. A possible rule for such cases would be a strict $P > 0.5$ rule that would require a plaintiff to prove *the entire case* by a preponderance of the evidence. If the plaintiff fails to discharge this burden, he or she will not be allowed to recover from the defendant. As mentioned above, this rule would certainly be desirable from a utilitarian perspective. It would discourage unmeritorious lawsuits and, thus, save litigation costs. It would reduce the number of verdicts that require enforcement, thereby saving enforcement costs. It also would acknowledge that for the average person, 'taking' is more harmful than 'not giving' because the bottom pound is of greater value to a person than the top pound. This saving of auxiliary costs arguably should be opted for when the probabilities are equal. For such cases, the equality principle prescribes indifference in regard to the primary cost of error, irrespective of whether this cost is to be sustained by the plaintiff or by the defendant. In view of this indifference, a decision rule saving auxiliary costs associated with litigation should be welcomed.

This *prima facie* appealing argument is flawed in one important aspect. From the equality perspective, a saving of auxiliary costs should be opted for not when the probabilities are equal, but when *everything* is equal. In the

[55] Cf. G. P. Fletcher, 'The Right and the Reasonable' (1985) 98 *Harvard L Rev* 949.

present case, the probabilities are equal, but everything else is not. Because the strict P>0.5 rule systematically favours defendants over plaintiffs in connection with any given issue that arises in litigation, it violates the equality principle. The equality principle therefore cannot embrace this rule. Because it cannot embrace this rule, the equality principle allocates risk of error *by dividing the discrete legal categories*, which pertain to specified classes of cases, between plaintiffs and defendants. As a result of this division, facts relevant to a legal category that is to the benefit of plaintiffs have to be established by the plaintiff as more probable than not. Facts pertaining to a category that benefits defendants (the 'affirmative defence' category) have to be established by the defendant at the same level of probability. Consequently, each litigant is exposed to the risk of error in relation to *his or her own allegations*, that is, only in relation to the facts making out his or her case under the controlling substantive law. For example, in a typical tort lawsuit, the plaintiff would have to establish, on a balance of probabilities, that his or her damage was negligently inflicted by the defendant; the defendant, in turn, would have to preponderantly establish contributory fault, should he or she raise this defence in order to absolve himself or herself from tort liability. Risk of error would thus be allocated between the parties in a roughly equal fashion.

According to Dale Nance, the existing burden of proof doctrine should be explained by another principle associated with fairness, namely, by the 'principle of civility', which presumes general compliance with the standards laid down by the law. A person who attributes non-compliance to her or his fellow has, therefore, to prove this allegation by a preponderance of the evidence.[56] This principled explanation of the burden-allocating framework is, indeed, appealing. As Nance rightly observes, a number of alternative explanations of this framework—which allude to the structure of pleadings, to unspecified policy considerations, or to the fact that affirmative defences are largely disfavoured[57]—should all be rejected as question-begging.[58] Equality and corrective justice are, therefore, the only competitors of the civility principle.

Nance's analysis, however, does not explicitly accommodate 'excuses' that function as defences in both civil and criminal law. When, for example, mistake is brought forth as a ground for escaping contractual liability, a person relying upon this defence does not invoke any civility-related imputation against her or his opponent. At the same time, this person cannot seriously claim that to enter into a contract upon unilateral (and purely subjective) mistake and subsequently to disavow any contractual responsibility is a conduct that squarely aligns with civility. This conduct falls below the general standard, and yet, as a matter of legal concession to human frailty, a person

[56] See D. A. Nance, 'Civility and the Burden of Proof' (1994) 17 *Harvard J L & Public Policy* 647.

[57] See, e.g., *McCormick* (n. 48 above) 510.

[58] See Nance (n. 56 above) 661–72.

responsible for it can, nevertheless, be excused. Any such excuse therefore needs to be proved by its proponent.[59] The civility principle can and should accommodate this requirement by removing its presumption from litigants relying upon excuses.

Application of this principle would, however, still be problematic. As widely acknowledged, strength of presumptions admits different degrees.[60] The civility principle certainly gives rise to its presumption, but this is not yet a justification for this presumption's strength. There appear to be no compelling reasons for applying this presumption when the probability of transgression is as high as 0.5 (that is, in the only case where the burden of persuasion comes into play). Founded upon good reasons for shifting the burden of producing evidence alone, the civility principle can, therefore, hardly justify its allocation of the risk of non-persuasion in cases where the evidence is balanced. Relatedly, when we know that the litigated damage did occur, and that either the plaintiff or the defendant is responsible for its occurrence, application of this principle might become arbitrary. By deciding that the plaintiff is not responsible, we uphold the civility presumption in relation to her or him, but hardly in relation to the defendant.

These difficulties are, admittedly, not fatal to the civility principle. They can be overcome by invoking the familiar line-drawing explanation. Based upon the premise that in practical matters a line must be drawn at some arbitrarily chosen point, this explanation would exempt the civility principle from justifying its perimeters. However, even if this explanation were to be accepted, lines drawn by the principle in order to fit into the existing burden-allocating framework would make this principle less attractive. These lines would cross a number of the most pivotal points of disagreement. Our explanation of the controlling burden of proof doctrine, as founded upon equality and corrective justice, does not suffer from such predicaments. This explanation must therefore be regarded as preferable amongst the fairness-based explanations of the doctrine.

D. SPECIAL CASES

The foregoing discussion has demonstrated the advantages of the burden of proof doctrine. This doctrine, however, also has its limitations: its application to particular categories of cases might frustrate both the deterrence and the corrective justice objectives of the law of torts. Take, for example, a scenario that, sadly, is typical of many medical malpractice lawsuits. Hospital patient P required urgent surgery, which would have given him a 60 per cent chance

[59] See Stein (n. 1 above) 337.

[60] For an illuminating discussion of this feature see E. Ullmann-Margalit, 'On Presumption' (1983) 80 *J Philosophy* 143.

of recovery. The doctors negligently delayed the surgery. The delayed surgery was performed impeccably, but it promised P only a 40 per cent chance of recovery. Ultimately, P did not recover, and he now attributes his terminal illness to his doctors' malpractice.[61] It is apparent, however, that P cannot establish the causation between the doctors' malpractice and his damage. A simple statistical analysis, which provides the strongest argument in support of P's lawsuit, reveals that the probability of the required causation equals here 0.33.[62] Under the general standard of proof doctrine, P's lawsuit must therefore be dismissed.

Dismissal of this and similar lawsuits, however, would be deeply problematic from both deterrence and corrective justice perspectives. As demonstrated above, this decisional strategy would minimize the *total* number of erroneous verdicts. At the same time, it would *totally* exempt the defendant and similarly situated actors from taking precautions. These actors would thus be able to externalize the risk associated with their actions. Specifically, these actors would be able to benefit from the indeterminate causation problem, by virtue of which plaintiff P was denied recovery. Aware of that problem—and cognizant of their consequent ability to find refuge in the shadows of uncertainty—these actors would feel free to add their negligence to the list of potentially damaging causes, thus exposing their patients to an increased risk of injury. This is exactly what happened in the case of patient P. Together with similarly situated defendants, P's doctors should therefore be blamed not only for their negligent activities that externalized the risk. They should also be blamed for the evidential damage that they negligently inflicted on P. Due to the negligence committed by such defendants, plaintiffs become unable to attribute their respective damages to the true causes of those damages. Such defendants, in other words, evidentially incapacitate their plaintiffs, and the law of torts should discourage such damaging behaviour. Application of the $P>0.5$ rule in such cases would therefore end up in both

61 These facts are adapted from the landmark House of Lords decision, *Hotson v East Berkshire Area Health Authority* [1987] 2 All ER 909 (HL) (holding that a patient's lost chances to recover do not constitute a damage actionable in torts). The Canadian Supreme Court delivered a similar holding in *Lawson v Laferriere*, 78 DLR 4th 609 (1991). For an American example, see *Herskovits v Group Health Cooperative of Puget Sound*, 664 P 2d 474 (1983) (holding that when medical malpractice reduces a patient's chances to recover, his lost chances constitute actionable damage). For an Israeli example, see *The General Trade Union Health Care Scheme v Fatach*, 42(3) Piskey Din 312 (1984) (Hebrew) (a patient's lost chances to recover are actionable in torts). For a full discussion of tort liability for lost chances, see Chapter IV below.

62 Under that argument, the doctors' negligence transferred P from one group of patients (group A) to another (group B). In group A, 60 out of 100 similarly situated patients recover from their illness. In group B, only 40 patients recover, while 60 do not. Since P did not recover, he belongs to the sub-group of 60 patients in group B. Amongst these 60 patients, 40 were initially doomed not to recover, while the remaining 20 were prevented from recovering due to their doctors' malpractice. The probability that P would turn out to be one of these 20 patients thus equals 20/60, that is, 0.33.

private and social losses. As explained in Chapters VI and VII, this would result in diluted deterrence and truncated corrective justice.

This morbid scenario justifies the adoption of a more refined approach to fact-determination in tort cases. In cases where application of the P>0.5 rule would unfold this scenario, other rules of decision would be more suitable. The subsequent chapters of this book identify those cases and divide them into paradigmatic categories. In cases falling under some of those special categories, substitution of the P>0.5 rule with a different decisional strategy would be justified on the grounds of deterrence. In other categories of cases, the same strategy would be justified by corrective justice. In most cases that fall under those categories, deviation from the P>0.5 rule would be justified by both deterrence and corrective justice. In such special cases, uncompromising application of the P>0.5 rule would both frustrate the compensatory objective of the law of torts and dilute the incentives that induce socially optimal behaviour. Thus, in the example involving patient P, denying remedy to the plaintiff would not merely weaken the relevant economic incentives; it also would leave P uncompensated for his evidential damage[63] and, arguably, for the risk to which he was negligently exposed by the defendants.[64]

These special cases are far from being exceptional. They are numerous, recurrent, and combine into several distinct categories, as identified in Chapter II. The evidence doctrine, as applied in tort litigation, must therefore continually seek an adequate trade-off between the objectives promoted by the P>0.5 rule and the substantive objectives of the law of torts (such as deterrence and corrective justice). Furthermore, a similar fusion of evidence and tort law policies is necessary for devising the internal criteria for fact-finding that will enable judges to answer the question 'What makes one factual scenario better than another?'. This is the issue to which we now turn.

E. TWO INTERPRETATIONS OF THE CIVIL STANDARD OF PROOF

1. The Standard of Proof and Criteria for Fact-Finding

As stated at the outset, understanding the civil standard of proof also depends on the question 'What makes one factual scenario comparatively better than another?'. At the case-specific level, the answer to this question is obvious: probative strength of a factual scenario depends on the strength of the evidence that supports it. However, evidential strength (also labelled as 'weight' or 'probative value' of the evidence) is an intrinsically ambiguous notion. The

[63] This issue is discussed below in Chapters VI and VII.
[64] This issue is examined below in Chapter IV.

meaning of that notion depends on the general criteria chosen for evaluating evidential strength.[65]

These criteria are unclear: the requirements set by the civil standard of proof are open to two conflicting interpretations, both equally plausible and appealing. Under the one interpretation, the standard refers to a frequentist type of probability. This probability may be calculated through enumeration of instances both favourable and unfavourable to the examined propositions, which, subsequently, is combined into a final probability assessment. The latter is generated mathematically by multiplying the probabilities of the propositions necessary for the verdict.[66] The required probability may be assessed experientially by the fact-finder, in which case it will also be reflective of frequencies, albeit unenumerated. These frequencies (identified as 'personalist' or 'subjectivist') should be reducible, in principle, to mathematical data that obey the ordinary rules of probabilistic calculus. Deviation from this condition would imply that the reasoning followed by the fact-finder was tainted by illogicality.[67] According to this interpretation of the civil proof standard, 'more probable than not' means that the chance that the finding fits the actual event is greater than the chance that the finding is wrong. Exhibiting calculus of chances, the logic embedded in this form of reasoning is *aleatory* in character.[68]

According to the second interpretation, the civil standard of proof refers to the degree of evidential support that underlies an examined proposition. More specifically, this interpretation refers to the extent to which facts pertaining to an examined proposition are specified in the evidence.[69] Measuring the ground covered by the evidence, this approach clearly favours case-specific (or 'individualized') proof over naked statistics. Under this approach, the strength of the evidential support for factual propositions is examined comparatively. It is determined by the gap between the existing and the ideal stock of evidence, with the latter representing the highest, albeit unreachable, level of evidential support. The evidential support gains strength as the gap narrows, and vice versa. Consequently, if there is more substantial evidence in support of a factual proposition than for its negation, then the proposition will be held to be more probable than not. Instead of assessing the favourable and the unfavourable odds under conditions of ignorance, this approach evaluates the scope of the existing body of knowledge. It does so by focusing upon the inductive justification extended by this knowledge to the inferences

[65] See A. Stein, 'An Essay on Uncertainty and Fact-Finding in Civil Litigation, with Special Reference to Contract Cases' (1998) 48 *U Toronto LJ* 299, 304–15.

[66] See B. Robertson and G. A. Vignaux, 'Probability—The Logic of the Law' (1993) 13 *OJLS* 457.

[67] Ibid.

[68] See L. J. Cohen, *An Introduction to the Philosophy of Induction and Probability* (1989) 13–27; ch. IV.

[69] Ibid. 4–13, ch. V.

that connect the evidence with the ultimate *probanda*. For this reason, this approach has been labelled 'inductivist'.

Under the aleatory framework of reasoning, the probability that event A either occurred or did not occur amounts to 1, when 1 stands for certainty and 0 for impossibility. Consequently, P(A)=1–P(not-A), which is known as the complementational principle for negation.[70] Under the inductivist framework of reasoning, meagre evidential support for proposition A does not entail, *ipso facto*, massive support for not-A, and vice versa. Evidential support is an empirical matter, also describable as a positive knowledge-factor. It derives from what the fact-finders actually have, not from what they do not have. Under the aleatory framework, the chances that A and another proposition (B) occurred jointly are not as good as the chances that only A (or B) occurred. Indeed, succeeding in a simple one-event gamble (with regard to A only) is much easier than succeeding in a compound gamble (with regard to both A and B). Consequently, P(A&B)=P(A)×P(B),[71] which is known as the multiplicational principle for conjunction.[72] Under the inductivist framework of reasoning, evidential support for proposition A&B is equal either to the support for A or for B, whichever is weaker.[73] Assessment of the known and gambling on the unknown are two logically distinct activities. Both are rational, but each is governed by its own, different type of logic.

Aleatory probabilities can be derived from any knowledge, however thin it may be. If we were to toss a coin without knowing whether or not the coin is rigged, it would be warranted for us to place 1:1 odds on either heads or tails. If later we were to discover that the coin is fair, we could justifiably make an identical bet. Under the aleatory framework, our first assessment of the odds is no less warranted than our second: if we happen not to know something, it is warranted for us to assume that the unknown possibilities, some favourable and some unfavourable to our hypothesis, are equally probable.[74] This assumption is known as the 'principle of indifference'.[75] This principle eliminates informational open-endedness that frustrates any attempt at determining probability. The principle of indifference replaces this open-endedness with informational closure, easily governed by mathematical logic. Consequently, probability is calculated on the assumption that facts relevant to the calculation are fully specified by the existing evidence. Artificial as it may sound, this assumption may be justified in the long run. The unknown possibilities, some favourable and

[70] Ibid. 17–18.

[71] To avoid an unnecessary complication, it is assumed that A and B are two mutually independent propositions. If no such independence is assumed, then P(A&B)=P(A)×P(B|A), which would have no impact on our discussion.

[72] Cohen (n. 68 above) 18–19.

[73] Once again, we assume that A and B are mutually independent and, thus, cannot corroborate one another.

[74] See Cohen (n. 68 above) 43–7; John M. Keynes, *A Treatise on Probability* (1921) 44.

[75] It also has been labelled 'the principle of insufficient reason'. See Keynes (n. 74 above).

some unfavourable to the examined hypothesis, can be expected to cancel each other out as the gambling proceeds. We can, therefore, exercise control over the ratio of right versus wrong decisions by ignoring these possibilities.

In contrast, the inductivist framework is based on the 'principle of difference'. Within this framework, a proposition supported by a high amount of evidence qualitatively differs from a proposition that rests on a slimmer evidential base. Fact-finders should treat the former proposition as more probable than the latter. This mode of assessing probabilities will apply even when an aleatory probability, constructed on a slim evidential base, is relatively high. In the coin example, if it were not known whether or not the coin is rigged, it would be inductively unwarranted to say that heads will come up in 50 per cent of the tosses (as indicated by placing 1:1 odds on either heads or tails). This prediction would have a far greater cogency if the coin were known to be fair. Within this framework, knowledge is not allowed to be procreated out of ignorance. If we were to have no reason for holding the coin either fair or biased, there would be no justification for us to ascribe equal incidence to its fairness and bias. Consequently, the extent to which facts pertaining to the decision are specified by the evidence becomes the key factor that needs to be examined by fact-finders.

Aleatory probability assessments may be accompanied by judgments regarding their resiliency. This resiliency will be contingent upon the survival of a given assessment in the event of change in its underlying informational base, which would be effected by the flow of new evidence. Because evidence is always lacking, the potential for the arrival of new evidence makes any probability assessment open to revision. An assessment's susceptibility to such revision will determine its resiliency and corresponding strength. It is obvious that some probability assessments are less open to revision than others, and there is a clear need to account for this factor. The greater the ability of an assessment to withstand potential changes in its informational base, the more resilient and, correspondingly, more reliable a probability assessment it is. To act upon this assessment in practical affairs consequently becomes a safer endeavour.[76] Introduction of this resiliency factor brings the aleatory and inductivist modes of reasoning closer to one another.

This fusion of the two modes of reasoning is, however, profoundly problematic. The resiliency of a probability assessment surely is an important factor, but setting an appropriate resiliency standard turns out to be a rather daunting task. If the standard is very demanding, it can be satisfied only when the examined proposition approaches either certainty or impossibility.[77]

[76] See, e.g., R. A. Fisher, *Statistical Methods for Research Workers* (7th edn., 1938) 120ff; N. B. Cohen, 'Confidence in Probability: Burdens of Persuasion in a World of Imperfect Knowledge' (1985) 60 *NYUL Rev* 385; J. Logue, *Projective Probability* (1995) 78–95.

[77] Impossibility, of course, is a form of certainty. To say that event E is impossible is tantamount to saying that it is certain that event E did not or will not occur.

Assessments that yield probabilities ranging between these two extremes would never satisfy such a standard. This would create a problem for cases that are evidentially deficient. If the probability of event A were to be assessed as amounting to, say, 0.6, the assessment could not be deemed sufficiently resilient. This would be due to the fact that we would have no significant clue (C) as to what would cause A to occur, as opposed to not-A. Our assessment would be sufficiently resilient only if we were to have this clue. But if we were to have this clue, we would have to transform our initial probability assessment, based upon the evidence previously available to us (E), into a new assessment of a considerably more refined and, therefore, altogether new proposition. Instead of talking about P(A|E), we would be talking about P(A|E,C). And if our clue were substantial enough, our assessment of P(A|E,C) would not only be more evidenced than that of P(A|E); indeed, if our knowledge of C were a real resiliency improvement, so that C could be causally associated with A, then P(A|E,C) would be much higher than 0.6.

Probabilities far removed from both certainty and impossibility therefore would not withstand a demanding resiliency standard. To keep these probabilities alive, the resiliency standard would have to be lowered. An undemanding standard, however, would not take us very far from unmitigated aleatory reasoning. There is room, of course, for setting a middle-ground standard, but it would only intensify the tension between the inductive component of a probabilistic assessment and its aleatory component. There is a perennial tension between the indifference principle and the resiliency requirement. The indifference principle promotes randomization, which is exactly the opposite of what is promoted by the resiliency requirement. The indifference principle allows for knowledge to be born out of ignorance, a move that the resiliency requirement rejects. The indifference principle and the resiliency requirement therefore cannot easily co-exist.[78]

More importantly, as we increase the demand for resiliency, our reasoning becomes more inductivist and less aleatory. To say that a judgment attaching a 0.7 probability to proposition A fails to meet the resiliency requirement is epistemically equivalent to saying that A is not sufficiently evidenced. When an assessment of probability is epistemically weak, its numerical content

[78] Inspired by W. Kneale, *Probability and Induction* (1949) 147–50, this point should not be understood as denying the validity of randomizing procedures. Numerous throws of a coin are likely to produce a roughly equal number of heads and tails, even when the attributes of the coin, along with the environmental conditions of each individual throw and the relevant laws of physics, are totally unknown. In resolving legal disputes, a roughly equal number of correct and incorrect decisions can be produced by following the same randomizing procedure or, more exotically, by allowing a monkey to choose between two equally appearing bananas, one of which bears the inscription GUILTY and the other NOT-GUILTY. In each of these cases, if we were to try to relate the resulting 0.5 probability to any individual trial or coin-tossing, we would find the probability disturbingly non-resilient (i.e., likely to be modified by virtually any addition of relevant information). Far from being weighty, this probability would still retain its validity as a randomizing device.

should make no epistemic difference. To disqualify a probability assessment for not passing the minimal resiliency threshold is tantamount to annulling its aleatory significance. Conversely, to say that a judgment attaching a 0.7 probability to proposition A satisfies the resiliency requirement is epistemically equivalent to asserting that proposition A is sufficiently supported by the evidence. Note that in this case, we would be unable to ascribe a 0.3 probability to A's negation. The gap left by adequate, although incomplete, evidential support cannot be filled by probabilistic inferences that run against the proposition favoured by the evidence. Any such inferences would have to satisfy the resiliency requirement with their own evidential support. Proposition P(not-A)=0.3 consequently cannot survive under a demanding resiliency standard, which is satisfied by P(A)=0.7. Because this demanding standard is satisfied by A, it cannot be satisfied by not-A. Therefore, in order to allow a proposition and its negation to cohabitate under one roof, we would have to accept abstract frequencies as epistemically sufficient for constructing resilient probabilities. Such a relaxation of the resiliency standard would take us back to aleatory reasoning. For supporters of trial by mathematics, a non-relaxation of the standard would be no more promising. It would prevent the ascription of a 0.3 probability to not-A, which would entail abandoning the complementational principle. The multiplicational principle, would also have to be discarded. If two independent propositions, P(A)=0.7 and P(B)=0.7, both satisfy the resiliency requirement, whereas their negations fail to satisfy it, to assert that P(A&B)=0.49 would be epistemically unwarranted. This would be so because the assertion ascribes a positive (0.3) value to unevidenced propositions P(not-A) and P(not-B). Abandoning the complementational and the multiplicational principles would constitute a decisive departure from the aleatory framework of reasoning.[79]

As may already be apparent, probability assessments depend on their resiliency not only in terms of cogency, but also in terms of content. Relaxation of the resiliency standard would permit construction of any probability estimate along the 0–1 continuum. Making this standard more exacting would exclude from consideration probability estimates that are far removed from both 0 and 1. Only those estimates that approach certainty (or impossibility) would survive. An increase in the flow of relevant information would not only enable the decision-maker to form a more resilient estimate of the probability, but it would also refine and, thus, modify the content of the proposition in question. The decision-maker would be forced to revise the proposition in question by ascribing the probability to a more refined factual proposition, which would be a new proposition, altogether different from the proposition initially considered. The decision-maker would have to

[79] See Cohen (n. 68 above) 104–9.

continue with this refinement process as the flow of information continues. In the end, she or he would determine the most elaborate proposition allowed by the information at her or his disposal. This proposition would be considerably more detailed and case-specific than the proposition originally examined. It would be more resilient and, therefore, less likely to be shaken by potential additions to its informational base. The probability estimate of this proposition would also come close to certainty.

This point requires some concretization. Let us assume that with regard to a tennis match played in good weather between A and B, we have been asked to assess the probability of A's victory. We have been given no information about A's and B's capacities as tennis players, and the outcome of the match is being kept secret. It is, we think, obvious that we will adequately discharge our task by assigning to A's victory a non-resilient probability of 0.5. A far more interesting question is whether this estimate of equiprobability can ever become resilient.

Let us now add the following to our original stock of information:

1. A and B played 10 matches in the past, of which 5 were won by A and 5 by B.
2. Both A and B were in excellent form shortly before the match in question.

This addition of relevant information certainly makes the assignment of a 0.5 probability to A's victory more resilient.[80] To maintain accuracy in our probability assignment, we now also have to modify the proposition in question. Our new assignment of probability no longer relates to A and B as totally unknown players. It relates to A and B as players in excellent form who have shown equal strength in the past, which is an altogether new proposition. Although more resilient than its predecessor, this assignment of probability is still deficient on the resiliency score. This deficiency is predicated on the absence of case-specific information to shed light on the match in question.

Let us now add a further item to our stock of information:

3. Shortly before the match, B appeared nervous and his leg slightly injured.

This addition allows us to raise the probability of A's victory from 0.5 to 0.6. As with the previous set of additional information, we are now required to introduce further refinement to the examined proposition. There is, however, still a problem with resiliency, because we have no relevant information about the match itself. The match was an individual event that must have been won by either A or B, and we need some information on that score as well in order to make our probability estimate more resilient. Let us therefore add the following information about the match:

[80] Cf. P. Gardenfors and N. E. Sahlin, 'Unreliable Probabilities, Risk Taking and Decision Making' (1982) 53 *Synthese* 361 (using an identical example to distinguish between 'risk of error' and 'epistemic risk').

4. A won the first set against B and was leading in the second.
5. At that stage, B's injured leg began to cause him pain.
6. B appeared very nervous, at times devastated, and lost his temper in two encounters with the umpire.

This information certainly makes our probability estimate sufficiently resilient. Concurrently, it requires that we raise the probability of A's victory from 0.6 to a level close to certainty. It also requires that we further refine the examined proposition. We no longer are talking about 'two equal players, A and B, playing against each other in good weather and in excellent form, subject to B's minor injury'. We have added to these facts A's interim score, as well as the aggravation of B's injury and his subsequent agitation. Once again, our previous proposition is transformed into an altogether new proposition that covers more particulars of the case at hand. Adherence to a strict resiliency standard makes this adjustment process both inevitable and desirable. Under such a standard, middle-range probability estimates made in relation to individual events will never be sufficiently resilient.

2. Low Evidential 'Weight' and Naked Statistical Evidence

This point has important implications for civil trials, where the 'more probable than not' standard allows reliance on middle-range probabilities in relation to individual events. The wording of this standard displays indifference towards the resiliency problem, which may suggest that adjudicators should do the same. This suggestion, however, adopts a rather narrow view as to what is required by the law. Ignoring the resiliency factor will not make the resiliency problem disappear. Reasons for being sceptical about non-resilient probabilities do not weaken simply because they are kept out of sight. These reasons must be considered seriously. Their role in adjudicative fact-finding must be determined. If the existing standard of proof does not determine this role explicitly, it must be determined by other legal principles or policies.

A choice between the aleatory and the inductivist modes of reasoning is, therefore, pivotal to understanding and administering the law of evidence.[81] As such, this choice has engendered a lasting and lively controversy in the

[81] Under another approach, facts should be determined holistically by evaluating the relative plausibility of the competing stories presented by the plaintiff and the defendant, respectively. There are indications that this approach is being adopted in positive law: see, e.g., *Old Chief v United States*, 117 S Ct 644 (1997). According to the most sophisticated version of this approach, plausibility of competing stories is not just a matter of inner coherence, but also of probabilities and evidential credentials. See R. J. Allen, 'Factual Ambiguity and a Theory of Evidence' (1994) 88 *Northwestern U L Rev* 604. This brings us back to the problems dealt with in this chapter. Yet another approach allows fact-finders to establish facts by their subjective experience-based beliefs. This approach does away with the justification requirement and, thus, allows liberties and properties to be taken away from people on the basis of whim and vogue.

legal literature, known as 'the probability debate'.[82] Focusing on both more and less important issues,[83] this debate has been framed and conducted as an

[82] For a brief survey of this debate, see W. L. Twining and A. Stein, *Evidence and Proof, The International Library of Essays in Law & Legal Theory, AREAS*, Vol. 11 (1992) xxi–xxiv; xxvii, n. 54. See also the symposium published in (1997) 1 *Int'l J Evidence & Proof* 253–360.

[83] One issue that has received an undue amount of attention is what is known as 'the conjunction paradox'. If, in order to succeed in a lawsuit, the plaintiff has to prove two mutually independent propositions, A and B, it would not suffice for her or him to establish that the probability of A and that of B equal 0.7. Under the conjunction rule, the overall probability of the plaintiff's case would amount to 0.49, which falls below the preponderance-of-the-evidence standard. Arguably, this strikingly counterintuitive outcome demonstrates that it would be anomalous to base judicial fact-finding upon mathematical calculus of chances. See L. J. Cohen, *The Probable and the Provable* (1977) 58–62.

This paradox is unreal. First, a distinction needs to be made between *elemental propositions* (such as formation of a contract, its breach by the defendant, and the ensuing damage) and *intermediary propositions* (such as those that specify the terms of the transaction offered by the plaintiff and accepted by the defendant). Elemental propositions refer to the lawsuit's constitutive elements, as determined by the controlling substantive law. Hohfeld termed them 'operative facts'. See W. N. Hohfeld, *Fundamental Legal Conceptions as Applied in Judicial Reasoning* (1923) 32–5. Intermediary propositions are propositions that establish elemental propositions. In order to establish an elemental proposition, one always needs more than one intermediary proposition. This distinction needs to be made, because the law requires each elemental proposition to be established separately (by the party upon whom the burden of proof lies). There is no requirement that the conjunction of the relevant elemental propositions be established as more probable than not. Consider a person who is seeking a declaratory judgment to the effect that there is a binding contract between her and another person. The probability of this allegation is subsequently established as equalling 0.7, and the judgment is rendered as requested. At some later stage, the same plaintiff comes to court complaining that the contract was breached by the defendant and requests another declaratory judgment that confirms this new allegation. The judge finds that the probability of this allegation is 0.7 and awards the plaintiff the requested judgment. Finally, the plaintiff sues the defendant for damages, and the probability of her allegations in this lawsuit is found by the judge also to equal 0.7. It seems obvious that the plaintiff should be awarded recovery, as it should be obvious that she should have been awarded recovery had the three issues been tried together. If the latter had been the case, the compensatory remedy sought by the plaintiff would have rested upon two interim declaratory judgments, as described above. Analytically, there would be three judgments, which combine into one for expediency reasons alone; and because each judgment would stand on its own proof as successfully provided by the plaintiff, the plaintiff would be entitled to the requested series of judgments. Hence, if the probability of litigated facts were to be determined mathematically, the conjunction rule would apply to intermediary propositions only, which is neither paradoxical nor overly demanding. Cf. R. Lempert, 'The New Evidence Scholarship: Analyzing the Process of Proof' (1986) 66 *Boston U L Rev* 439, 452 n. 42. Richard Lempert draws a distinction that is almost identical to ours, but argues that the conjunction paradox still retains its force because the law's refusal to apply the conjunction rule undermines the decisional accuracy in the long run. See also M. Bar-Hillel, 'Probabilistic Analysis in Legal Factfinding' (1984) 56 *Acta Psychologia* 267.

Second, as Ronald Allen explains, the conjunction rule has no scope for application at trials because a disjunctive argument that relies upon statistical cumulation of doubts is illegitimate in adjudication. Both the plaintiff and the defendant must present before the court their competing accounts of events as coherent stories, and disjunctive arguments uniformly fail to satisfy this criterion. Thus, a defendant must not be allowed to benefit from the combined probability of a proposition 'I did not do what the plaintiff says I did; and if I did it, then the plaintiff did not sustain any damage; and if he did sustain it, then what I did is causally unrelated to the damage'. R. J. Allen, 'The Nature of Juridical Proof' (1991) 13 *Cardozo L Rev* 373. Allen's theory is, indeed, well-supported by the equality rationale for the burden of proof doctrine. To justify it economically is more difficult, but there are other economic arguments that run against the idea uncompromising clash between the two modes of reasoning. However, in practical reasoning, to which fact-finding in adjudication belongs, this clash should be treated as spurious. We therefore suspect that the probability debate has posed a false dichotomy.

By using the terminology offered by John Maynard Keynes, we are now in a position to observe that uncertain reasoning has two *separate* dimensions, 'probability' and 'weight', and that neither of these dimensions can be

of applying the conjunction rule in adjudication. As claimed by one of the present authors, suppression of that rule is economically efficient because it helps to align the fact-finder's *ex post* information with the information reasonably available to the defendant at the time that he contemplated the litigated action. Stein (n. 13 above). For attempted reconciliations between the conjunction rule and the conventional proof methods, see R. A. Posner, 'An Economic Approach to the Law of Evidence' (1999) 51 *Stanford L Rev* 1477, 1512–14; and S. Levmore, 'Conjunction and Aggregation', (2001) 99 *Michigan L. Rev.* 723.

Another paradox, which we also consider spurious, points to the difficulty of combining mutually corroborating pieces of evidence. This difficulty is related to an analysis of corroboration originally provided by Bernoulli. In this analysis, the probability that witness A speaks the truth is denoted as p; the probability that witness B speaks the truth is denoted as q; and the fact-finder's task is to determine the probability that A and B both speak the truth when they converge in a statement. This probability (w) is equal to $pq / pq + (1–p) (1–q)$, which demonstrates that the corroboration will not work when either p or q falls below 0.5. Therefore, when both A and B appear as rather unreliable—one because of a prior conviction for perjury, the other because of poor eyesight—their testimonies will not corroborate one another, even though they testify independently to the same facts. If we estimate both p and q as amounting to 0.4, w would be equal to 0.31. This reduction of the probative force of mutually corroborating pieces of evidence is plainly counterintuitive. See Cohen (n. 83 above) 95–6.

In judicial fact-finding, however, corroboration is employed *as a matter of caution* rather than cumulation. For the proponent of A and B, it would be enough if *either* one of these witnesses tells the truth. Therefore, as explicated by John Stuart Mill, the probability that should interest us is that of the disjunctive inference that either A or B is a truthful witness. J. S. Mill, *A System of Logic Ratiocinative and Inductive* (1891) 391. In our example, this probability amounts to $(p+q)–(pq)$, i.e., to 0.64 (the co-occurrence probability pq was detracted in order to avoid double-counting). Jonathan Cohen did not ignore this interpretation of the corroboration notion, although he attributes it, instead of to John Stuart Mill, to P. Olof Ekelof, 'Free Evaluation of Evidence' (1964) 8 *Scandinavian Studies in Law* 47, 58 (see Cohen (above) 99). In Cohen's view, by explaining away the Bernoulli paradox, this interpretation engenders another difficulty, describable as 'the opposite-direction convergence paradox'. Returning to our example, since both p and q equal 0.4, the probability that A did not tell the truth amounts to 0.6, which holds true also with regard to the probability that B testified untruthfully. Because these latter probabilities are also mutually corroborating, their combined force amounts to 0.84.

This critique is misdirected, for it conflates the tasks faced by a proponent of mutually corroborating pieces of evidence and by the opponent of that evidence. For the proponent of A and B in our example, it would be sufficient to establish that either of those witnesses testified truthfully. For the opponent of this evidence, to establish that either A or B testified untruthfully would not be sufficient. If one of these witnesses testified truthfully, the opponent's case would be lost. The opponent's burden is conjunctive in nature, not disjunctive, as in the proponent's case. The probability of the opponent's case will, therefore, amount to $(1–p)(1–q)$, i.e., to 0.36, not to 0.84. For different (and more complex) analyses of the same problem, see R. Eggleston, 'The Mathematics of Corroboration' (1985) *Crim LR* 640; A. P. Dawid, 'The Difficulty about Conjunction' (1987) 36 *The Statistician* 91.

Less threatening to the mathematical project on their own terms, other difficulties and paradoxes have been explained away by numerous writers, most convincingly (in our opinion) by F. Schoeman, 'Cohen on Inductive Probability and the Law of Evidence' (1987) 54 *Philosophy of*

neglected.[84] Probability should reflect the chance that the proposition at hand fits the actual event, which will be worked out from the existing evidence. The contents of a probability assessment will, thus, derive from the *insides* of its informational base. In terms of its weight or cogency, a probability assessment will be conditioned upon the *size* of its informational base. The weight of a probability assessment will be determined by the size of the ground covered by the evidence, that is, by the extent to which the existing evidence encompasses the facts necessary for decision. Therefore, probability assessments will vary in their respective weight. Some probability assessments will be weightier and, correspondingly, more reliable than others.[85]

Neither of these two factors can be ignored in adjudication. To base a judgment on a probabilistic assessment that does not carry much weight is obviously risky, even when the probability is high. If constructed on a slim evidential base, such high probability may be misleading; and, as such, it may lead to a wrong decision. Yet to ignore a substantial probability that rests on an evidentially deficient base is equally risky. A decision that disregards this probability is likely to be erroneous. Missing evidence holds a mystery that may unfold in various ways. Both reliance on a low-weight probability as well as refusal to rely upon it involve risk of error. Because adjudicative fact-finding cannot be halted in indecision, one of the possible decisions has to be accorded preference, and any chosen decision will allocate the risk of error between the parties in dispute.

This point requires elaboration. Scarcity of evidence is a commonplace phenomenon in practical affairs, and adjudication is no exception in this respect. In many cases, fact-finders are presented with less evidence than desired, which does not absolve them from the duty to decide the case one way or another. Evidence used in practical affairs has to be processed and evaluated 'as is'. If the evidence is slim, this slimness should be accounted for

Science 76. Broadly speaking, implementation of the mathematical probability principles in judicial fact-finding is systematically frustrated by: (1) a lack of credible statistical data; (2) severe computational problems; and (3) moral difficulty in determining a person's liability by framing him into some statistically significant group of people, which would be especially problematic in criminal cases. See L. Tribe, 'Trial by Mathematics: Precision and Ritual in the Legal Process' (1971) 84 *Harvard L Rev* 1329; J. J. Thomson, 'Liability and Individualized Evidence' (1986) 49 (3) *Law & Contemporary Problems* 199; C. R. Callen, 'Notes on a Grand Illusion: Some Limits on the Use of Bayesian Theory in Evidence Law' (1982) 57 *Indiana LJ* 1. For these reasons and also in order to escape the above-mentioned difficulties and paradoxes, some supporters of the mathematical project have turned to subjectivist probabilities. See, e.g., Robertson and Vignaux (n. 66 above). The subjectivist approach, however, appears tautological, in the sense that its application can produce no inferential progress. See A. Stein, 'Judicial Fact-finding and the Bayesian Method: The Case for Deeper Scepticism about their Combination' (1996) 1 *Int'l J Evidence & Proof* 25; A. Stein, 'Bayesioskepticism Justified' (1997) 1 *Int'l J Evidence & Proof* 339.

[84] Keynes (n. 74 above) 71–7.

[85] Charles Peirce is another source who can be traced back to in this connection. He wrote that 'to express the proper state of belief, not *one* number but *two* are requisite, the first depending on the inferred probability, the second on the amount of knowledge on which that probability is based'. C. Hartshorne and P. Weiss (eds.), *Collected Papers of Charles Sanders Peirce*, Vol. II (1932) 421.

in the final judgment. If the probability deriving from a slim evidential base is substantial, this probability also should be accounted for in the final judgment. Such an all-things-considered judgment is the very essence of practical reasoning, an enterprise that seeks the optimal decision in a world of imperfect information. In the trial context, the optimal decision about uncertain facts is that which identifies the risk of error and allocates it in an appropriate way. Risk of error dealt with in adjudication is a risk that materializes in the form of deprivation of a person's liberty or property. Severity of the loss to be sustained by a litigant upon materialization of this risk is, therefore, yet another factor that needs to be taken into account. Unlike probability and weight, this factor is not epistemic. Probability and weight epistemically determine the potential error, but the latter's consequences are not an epistemic notion. As already mentioned, the risk-of-error factor is determined by a moral assessment of the error's consequences. Situated in the domain of political morality, this factor ascribes to the final verdict a distinctively moral and political nature. This nature is not only moral, but also political, because any verdict, erroneous or not, will forcefully protect and enforce the recognized entitlement by directing the coercion mechanism, sponsored by the state, to operate in a particular way and against particular individuals.

To decide in advance that low-weight probabilities, which are otherwise substantial, will be excluded from consideration is to allocate the risk of error in a way that will not always be desirable. An advance ruling that substantial probabilities alone, irrespective of their weight, will be sufficient for rendering verdicts is equally problematic. This allocation of the risk of error carries no promise of producing more good than harm. Both of these hard-and-fast rules are bound to produce serious damage, which can be avoided by adopting a more refined approach. This prediction can be substantiated without difficulty. Each of the above rules offers an epistemically plausible solution to what it incorrectly identifies as an epistemic problem. The problem at hand is not epistemic. It originates from a slim evidential base that produces epistemic deficiency, but the latter does not determine the ultimate nature of the problem. If the problem were epistemic, its epistemically best solution would be to reserve judgment in any case where adequate knowledge is unavailable. This solution is epistemically more accurate than any other solution to the problem. It is not, however, allowed by the law. Thus, the nature of the problem at hand is ultimately determined by the rule that does not allow fact-finders to treat epistemic deficiency as grounds for not deciding a case. Forthrightly contradicting the epistemological principle that requires a person to withhold judgment in the absence of adequate knowledge, this rule is not surprising. In the trial context, to withhold judgment (the verdict) by not deciding the case is to uphold the *status quo ante*, which is tantamount to making a substantive decision. Allocation of the risk of error under uncertainty therefore cannot be avoided. Situated in the domain of political morality, allocation of this risk can be made only on moral grounds. Rules driven by epistemic concerns, which either discard low-weight probabilities or accept any substantial probability, regardless of its weight, are therefore misdirected.

In torts, low-weight probabilities should, indeed, be allowed to be used as a basis for judgments under various risk-allocating principles. They can be utilized for promoting a long-term efficiency in cases involving a recurrent wrong pattern. This can be done by applying the P>0.5 rule on the basis of any probability, irrespective of its weight,[86] or by treating bare statistical risk as a harmful externality.[87] This can also be done in cases where the low weight, from which the relevant probabilities suffer, results from an infliction of evidential damage by the defendant.[88] In such cases, reliance on low-weight probabilities would be justified not only on the grounds of deterrence, but also by equality and corrective justice. The legal system's choice of its evidential strategy must always accommodate the objectives of the relevant substantive law. This, indeed, is one of the principal theses of the present book.

More fundamentally, under the equality principle, scarcity of evidence must not work to the plaintiff's detriment more than it works to the disadvantage of the defendant. There is no general reason for holding the plaintiff more responsible than the defendant for the fact that some important evidence is missing. From this perspective, the hostility that the settled law generally exhibits towards naked statistical evidence[89] can therefore be justified only on special grounds. In principle, such evidence can serve as a basis for judicial verdicts in civil trials. Deviation from this principle would be legitimate only as a means for promoting some overriding legal objective.

86 See Levmore (n. 36 above).

87 See Chapters IV and V below.

88 See Chapters III, VI and VII below.

89 This hostility is exemplified by cases such as *Smith v Rapid Transit*, 58 NE 2d 754 (1945) and *Rhesa Shipping Co. v Edmunds (The Popi M)* [1985] 2 All ER 712 (HL). For references to further cases, see M. Dant, 'Gambling on the Truth: The Use of Purely Statistical Evidence as a Basis for Civil Liability' (1988) 22 *Columbia J Law & Social Problems* 31, 31 n. 1.

II

The Tension between the Burden of Proof and Tort Law Objectives

CHAPTER I established that the basic civil proof requirement, labelled the P>0.5 rule, is both generally efficient and justified on grounds of equality and corrective justice. We did, however, also point out that there are cases in which a simple application of this requirement would produce injustice as well as inefficiency. In such cases, this requirement would systematically deny recovery to plaintiffs who failed to satisfy its demands, while the substantive objectives of the law of torts, such as deterrence and corrective justice, demand that such plaintiffs be allowed recovery. If the basic civil proof requirement were allowed to prevail in this clash, these substantive objectives would be systematically frustrated.

For such cases, the law of torts therefore attempts to furnish more sophisticated solutions that aim both at satisfying the demands of justice and efficiency and being integrated into the positive law in a coherent fashion. However, the traditional tort law tools are also not altogether satisfactory for achieving these goals. There are numerous cases in which both the basic civil proof requirement as well as tort law's supplementary doctrines fail to satisfy the demands of efficiency and justice. A need therefore arises to develop new doctrinal solutions. In this chapter, we examine the solutions furnished by the law of torts to supplement the basic civil proof doctrine. These solutions target cases that are factually uncertain and where uncertainty is a recurrent feature. We discuss five categories of cases in which these special solutions still do not provide a satisfactory response to the uncertainty problem. In the following chapters, we will propose a number of solutions for the cases presented here.

The five categories of cases are as follows:

(1) cases of wrongful damage where the wrongdoer is unidentifiable;
(2) cases of wrongful damage where the injured party is unidentifiable;
(3) cases of wrongful conduct that may or may not have resulted in damage;
(4) cases of damage wrongfully inflicted by separate wrongdoers, where it cannot be determined which part of the damage was caused by each wrongdoer;
(5) cases of damage originating both from a wrongdoer and a non-wrongful cause, in which it cannot be determined which part of the damage was caused by the wrongdoer.

The common denominator in these and other cases discussed in the book is indeterminate causation.

A. CASES OF WRONGFUL DAMAGE WHERE THE WRONGDOER IS UNIDENTIFIABLE

1. Cases Comprising the Category

This first category comprises cases where it cannot be established on a balance of probabilities that the defendant wrongfully caused the plaintiff's damage, but it can be established that the defendant belongs to a group of people that includes the actual, albeit unidentifiable, wrongdoer. There is, therefore, a statistical probability that the defendant is the one who wrongfully inflicted the plaintiff's damage.

It is useful to divide this category of cases into three sub-groups. The *first sub-group* comprises cases in which the defendant acted wrongfully, but his act cannot be proved to be the cause of the damage. Let us take two paradigmatic examples. The first is the *Hunters' Case*, which our book discusses on numerous occasions:

> *The Hunters' Case*. Three people participated in quail hunting. One of them (the plaintiff) was shot in the eye by a stray bullet negligently fired by one of the other hunters (the defendants). The defendants pulled their triggers simultaneously, so it could not be determined whose bullet injured the plaintiff.[1]

The second example is the well-known *DES Case*.

> *The DES Case*. DES, a drug designed to prevent miscarriages and which was manufactured by hundreds of companies, turns out to be latently carcinogenic to female foetuses. Twenty-five years later, many of the women whose mothers took the drug have been diagnosed with uterine cancer. Unfortunately, none of the plaintiffs can evidentially link the specific pills their mothers took to a specific manufacturer. However, it is established by a preponderance of the evidence that the drug was not tested properly prior to its marketing and that the manufacturers ignored certain findings that had pointed to the risk of cancer. Furthermore, the plaintiffs' mothers were never cautioned against this potential risk. Finally, the drug was marketed under its generic rather than brand name, which has foiled the attempt to trace each pill back to its actual manufacturer.[2]

[1] An adaptation of *Summers v Tice*, 199 P 2d 1 (1948).

[2] An adaptation of *Sindell v Abbott Laboratories*, 607 P 2d 924 (Cal 1980).

The *second sub-group* comprises cases in which it is preponderantly clear that the defendant caused the damage, but his act cannot be proved to be wrongful. This sub-group is exemplified by the *Two Cars Case*.

> *The Two Cars Case.* Two cars were involved in a road accident in which a pedestrian was killed. Although it is preponderantly established that one of the two drivers was negligent, it is unknown who this is. There is equal probability that either of them was negligent.

The *third sub-group* comprises cases in which it cannot be proved on a balance of probabilities that the defendant acted wrongfully and that he actually caused the damage. The defendant, however, clearly belongs to a particular group of people of whom one wrongfully caused the damage. Here, the following two examples are illustrative:

> *The Injured Shoulder Case*. The plaintiff is admitted into hospital to have his appendix removed. In the course of treatment, the plaintiff's shoulder is injured. His injury is caused negligently by one of the eight people on his attending medical staff. The identity of that wrongdoer is unknown.[3]

> *The Cargo Case*. The plaintiff imports goods by sea. Upon receiving a certain shipment, he finds the goods damaged. The wrongdoer cannot be identified, but he is evidently one of the following two: either the shipping company that transported the cargo or the port authority that received the cargo from the shipping company and subsequently delivered it to the plaintiff. The probabilities of each of these scenarios are equal. Damaging events of this type occur quite frequently, and in many cases, the identity of the wrongdoer cannot be determined.[4]

2. The Doctrinal Solutions

(a) Sub-Group I: Indeterminacy in Causation

One possible solution to the cases in sub-group I can be found in the framework of the joint tortfeasor doctrine. Under this doctrine, joint tortfeasors—including those who aided and abetted in the wrongful act—are responsible for the resultant damage both jointly and severally.[5] This solution, however,

[3] An adaptation of *Ybarra v Spangard*, 154 P 2d 687 (1944).

[4] An adaptation of *Zim Israeli Sailing Co. Ltd. v Hamagen Insurance Co. Ltd.*, 39 (1) Piskey Din 640 (1985) (Hebrew). For other cases that fall into the second sub-group, see *Aruji v Fink*, 27 (2) Piskey Din 547 (1973) (Hebrew); *Amir v Conffino*, 46 (3) Piskey Din 233 (1992) (Hebrew). For a discussion of these cases, see A. Porat, 'Collective Liability in the Law of Torts' (1994) 23 *Mishpatim* 311, 316–21 (Hebrew).

[5] P. Keeton (ed.), *Prosser and Keeton On Torts* (St. Paul, 5th edn., 1984) 322–4; W. V. H. Rogers (ed.), *Winfield and Jolowicz On Tort* (London, 15th edn., 1998) 729–33.

cannot resolve the *Hunters' Case* problem. The rule that imposes liability upon joint tortfeasors is applicable only in those instances where two or more individuals joined each other in committing a wrongful act. This rule does not apply in cases where a number of people jointly engaged in a non-wrongful activity and, in the course of that activity, only one of them perpetrated a tort. In the *Hunters' Case*, the two hunters set out together to hunt, which created a certain risk for the ultimately injured plaintiff. Hunting, however, even when it does pose risks, is not a wrongful act. Risks associated with hunting *per se* are, therefore, not actionable in torts. As for the wrongful risk that ensued from the hunters' *negligent* actions, this risk was created by each of them separately. The plaintiff therefore was injured pursuant to the materialization of the risk created by only one of the hunters.[6] Accordingly, the two hunters cannot be held responsible as joint tortfeasors. Holding differently would produce the result that any individual who engages in any activity that generates any kind of risk would be liable for the damage wrongfully caused by any person participating in that same activity. This outcome is both far-fetched and incompatible with the traditional conceptions of tort liability.[7]

In our second example—the *DES Case*—the joint tortfeasor doctrine might actually produce the desired results. This would happen if we were to assume that all the defendant firms wrongfully harmed society by withholding the information about the DES risks. All DES manufacturers, including those whose drugs actually caused cancer, would thus be found responsible for withholding that information. They were all associated in creating an atmosphere of confidence with regard to their products, so no manufacturer should, arguably, be allowed to disassociate itself from the outcome of the DES marketing.[8] Under this solution to the problem, every manufacturer would be held liable for the entire damage sustained by each of the plaintiffs.[9]

[6] Even if the mere creation of a wrongful risk were to be considered a damage, the injured plaintiff would be entitled to compensation from each hunter by virtue only of the creation of a risk and not due to the physical damage sustained. The latter is the product of the risk created by one of the two hunters, whose identity cannot be ascertained. See Chapter IV below.

[7] The American joint-venture doctrine also is not applicable in the *Hunters' Case*. See *Prosser and Keeton* (n. 5 above) 516–22.

[8] Although the question may arise as to whether each of the manufacturers is a *sine qua non* factor in the damage. See below p. 186.

[9] In *Collins v Eli Lilly*, 342 NW 2d 37 (Wis 1984), *cert. denied*, 469 US 826 (1984), the Wisconsin Supreme Court based the liability of the manufacturers of DES on their contribution to the risk that caused the plaintiffs' damage. As a result, all the manufacturers were held liable for the entire damage, jointly and severally. It was determined, however, that if a manufacturer could prove that its product did not cause the damage in a specific case, it would be relieved of liability. On creation of risk as normative grounds for imposing collective liability, see G. O. Robinson, 'Probabilistic Causation and Compensation for Tortious Risk' (1985) 14 *J Legal Studies* 779. On basing the market share liability doctrine (explained below) on the fact that the manufacturers were co-producers of the risk and thereby causes-in-fact of the damage, see N. L. Firak, 'Alternative Forms of Liability: Developing Policy Aspects of the Cause-in-Fact Requirement of Tort Law' (1988) 20 *Arizona State LJ* 1041.

Still, this solution is artificial. American courts have, therefore, rightly rejected it.[10] Thus, the traditional tort law does not offer a clear systematic solution to cases falling under sub-group I. However, both the *DES Case* and the *Hunters' Case* were resolved in the United States by imposing tort liability on the defendants. The courts arrived at this outcome by developing two independent legal doctrines designed to resolve the problem at hand. The *Hunters' Case* was resolved by establishing the 'alternative liability' principle, which shifts the burden of persuasion to the defendant 'to absolve himself, if he can'.[11] Defendants unable to disassociate themselves evidentially from the damage are, therefore, held liable for the entire damage. Originally adopted by a Californian court,[12] this principle ultimately found its way into the Second Restatement of Torts.[13]

The *DES Case* was resolved in a number of American states on the basis of another innovative doctrine, labelled Market Share Liability (MSL). Like its 'alternative liability' predecessor, the MSL doctrine was born in a California court.[14] Under this doctrine, each of the defendants would be held liable for the plaintiff's damage unless each successfully proved that he did not manufacture the drug taken by the plaintiff's mother. As further clarified by the court in *Sindell*, this liability would be imposed only on those manufacturers who

[10] *Sindell v Abbott* (n. 2 above); *In the Matter of New York State Silicone Breast Implant Litigation*, 631 NYS 2d 491 (1996). But see n. 9 above.

[11] *Summers v Tice* (n. 1 above). See also *Copley v Putter*, 207 P 2d 876 (1949), a case decided under the same principle. In this case, each of the two defendant drivers negligently collided with the plaintiff's car. As a result of one of these collisions, or both, the plaintiff sustained severe injuries, and there was no evidence individually attributing any of those injuries to either the first or the second defendant. The court held both defendants liable for the plaintiff's entire damage, both jointly and severally.

[12] *Summers v Tice* (n. 1 above). This solution was also adopted in Canada, in a surprisingly similar case: *Cook v Lewis* [1952] 1 DLR 1.

[13] Restatement (Second) of Torts, § 433B & Ill 9.

[14] *Sindell v Abbott* (n. 2 above); *Collins* (n. 9 above); *Martin v Abbott Laboratories*, 689 P 2d 368 (Wash 1984); *Hymowitz v Eli Lilly & Co.*, 539 NE 2d 1069 (NY 1989). On the adoption of MSL in the Netherlands, see J. G. Teulings, 'D.E.S. and Market Share Liability in the Netherlands', (1994) 110 *LQR* 228. On the rejection of the MSL in Ohio law, see *Kurczi v Eli Lilly & Co.*, 113 F 3d 1426 (6th Cir 1997). In the *Sindell* decision, the California Supreme Court examined a number of legal doctrines that could have led to imposing liability on the manufacturers, but it rejected each doctrine, one by one. The principle that was established in *Summers* was determined as not directly applicable in this case, since there was only a slight chance of each defendant having wrongfully caused the damage, whereas in *Summers*, there was a 50% chance with regard to each defendant. The doctrine of joint tortfeasors was found to be inapplicable here as well, primarily since it could not be proven that the defendants had come to a common understanding or had jointly planned not to properly test the drug and not to warn against the risks inherent to the drug. The Court also rejected the applicability of the enterprise liability doctrine, discussed below. The Court ruled that this doctrine was not applicable in cases where the industry comprised a great number of manufacturers and where these manufacturers acted in accordance with standards adopted by the industry's supervisory authorities. Such was the case in this instance, even though adhering to standards adopted by the authorities does not, *per se*, release defendants from liability in torts.

produced a substantial proportion of the DES drugs in the relevant market.[15] The *Sindell* court ultimately decided that the burden of compensating each plaintiff for her damage would be allocated between the manufacturers in accordance with their respective shares in the DES market that supplied the plaintiff's mother with the drug.[16] The court's principal justification for developing this doctrine was similar to the rationale underlying the *Hunters' Case* decision, namely, the moral preference accorded to the faultless plaintiff over the negligent defendants. The *Sindell* court also emphasized that the defendants should bear the responsibility for creating the indeterminate causation problem. According to the court, the defendants should bear that responsibility because they had wrongfully externalized a risk that materialized only after a lengthy period of time.[17] Finally, the court reasoned that holding the manufacturers liable could also be justified by the loss-spreading policy, as well as deterrence.[18]

[15] The reason given in the decision for setting this condition (hereinafter 'the substantial market share condition') is the desire to avoid a situation whereby the real wrongdoer could have a good chance of escaping all legal liability.

This condition of a substantial market share can be easily understood if we interpret the *Sindell* case as imposing liability on each defendant for all the plaintiff's damage (while the allocation of this damage among defendants according to their market share will be achieved through indemnification claims between themselves). Absent this condition, a defendant with a very small share of the market is under risk of bearing a significant part of the damage in the long run. This risk would materialize if he were to fail in collecting from other wrongdoers. If, on the other hand, we interpret the *Sindell* case as imposing liability on each defendant for only part of the plaintiff's damage (in accordance with each defendant's market share), there seems to be no reason for imposing the condition of substantial market share, since the allocation of the damage among the defendants will not be influenced by his ability to collect from other wrongdoers. Therefore, the fact that this condition was imposed in *Sindell* seems to support the claim for adopting the first interpretation of the ruling. See A. D. Twerski, 'Market Share—A Tale of Two Centuries' (1989–90) 55 *Brooklyn L Rev* 869, 874 n. 16.

It should be noted that it is possible to conceive of another variation of the market share liability doctrine, according to which each defendant will be liable for only part of the plaintiff's damage, but not according to market share; instead, the damage will be allocated according to the market share of each defendant relative to that of his co-defendants and in such a way that the plaintiff will receive full compensation for her damage. Let us assume that the damage is 1,000 and that there are 5 defendants, each one with a 10% share of the market. Under this variation of MSL, each defendant will be held liable towards the plaintiff for 200 (and not 100). The plaintiff will be awarded full compensation for all her damage and not for only half of that damage. This variation of the doctrine apparently mandates the adoption of the substantial market share condition, and there are those who even maintain that this variation actually was adopted in *Sindell*: see J. J. Thomson 'Remarks on Causation and Liability' (1984) 13 *Philosophy & Public Affairs* 101, 120–4.

[16] It is not clear whether this decision should be interpreted as imposing liability on each defendant for all the plaintiff's damage (and then the allocation is achieved through indemnification claims between the co-defendants) or as imposing liability on each defendant only for part of the damage. As noted, the fact that the Court invoked the condition of substantial market share supports the first interpretation of this ruling; n. 2 above. There are those who prefer the second interpretation, as eventually was the case in California in *Brown v Superior Court*, 751 P 2d 470, 485–7 (Cal 1988).

[17] *Sindell v Abbott* (n. 2 above).

[18] The Court noted that in the long run, each manufacturer would bear, more or less, the damage caused by the drug that he had produced. *Sindell*, ibid. 937. See discussion below.

Decisions subsequently made by American courts on the basis of MSL did not exhibit a uniform approach to the problem.[19] Some of these decisions allowed the plaintiff to recover her entire damage from each of the defendants. This was done in order to impel the *defendant* manufacturers to locate the other manufacturers of the drug and seek indemnification or even implead them as co-defendants.[20] Other decisions sanctioned only partial recompense for the plaintiff, according to the defendants' shares in the market.[21] Yet other decisions allowed the defendants to release themselves from liability by adducing evidence that convincingly disassociated them from the litigated damage;[22] other decisions, however, declined to allow the defendants such leeway.[23] In some cases, the defendants' market share was determined by focusing on the nation-wide market[24] while, in others, smaller regional

[19] The conceptual basis was not always identical in these rulings. Some courts rejected the conceptual basis of *Sindell* (n. 2 above) and based their rulings on different rationales, although they also resulted in liability being allocated according to market share (or a similar method). Because the conceptual grounds varied, there were also certain differences in the outcomes in certain matters to the *Sindell* case; see, e.g., *Collins v Eli Lilly* (n. 9 above); *Martin v Abbott Laboratories* (n. 14 above). In some states, the courts completely rejected the doctrine in their rulings, usually on the grounds that this is a matter for the legislature, and not the judiciary, todetermine, as well as due to the exorbitant administrative costs involved in applying the doctrine; *Zafft v Eli Lilly & Co.*, 676 SW 2d 241 (Mo 1984); *Mulcahy v Eli Lilly & Co.*, 386 NW 2d 67 (Iowa 1986); *Smith v Eli Lilly & Co.*, 560 NE 2d 324 (Ill 1990).

[20] *Collins v Eli Lilly Co.* (n. 9 above); *Abel v Eli Lilly & Co.*, 343 NW 2d 164 (Mich 1984). In *Collins v Eli Lilly Co.*, ibid. 52–3, the Court ruled that the damage would be allocated between the defendants according to principles of comparative fault and not according to market share, the latter being merely one, and not the only, relevant factor.

[21] *Brown v Superior Ct.* (n. 16 above) 485–7; *Martin v Abbott Laboratories* (n. 14 above) 383; *McCormack v Abbott Laboratories*, 617 F Supp 1521 (Mass 1985); *Hymowitz v Eli Lilly Co.* (n. 14 above). In *Hymowitz*, the Court ruled that the criterion for the allocation of damage is the relative fault of each defendant, which is measured according to the extent of risk to the public created by each defendant.

Difficulty often is encountered in proving the market share of each defendant. Consequently, some courts have established a presumption of equal allocation of the market between the defendants. This presumption, however, is not irrefutable, and defendants can try to prove that they have smaller market shares. *Martin v Abbott Laboratories* (n. 14 above) 383; *Conley v Boyle Drug Co.*, in A. B. Nace, 'Market Share Liability: A Current Assessment of a Decade-Old Doctrine' (1991) 44 *Vanderbilt L Rev* 395, 409.

[22] This was the ruling in *Sindell* (n. 2 above) 937, and, indeed, in this case one of the defendants succeeded in thus releasing himself from liability. See also *Collins v Eli Lilly Co.* (n. 9 above) 52; *Martin v Abbott Laboratories* (n. 14 above) 382.

[23] *Hymowitz v Eli Lilly & Co.* (n. 14 above) 1078. The rationale offered for this approach was that the alternative solution would result in a windfall for any defendant whose drug could easily be identified or who had marketed his drugs to specific drugstores (however, liability would not be imposed on a manufacturer who could prove that he did not sell the drug for use by pregnant women during the time that the mother of the plaintiff was pregnant; ibid., 1078 and n. 2). This ruling must be understood in the context of the legal principle laid down by the New York Court of Appeals in its decision in this case. Under this principle, liability arises for each of the defendants because of their participation in the negligent creation of risk to the public. For support of this approach, see Nace (n. 21 above) 426–8.

[24] *Hymowitz v Eli Lilly & Co.* (n. 14 above) 1078. For support of this approach, see Nace (n. 21 above) 425–6; Twerski (n. 15 above) 870–2; D. A. Fischer, 'Products Liability—An Analysis of Market Share Liability' (1981) 34 *Vanderbilt L Rev* 1623, 1644.

markets were used as the baseline.[25] In some cases, plaintiffs were allowed to sue only those defendants who controlled a considerable share of the market,[26] while in other cases, no such preconditions were set.[27]

Blasting cap cases, similar in many respects to the DES cases, are equally illustrative examples. In different places across the United States, children playing with blasting caps sustained injuries, and it was usually impossible to identify the manufacturers who had produced the caps that actually caused the injuries. The only thing that was possible to identify was the group of manufacturers to which the actual wrongdoer belonged. In a decision dealing with a number of such blasting cap injuries, the court shifted the burden of persuasion to each member of that group. The court required each defendant preponderantly to establish that its caps did not actually cause the injury: thus, a defendant who could not discharge this burden would bear full responsibility for the damage. These decisions preceded *Sindell* and were grounded on the 'Enterprise Liability' doctrine. This doctrine was held to be applicable when the following two conditions are satisfied:

(1) the group of defendants must not comprise too large a number of manufacturers (for this very reason American courts declined to apply the Enterprise Liability doctrine in DES cases); and
(2) the plaintiff must prove on a balance of probabilities that the damaging product was manufactured by one of the members of this group (although the identity of the actual wrongdoer cannot be established).

The official rationale for adopting this doctrine was as follows: since all the defendants adhered to the defective safety standards in their industry and commonly practised those standards, they ought to be regarded as partners in the ensuing tort, analogous to joint tortfeasors. Each defendant must, therefore, be regarded as responsible for both creating and exercising control over the risk associated with its product and those similar to it.[28] Indeed, it is possible to perceive this doctrine as an extension of the joint and several liability imposed upon joint tortfeasors. By this perception, the Enterprise Liability doctrine made progress towards resolving the indeterminate causation problem in torts, but this progress was limited. The *Sindell* decision, along with subsequent rulings, took a further and far more substantial step in that direction.

Since the adoption of the MSL doctrine in a number of DES decisions, plaintiffs have attempted to apply the doctrine in other types of cases. The courts, however, have usually refused to expand the doctrine's scope, based on the theory that the allegedly defective products are not identical or fungible, as was

[25] In a Florida decision, the Court narrowed the market to as great an extent as possible. The Court regarded even the state-wide Florida market as too broad for its purposes. *Conley v Boyle Drug Co.*, in Nace (n. 21 above) 408–9.

[26] *Sindell v Abbott* (n. 2 above) 937.

[27] *Collins v Eli Lilly Co.* (n. 9 above) 48; *Martin v Abbott Laboratories* (n. 14 above) 382.

[28] *Hall v E. I. Du Pont De Nemours & Co., Inc.*, 345 F Supp 353 (NY 1972).

the case with the DES drug. Thus, the courts refused to apply the doctrine in cases where workers exposed to asbestos contracted cancer and could not identify the specific asbestos manufacturer whose product had caused the cancer. These cases were distinguished from the DES cases by the fact that the asbestos products were not identical and that the complexity of the asbestos market made it difficult to determine each manufacturer's share in the market.[29]

The courts also refused to apply the MSL doctrine in cases where people were injured by a defective vaccine produced by different manufacturers. The plaintiffs failed to prevail in these cases because they were unable to identify the manufacturer who had produced the vaccine that had actually been administered to them. Those cases were distinguished from the DES cases on several grounds. First, those cases involved a defect in the manufacturing process and not a design defect, and thus the basic condition for applying the MSL doctrine—negligence of each defendant manufacturer—was not established. Second, injuries from the defective vaccine were discovered fairly soon after its administration, and in such cases, evidence pertaining to individual injuries must, presumably, be found. The third and final ground was overdeterrence: according to the court, imposition of tort liability on the manufacturers would create a disincentive for developing new vaccines.[30] In one such case, however, the court ruled that the MSL doctrine was applicable, because the vaccine design had been defective.[31]

Courts also refused to apply the MSL doctrine in silicone breast implant cases. These decisions rested on two factors: (1) the products complained against were not identical; and (2) individual manufacturers of the implants can often be identified. The courts also emphasized that 'there are differences in the design and composition of the implants'; 'the warning inserts in each of the products vary'; 'the products are not generally marketed'; and that 'the majority of the women involved in the breast implant litigation have been able to identify all or some of the manufacturers of their implants'.[32]

In a lawsuit against several cigarette manufacturers, brought by smokers who allegedly contracted cancer and other diseases as a result of prolonged cigarette smoking, the court ruled against applying the MSL doctrine. According to this decision, each individual plaintiff is allowed to sue only the specific manufacturer whose cigarette brand was used by that plaintiff. The

[29] See *Goldman v Johns Manville Sales Corp.*, 514 NE 2d 691 (Ohio 1987); *Case v Fibreboard Corp.*, 743 P 2d 1062 (Okla 1987); *White v Celotex Corp.*, 907 F 2d 104 (9th Cir 1990). For cases involving asbestos-lined brake pads, in which courts in California applied MSL, see *Wheeler v Raybestos-Manhattan*, 11 Cal Rptr 2d 109 (1992); *Richie v Bridgestone/Firestone, Inc.*, 27 Cal Rptr 2d 418 (1994).

[30] See *Sheffield v Eli Lilly & Co.*, 192 Cal Rptr 870 (1983); *Shackil v Lederle Laboratories*, 561 A 2d 511 (NJ 1989).

[31] *Morris v Parke, Davis & Co.*, 667 F Supp 1332 (Cal 1987).

[32] *In the Matter of New York State Silicone Breast Implant Litigation* (n. 10 above). See also *Lee v Baxter Health Care Corp.*, 721 F Supp 89 (D Md 1989), *aff'd*, 898 F 2d 146 (4th Cir 1990).

court reasoned that cigarette brands are readily identifiable and not identical; therefore, the case at hand was substantively different from DES cases.[33]

In yet another case, homeowners suffered substantial property damage caused by defective pipes that were installed in their houses. Although they could identify the manufacturers of the pipes, as well as the contractors who installed them, they were unable to identify the wholesalers who distributed the pipes. Consequently, they filed suits against the manufacturers, contractors, and wholesalers. The court refused to apply MSL and the alternative liability doctrines against the wholesalers who negligently distributed the pipes to the pipe-installing contractors. It reasoned that in contrast to the DES cases and the *Hunters' Case*, the plaintiffs were not left without remedy since the pipe manufacturers and the pipe-installing contractors were both easily identifiable defendants. The court also emphasized that, unlike DES, the pipes installed in the plaintiffs' homes were not fungible products and the defects in those pipes were manufacturing, rather than design, defects.[34] Courts resorted to the non-fungible nature of defective products also on other occasions as a reason for not applying the MSL doctrine.[35]

Blood product litigation is one area outside of the DES cases where a tendency to apply the MSL doctrine is discernible.[36] Paint cases are another area where some courts have been willing to apply the doctrine. In one such case, the plaintiff sustained injuries after ingesting white lead pigment that was in the paint used in his home. It was impossible to identify the manufacturer who had produced the specific paint used: there were far too many manufacturers who produced paint containing white lead. At the same time, it was certain that all white lead agents are identical in their chemical composition, so the court decided that the MSL doctrine must be activated against the relevant manufacturers. In this decision, the court pointed to the similarity between lead paint and DES. Similar to DES, white lead was a generically marketed fungible product, which led to the defendant identification problem. In addition, as in the DES cases, there was a substantial latency period between the use of the paint containing lead pigment and the ingestion of paint chips by the plaintiff.[37]

An American federal court recently applied the MSL doctrine against the gun industry. In that case, the relatives of six people killed by handguns,

[33] *Rose v The American Tobacco Co.*, 1997 NY Misc Lexis 662 (1997).

[34] *Edwards v A. L. Lease & Co., Inc.*, 54 Cal Rptr 2d 259 (1996).

[35] E.g., *Kennedy v Baxter Healthcare Corp.*, 50 Cal Rptr 2d 736 (1996) (injuries sustained due to an alleged allergic reaction to latex gloves); *Kinnett v Mass Gas & Electric Supply Co.*, 716 F. Supp. 695 (D.N.H. 1989) (fire damages allegedly caused by heat tapes).

[36] *Doe v Cutter Biological*, 971 F 2d 375 (9th Cir 1992); *Ray v Cutter Lab.*, 754 F Supp 193 (MD Fla 1991); *Smith v Cutter Biological*, 823 P 2d 717 (Haw 1991).

[37] *Brenner v American Cyanamid Co.*, 1999 NY Misc Lexis 440 (1999). See also *Jackson v Glidden Co.*, 647 NE 2d 879 (Ohio 1994). But see another case, in which the plaintiff could not identify the specific chemicals or toxics involved in his injury, and consequently, his suit against several manufacturers of paint, solvents, strippers, and glue was rejected, under both alternative liability and MSL; *Setliff v E.I. Du Pont De Memours & Co.*, 38 Cal Rptr 2d 763 (1995).

together with one injured survivor, sued twenty-five handgun manufacturers for negligence. The plaintiffs contended that the defendants marketed and distributed handguns negligently and that this negligence was responsible for each of the shootings at issue. Specifically, the plaintiffs claimed that 'the manufacturers' indiscriminate marketing and distribution practices generated an underground market in handguns, providing youths and violent criminals like the shooters in these cases with easy access to the instruments they have used with lethal effect'. The court found that some of the manufacturers had, indeed, been negligent. Based on this finding, the court applied the MSL doctrine and held liable the negligent manufacturers who could have manufactured the guns used by the shooters. The specific liability of each of those manufacturers was determined in accordance with its share in the handgun market. The court clarified that the MSL doctrine would apply to *all* negligent handgun manufacturers only when the gun that fired the injuring shot could not be identified. If it were possible to identify the individual features of the gun, such as its calibre, then only those negligent manufacturers who produced guns with those features would be held liable.[38]

To sum up, in cases falling under the present sub-group, plaintiffs receive no redress in virtually all common law jurisdictions, except in the United States. The subsequent chapters of this book demonstrate that this absence of liability creates serious problems in terms of both deterrence and corrective justice. They also demonstrate that the solutions to the problem at hand that have been adopted by American law are unduly limited in scope. As a consequence, wrongdoers escape liability in many cases where it ought to be imposed under the principles of deterrence and corrective justice.

(b) Sub-Group II: Indeterminacy in Wrongfulness

English courts have dealt with cases falling into this sub-group on more than one occasion. In cases similar to our *Two Cars Case*, there is a clear tendency at common law to shift the burden of persuasion to the defendants, so that each of them has to prove that he drove his car faultlessly. If the driver fails to discharge this burden, he is held liable for the entire damage sustained by the plaintiff. In most decisions that have reflected this trend, the courts have reasoned that there is a possibility that both drivers were negligent, which must be combined with the 'only one negligent driver' scenario and its likelihood with respect to each driver. If so, then the probability of the proposition ascribing negligence to each driver is above 50 per cent.[39] According to these

[38] *Hamilton v Accu-Tek*, 62 F Supp 2d 802 (EDNY 1999). On appeal, the United States Court of Appeal for the Second District decided to forward the legal question that arose in this case to the New York Court of Appeals: 222 F 3d 36 (2d Cir 2000).

[39] *Bray v Palmer* [1953] 2 All ER 1449 (CA); *France v Parkinson* [1954] 1 All ER 739 (CA). See, especially, the decision in *Baker v Market Harborough Industrial Co-operative Soc. Ltd.* [1953] 1 WLR 1472. In this decision, Lord Justice Sommerville expressed the opinion that the plaintiff's

courts, this satisfies the 'proof on a balance of probabilities' requirement. These decisions thus deviate from the general principle under which litigated facts cannot be determined by naked statistics. This technique is also problematic on its own terms. Indeed, it would be inapplicable in numerous other cases where three or more vehicles are found to have been involved in an accident. In any such case, since the probability of negligence goes below (and, in some cases, far below) 50 per cent, no liability would be imposed. In many such cases, however, as we explain in Chapter V, imposition of liability would be necessitated (at least) by reasons of deterrence.

(c) Sub-Group III: Indeterminacy in both Wrongfulness and Causation

In a legal system where tort liability is conditioned upon fault and causation, none of the defendants in the *Injured Shoulder Case* and *Cargo Case* examples can apparently be held liable.

The *Injured Shoulder Case* was famously solved by a California court in *Ybarra* by imposing liability on the entire medical staff. This outcome, however, was predicated on the court's creation of a new doctrine. The court expanded the ambit of the *res ipsa loquitur* presumption and reversed the burden of adducing evidence: it ruled that in order to exempt himself from liability, each defendant must come forward with exonerating evidence. Because none of the defendants possessed such evidence, the court found all the defendants liable (both jointly and severally) for the plaintiff's damage. As explicitly indicated in the decision, the main reason for this finding was the obvious evidential inferiority of the plaintiff relative to the defendants. The defendants had incomparably better access to information that could shed light on the actual events that had transpired. In this context, the court regarded as pivotal the fact that the plaintiff had been unconscious throughout his treatment and that his body had been under the defendants' control. The court also treated as unreasonable the possibility that a patient who has sustained injury due to negligence committed by an unidentified medical staff member will go uncompensated.[40] This decision is both unusual and

claim must be dismissed when it is clear that only one of the two drivers was negligent, and not both. Lord Justice Denning, on the other hand, maintained that in this type of case, the court must decide upon which of the two drivers to impose liability. All the justices did agree that in the case before them, there was a possibility that both drivers had been negligent and, therefore, both must be held liable. In a later decision, which dealt with medical malpractice, Lord Justice Denning expressed the opinion in *obiter dictum* that when damage was wrongfully caused to the plaintiff by one of two defendants, the injured party has a cause of action against both of them, and the burden shifts to each of the defendants to explain why he could not be the wrongdoer; *Roe v Ministry of Health* [1954] 2 All ER 131, 137 (CA).

In American case law, there has been a tendency to release drivers involved in an accident from liability when it is unclear which driver was negligent. *Prosser and Keeton* (n. 5 above) 251–2. None the less, there are also decisions in which the burden was shifted to the defendant drivers to prove that they had not been negligent; *Vahey v Sacia*, 178 Cal Rptr 559 (1981).

[40] *Ybarra v Spangard* (n. 3 above).

doctrinally problematic. As such, it has been widely criticized and American courts generally decline to follow it.[41] English courts have refused to apply a principle similar to that set out in *Ybarra*. They have, however, developed their own solution for the problem at hand by applying the doctrine of vicarious liability. Under that doctrine, a hospital administration is held responsible for torts committed by unidentified members of the medical team that treated the injured plaintiff. The identity of the actual wrongdoer thus becomes immaterial.[42] However, this solution of the problem has a limited scope of application: in the absence of an institution or an employer that can be held accountable for the actions of its employees, the injured plaintiff will be left without redress.

In *Zim*, the *Cargo Case* was brought before the Israel Supreme Court, which found one of the defendants individually liable. The Court stated that since liability in torts can be imposed only on individualized, rather than collective, grounds, in the absence of proof singling out one of the defendants as liable on a balance of probabilities, there is no other choice but to dismiss the lawsuit.[43] This decision followed the path first taken by the Court in *Aruji*, when it foiled an attempt to establish collective liability.[44]

In sum, the existing doctrinal approach, once again, is too restrictive. In the subsequent chapters, we will demonstrate that the courts' refusal to impose liability in certain types of cases that fall into the present sub-group is unjustified from the perspectives of both deterrence and corrective justice.

[41] For criticism of this ruling and of the application therein of the *res ipsa loquitur* doctrine, see W. A. Seavy, 'Res Ipsa Loquitur: Tabula in Naufragio' (1950) 63 *Harvard L Rev* 643. Subsequent American case law tended not to follow the *Ybarra* ruling (*Prosser and Keeton* (n. 5 above) 253), although a few rulings did indeed adopt it (S. A. Spitz, 'From *Res Ipsa Loquitur* to Diethylstilbestrol: The Unidentifiable Tortfeasor in California' (1990) 65 *Indiana LJ* 591, 606 and n. 100).

[42] For the application of vicarious liability in this context, see, for example, *Lindsey County Council v Marshall* [1936] 2 All ER 1076 (HL); *Gold v Essex County Council* [1942] 2 All ER 237 (CA); *Collins v Hertfordshire County Council* [1947] 1 All ER 633; *Cassidy v Ministry of Health* [1951] 2 KB 343; *Roe v Ministry of Health* (n. 39 above). For a rejection of a plaintiff's claim when it was unclear which member of the medical team had caused the injury and there was no responsible entity to bear vicarious liability for all members of the team, see *Morris v Winsbury-White* [1937] 4 All ER 494; *Mahon v Osborne* [1939] 1 All ER 535 (CA). In *Roe v Ministry of Health* (ibid. 137), Lord Justice Denning indicated, in *obiter dictum*, a willingness to shift the burden of adducing evidence onto the shoulders of each of the defendants, of which only one wrongfully caused damage (n. 39 above).

[43] *Zim Israeli Sailing Co. Ltd. v Hamagen Insurance Co. Ltd.* (n. 4 above).

[44] *Aruji v Fink* (n. 4 above).

In a third Israeli Supreme Court ruling regarding the third sub-group, one of the Justices (though in *obiter dictum*) favoured the possibility of imposing collective liability in certain situations; *Amir v Conffino* (n. 4 above). For this point, see A. Porat (n. 4 above) 319–21.

B. CASES OF WRONGFUL DAMAGE WHERE THE INJURED PARTY IS UNIDENTIFIABLE

1. Cases Comprising the Category

This category consists of cases where it is preponderantly proved that the defendant wrongfully inflicted damage upon certain unidentifiable people. The latter, together with others who sustained similar—but not wrongful—injuries, form an identifiable group. Hence, there is no proof that the defendant wrongfully injured any specific member of this group, whose damage could equally have originated in some other course of events that involved no tort. One of these group members is the plaintiff who is suing the defendant for his injuries.

The problem of proof that arises in this category of cases is transparently clear. In any such case, there is a statistical probability that it was, indeed, the defendant who wrongfully caused the plaintiff's damage. At the same time, this probability may be insufficient; and even if it were sufficient, naked statistical evidence generally would not be sufficient to establish the plaintiff's case.[45]

The following example is representative of this category of cases.

> *The Radiation Case*. The defendant's factory emits carcinogenic radiation. In the area affected by the radiation, the incidence of cancer rises by 25%: while prior to the factory's operation, only 80 people contracted cancer each year, 100 people now become afflicted each year.[46] There is, however, no evidence that could preponderantly identify those people who actually contracted cancer as a result of exposure to the radiation, as opposed to those who are simply victims of misfortune. All 100 people file lawsuits against the factory's owner.[47]

Another illustrative example is provided by the Israeli *Ringworm Case*, which involved radiation therapy wrongfully administered to immigrants from North Africa. There is no doubt that this therapy damaged certain people, but they were pooled together with others who suffered from similar diseases that did not originate in a tort. The relevant diseases were attributable to radiation. But since they also could have developed independently, they could equally be attributed to a variety of non-wrongful causal factors.[48]

[45] See Chapter III below.

[46] For the sake of simplicity, we shall assume that whoever did not contract the disease within a year of exposure would not contract it in the future. See discussion below.

[47] For a well-known case belonging to this group and in which a settlement was reached, see *In re 'Agent Orange' Product Liability Litigation*, 597 F Supp 740 (EDNY 1984), *aff'd*, 818 F 2d 145 (2d Cir 1987).

[48] The Israeli legislator provided an ad hoc solution to the *Ringworm Case*, by alleviating the burden of proof requirement; Compensation for Ringworm Injuries Law 1994.

There is a certain resemblance between this and our first category of cases. Both include cases where the specific wrongdoer who caused the plaintiff's damage cannot be identified on a balance of probabilities. But the two categories also differ from each other: while plaintiffs belonging to the first category were undoubtedly damaged by a wrongful act, plaintiffs in the second category may have sustained their damage non-wrongfully. This distinction has bearing on the corrective justice principles, applicable in both categories of cases.[49]

2. The Doctrinal Solutions

One possible solution to the problem at hand is simply to rule against the plaintiff. Alternatively, plaintiffs may be allowed to establish their cases on naked statistics, so that a plaintiff would succeed in his lawsuit when its statistical probability exceeds 0.5. If this probability falls below the 0.5 level, then the lawsuit should be dismissed, as prescribed by the burden of proof doctrine. Under each of these two approaches, lawsuits brought in cases similar to the *Radiation Case* example would be doomed to failure. Consequently, the plaintiffs would be left without redress and defendants without deterrence.

Another possible solution is to compensate each plaintiff who sustained the relevant injury for exposure to risk or for loss of chances.[50] Under this approach, each plaintiff in the *Radiation Case* would recover compensation for 20 per cent of his damage (since only 20 people out of 100 can attribute their affliction to the radiation). The exposure to radiation increased each plaintiff's chances of contracting cancer (in terms of the lost chance doctrine, it reduced each plaintiff's chances of not contracting the disease). The magnitude of the loss inflicted by the defendant equals 20 per cent of the total damage. This approach, however, would be highly controversial. Under the traditional tort liability doctrine, bare risk is not a damage. If a person was wrongfully exposed to risk, but the risk did not materialize in reality, this person has no cause of action against the risk-creator.[51] This person was lucky, and the same description would also be applicable to the risk-creator. Luck for the former entails luck for the latter: when a person exposed to risk does not incur any tangible damage, the risk-creator does not incur liability in torts. For these reasons, grounding tort liability in the *Radiation Case* on the exposure-to-risk theory is rather problematic.

[49] See Chapter VII below. Occasionally, the two groups may merge into one if, for example, the damage might have been created by either a non-wrongful cause or by one of several identifiable wrongful causes. This would have been true in the *Radiation Case* had several other radiation-producing factories existed in the area. The *Radiation Case* could have been further complicated had there been a possibility that the damage resulted from several, cumulative causes.

[50] For a solution involving a class action, see R. Delgado, 'Beyond Sindell: Relaxation of Cause-In-Fact Rules for Indeterminate Plaintiffs' (1982) 70 *California L Rev* 881, 899–902.

[51] See below 101–15.

Even if a person's exposure to risk could be construed in terms of lost chances that, arguably, constitute damage,[52] we would still be faced with an obstacle: could it be maintained that the radiation increased the likelihood of contracting cancer for all the plaintiffs, and not just for some of them? If this question were considered *ex post*, that is, after the event, then it should be obvious that 80 per cent of the plaintiffs would have contracted the disease in any event; so their chances of escaping cancer were unaffected by the radiation. If the question were considered from an *ex ante* perspective, the inevitable conclusion would be that all plaintiffs were exposed to the risk of contracting the disease. However, the risk to which the plaintiffs were exposed would then be much lower than 20 per cent. From an *ex ante* perspective, the plaintiffs' group does not exclusively represent all those who were actually exposed to the risk, since many people who did not develop cancer were equally exposed to it. In the *Radiation Case*, for example, an assumption that 100,000 people were exposed to the radiation would require the conclusion that the chances of escaping cancer were decreased only by 0.02 per cent for each individual. Compensation for each plaintiff would thus amount to only 0.02 per cent of his total damage. Furthermore, making the prospect of becoming injured actionable in torts would allow recovery for plaintiffs who did not sustain tangible damages. Such plaintiffs would have to be compensated similarly to those who sustained injuries, which plainly would be anomalous.[53]

These difficulties stem from the fundamental difference between risk and damage. Risk is a purely epistemic notion that determines the fact-finder's balance of knowledge versus ignorance. Damage, in contrast, is a tangible factor that reflects the plaintiff's welfare. A plaintiff may, thus, justifiably be held to have sustained an actionable damage when he is wrongfully forced to live in the shadow of some risk that may or may not materialize in the future. In such forward-looking cases, courts should award damages for lost chances, and actually do so.[54] After the event, however—when the fact-finder positively knows that the plaintiff either sustained the litigated damage or did not sustain it—compensation for an 'increased risk' and for 'lost chances' would be misdirected.[55]

In a fairly recent American judgment, Richard Posner offered yet another solution to the problem at hand by drawing an analogy to DES cases. According to Judge Posner, all people who have the potential to be the victims of the given wrongdoing will be entitled to damages that would cover their aggregate loss as a class. Subsequently, the recovered amount would be divided between the members of the class in accordance with the probability of each

[52] See below 125–9.

[53] On the problematics of finding a solution for such cases, see Delgado (n. 50 above); D. Rosenberg, 'The Causal Connection in Mass Exposure Cases: A "Public Law" Vision of the Tort System' (1984) 97 *Harvard L Rev* 849.

[54] See below 114–15.

[55] See Chapter IV below.

person's case.[56] This opinion was delivered in a claim brought by employees against their employer. The employees contended that they had worked overtime and were therefore entitled to a statutory amount of extra-work compensation. The court found that on most of the occasions, the plaintiffs had been engaged in work to which the statute did not apply. The plaintiffs were entitled to compensation only for the work protected under the statute, which they performed on other occasions. None of the plaintiffs, however, was able to prove on a balance of probabilities his or her individual entitlement, because the workers had been engaged in both protected and unprotected overtime work and there was no evidence that could establish who did what.

Judge Posner delivered the opinion of the Federal Court of Appeals for the Seventh Circuit, which remanded the case, with instructions, back to the District Court. Judge Posner decided that 'it might be enough for the plaintiffs to show that, given work patterns and assignments, 10 per cent, say, of [the employer's] workers probably did some nonexempt work during their overtime weeks, even if it were impossible to prove which workers they were; and then perhaps all the workers in the class could divide the pie . . . Each would have suffered a probabilistic harm measured by his fractional share of the total amount of nonexempt work done by [the employer's] work force.'[57] He also noted that if it were feasible for the employer to keep records that could enable identification of workers who perform non-exempt work, then failure to keep those records would be a potent argument for resolving all reasonable doubts about an award of damages against the employer.[58] This point comes close to recognizing the possibility of imposing liability for evidential damage, as proposed in Chapters VI and VII.

Apart from Judge Posner's revolutionary decision, there is no hard support in American (or other) case law for the above solution to the problem. If other courts refuse to follow Judge Posner's path, cases falling under the present category will generally be governed by the no-liability principle. Consequently, even wrongdoers positively known to have inflicted damage will be absolved from liability. As demonstrated in the following chapters, this outcome would be profoundly problematic both in terms of deterrence and corrective justice.

C. CASES OF WRONGFUL CONDUCT THAT MAY OR MAY NOT HAVE RESULTED IN DAMAGE

1. Cases Comprising the Category

This category comprises cases where it is adequately established that the defendant wrongfully exposed the plaintiff to a risk that may have materialized

[56] *Adkins v Mid-American Growers, Inc.*, 167 F 3d 355 (7th Cir 1999).
[57] *Adkins v Mid-American Growers, Inc.*, ibid. 359–60.
[58] *Adkins v Mid-American Growers, Inc.*, ibid. 360.

as the litigated damage. However, at the same time, it cannot be established that the defendant's conduct actually produced any damage (either to the plaintiff or to anyone else). The litigated damage therefore could be the result of a non-wrongful causal factor (such as natural forces).

Facially, this category of cases is identical to the second category: in both categories, the defendant wrongfully exposed the plaintiff to a risk that may or may not have materialized. The two categories, however, differ from each other in one important aspect. In the second category of cases, the defendant's conduct undoubtedly inflicted damage (to a victim whose identity cannot be determined), while in cases belonging to the third category, it is unclear whether the defendant caused any damage at all. From the corrective justice perspective, this difference is significant.[59]

This category of cases is exemplified by the *Thigh Case*.

> *The Thigh Case*. The plaintiff was admitted to hospital with a thigh injury, and his doctors negligently failed to detect the gravity of his condition until it was too late. The plaintiff sustained permanent disability, which could have had a 25% chance of being prevented had the plaintiff's dangerous condition been properly diagnosed. Arguably, the doctors' negligence deprived the plaintiff of his 25% chance of recovery.[60]

2. The Doctrinal Solutions

Cases belonging to this category can be resolved by ruling against the plaintiff. Alternatively, they can be resolved by ruling against the plaintiff when the probability favouring his case does not exceed the 0.5 threshold. If that probability does exceed the 0.5 threshold, the plaintiff should be awarded recovery. These solutions are anchored in the general proof requirement, under which the plaintiff will succeed when his case is more probable than not.

There is a clear tendency to adopt this solution at common law. The House of Lords seems to have adopted it in deciding a variation of the *Thigh Case* paradigm.[61] The same path has been taken by the Supreme Court of Canada[62] and by many American courts.[63]

[59] See Chapter IV below.

[60] An adaptation of *Hotson v East Berkshire Area Health Authority* [1987] 2 All ER 909 (HL).

[61] Ibid. Although the possibility of compensation for lost chances in medical malpractice cases was not rejected altogether, the specific facts of the case under consideration did not warrant such compensation. See also *Wilsher v Essex Area Health Authority*, [1988] 1 All ER 871 (HL), a case which was brought before the House of Lords and likewise dealt with medical malpractice. This case involved damage that could have been caused by either medical malpractice or several other, non-wrongful factors. The Court ruled against the plaintiff, for no causal connection could be proved between the malpractice and the damage.

[62] *Lawson v Laferriere*, 78 DLR (4th) 609 (1991).

[63] E.g., *Grant v American National Red Cross*, 2000 DC App Lexis 35 (2000). For cases following the same line, rejecting the lost chance solution described below, see also *Weymer v Khera*, 563 NW 2d 647, 653 (Mich 1997); *Jones v Owings*, 456 SE 2d 371, 374 (SC 1995); *Kilpatrick v Bryant*, 868 SW 2d 594, 602 (Tenn 1993); *Dumas v Cooney*, 1 Cal Rptr 2d 584 (1991).

Re-allocation of the burden of proof is another way of resolving the problem. Based upon justice considerations that favour an innocent plaintiff over the guilty defendant, this approach has frequently been followed by English courts. It was decisively applied in lawsuits filed against employers for exposing their employees to hazardous substances. As decided by the House of Lords, if an employer wrongfully exposed its employees to a risk and if an employee's damage could have resulted from exposure to that risk, then the employer will be held liable for the entire damage. The employer will be released from that liability only upon proof by a preponderance of the evidence that the damage sustained by the employee was rooted in a different cause.[64]

American courts, too, have alleviated the plaintiff's proof burden with regard to the causation issue in hazardous substances cases, but only occasionally.[65] In one American case, where it could not be determined whether the plaintiff actually had sustained his damage due to the defendant's wrongful omission, the court imposed full liability on the defendant, who could not positively disassociate the damage from his omission. One of the reasons leading to this decision was the fact that the defendant's wrongful omission had turned the causation issue into an irreducible complexity.[66] This is yet another decision that came close to explicitly recognizing liability *for* uncertainty, identified in this book as liability for evidential damage.

A further solution to the problem at hand can be found in the doctrine that treats the plaintiff's lost chances of not being damaged as an actionable loss. In both the United States and Israel, this solution has been adopted in medical malpractice litigation, and it has afforded compensation to American and Israeli plaintiffs in cases similar to our *Thigh Case* example.[67] While English

[64] *McGhee v National Coal Bd.* [1972] 3 All ER 1008 (HL). See also *Bryce v Swan Hunter Group* [1988] 1 All ER 659 (following the same line of reasoning).

[65] See, for example, *Allen v U.S.*, 588 F Supp 247 (D Utah 1984). On adopting this solution in a malpractice case, when it was unclear whether the patient's death due to consuming a specific drug was caused by the wrongly-prescribed excessive dosage of the drug, see *Zuchowicz v U.S.*, 140 F 3d 381 (2d Cir 1998).

[66] *Haft v Lone Palm Hotel*, 478 P 2d 465 (Cal 1970). This case involved the drowning deaths of a father and son in a hotel swimming pool. It was argued that had the hotel met its legal duty to assign lifeguards at the relevant time, the accident would not have happened. However, since the circumstances of the accident could not be determined, it also could not be determined whether the presence of a lifeguard would have prevented the accident. None the less, the court imposed full liability on the hotel, reasoning that the duty to assign lifeguards to pools was intended not only to prevent drowning, but also to provide the means for ascertaining the causes of such damaging events. The plaintiffs' difficulty in proving their case was, therefore, caused by the hotel's breach of its duty, justifying imposition of full liability for the damage on the hotel. For analysis and criticism of this case, see S. Levmore, 'Probabilistic Recoveries, Restitution and Recurring Wrongs' (1990) 19 *J Legal Studies* 691, 705–10.

[67] See *Kupat Holim of the General Federation of Labour v Fatach*, 42(3) Piskey Din 312 (1988) (Hebrew); *Herskovits v Group Health Cooperative of Puget Sound*, 664 P 2d 474 (Wash 1983); *Perez v Las Vegas Medical Center*, 805 P 2d 589, 592 (Nev 1991); *Falcon v Memorial Hosp.*, 462 NW 2d 44, 56–7 (Mich 1990) (the lost chance doctrine was later abolished by the Michigan legislature. MCL 600.2912a(2); MSA.2912(1)(2).); *Delaney v Cade*, 873 P 2d 175 (Kan 1994) (The court held that in order to recover damages for the loss of chances for a better recovery, the

courts have not ruled this solution out,[68] they have exhibited a clear tendency to deciding such cases on an 'all-or-nothing' basis. They do so simply by applying the burden of proof so that the plaintiff either totally loses his case or else receives full compensation for his damage.[69] In England, probability-based compensation is recognized in contracts.[70] In torts, it has been recognized only in assessing future (or potential) losses that are yet to be incurred.[71] English courts have repeatedly declined to determine past events on the basis of naked statistics.[72]

Application of the 'all-or-nothing' recovery principle to cases falling under the present category would lead to both insufficient deterrence of wrongdoers and inadequate compensation for their victims. As demonstrated in Chapters IV, VI, and VII, the deterrence objectives of the law of torts would be promoted better if plaintiffs were compensated for their lost chances. This form of compensation, however, would be problematic from the corrective justice viewpoint and also would be faced with the customary reluctance of common law judges to treat bare risk as actionable damage. Chapters VI and VII offer a new doctrinal solution that both fits the traditional approach to tort liability and mediates between the two competing objectives of the law of torts.

D. CASES OF DAMAGE WRONGFULLY INFLICTED BY SEPARATE WRONGDOERS

1. Cases Comprising the Category

This category comprises cases in which the defendant undoubtedly inflicted some part of the damage to the plaintiff, but the size of this part cannot be

diminished degree of recovery must be a substantial one. In *Perez v Las Vegas Medical Center*, above, the court held that a 10% probability constitutes a substantial diminished degree of recovery.); *Ehlinger v Sipes*, 454 NW 2d 754, 759 (Wis 1990). Some courts have adopted the lost chance doctrine in cases of the victim's demise only, rejecting it in other cases. For the application of the lost chance doctrine in cases of the victim's demise, see *Falcon v Memorial Hosp.*, above. For the rejection of the doctrine in non-demise cases, see *Weymer v Khera* (n. 63 above) and references therein. See also D. B. Dobbs, *Law of Remedies* (2nd edn., 1993) 238. For straightforward support of this solution, see J. H. King, 'Causation, Valuation, and Chance in Personal Injury Torts Involving Preexisting Conditions and Future Consequences' (1981) 90 *Yale LJ* 1353; *Doll v Brown*, 75 F 3d 1200 (7th Cir 1996). In *Doll*, Judge Posner supported extending the lost chance principle to areas beyond malpractice. Specifically, he instructed the court of the first instance to consider the possibility of awarding the plaintiff in an employment discrimination suit damages calculated according to the plaintiff's chances of having housing been discriminated against by the defendant.

[68] See *Hotson v East Berkshire Area Health Authority* (n. 60 above) 916–19.

[69] See above 74–5.

[70] *Chaplin v Hicks* [1911] 2 KB 786. See also M. A. Eisenberg, 'Probability and Chance in Contract Law' (1998) 45 *University of California Los Angeles L Rev* 1005.

[71] *McGregor On Damages* (London, 16th edn., 1997) 246–59.

[72] On this distinction, see *Hotson v East Berkshire Area Health Authority* (n. 60 above) 915.

adequately established. Another wrongdoer caused the remainder of the plaintiff's damage.

Two examples will serve us here:

> *The Dogs Case.* Two dogs, each of which belongs to a different wrongdoer, simultaneously attacked the plaintiff. The ensuing damage is evidentially indivisible, for it is impossible to establish which dog did what.[73]
>
> *The Cattle Invasion Case.* Cattle invaded the plaintiff's field for three consecutive days and damaged his crops. The defendant's cattle did so during only one of those days. The herd belonging to another person did so during the other two days.[74]

This category of cases bears some resemblance to the first category. In both categories, the plaintiff's entire damage was inflicted wrongfully.[75] In the first category of cases, however, the damage was, without a doubt, inflicted by a single, unidentified wrongdoer, who belongs to a well-defined class of potential wrongdoers. In the fourth category of cases, on the other hand, all the actual wrongdoers have been individually identified: it is positively known that each of them caused a fraction of the plaintiff's damage. The size of each respective fraction, however, remains uncertain, so we cannot tell which wrongdoer did what. At the same time, the two categories would completely overlap each other if we could decompose the plaintiff's damage into discrete ingredients: in such a case, we would only have the potential, rather than actual, wrongdoers vis-à-vis each ingredient of the damage, which would transfer the case to our first category.[76]

[73] This is an adaptation of *Melech v Cornhauser*, 44(2) Piskey Din 89 (1990) (Hebrew).

[74] This is an adaptation of *Genosar v Dchabra*, 23(1) Piskey Din 366 (1969) (Hebrew).

[75] This distinction also differentiates the first and fourth categories from the second and third categories, the latter two including cases where it cannot be positively determined whether the cause of the plaintiff's damage was wrongful or non-wrongful.

[76] The resemblance between fourth-category cases and first-category cases would become even more transparent if we compare the former with sub-group I cases of the first category in which all defendants acted wrongfully. In cases belonging to sub-groups II and III of the first category, on the other hand, most defendants, with the exception of those who actually caused the plaintiff's damage, did not act wrongfully (although they sometimes wrongfully created evidential damage, see Chapter VII below). The similarity between the two categories can be demonstrated by *Fitzgerald v Lane* [1987] 2 All ER 455 (CA), a case that can be equally categorized under both paradigms. The plaintiff in this case was injured successively by two cars. The question was who should be held liable for the main and distinct part of the plaintiff's damage. Three scenarios were raised for explaining the cause of that part of the damage, two relating to the first vehicle and one to the second vehicle. The Court of Appeal was willing to impose liability for that damage on the second driver, despite the fact that he could only be responsible if one of the three scenarios had actually occurred. On the one hand, this case could be categorized under the fourth category: two wrongdoers caused the plaintiff's entire damage, the specific parts of which cannot be traced to either wrongdoer. On the other hand, the main and distinct part of the damage could be viewed as separate from the rest of the damage. This part of the damage raises a first-category question: Which of the two defendants wrongfully inflicted it? Note that the uncertainty with regard to causation in this case exists only with regard to the second driver's part in the damage. The first driver is *causa sine qua non* of the entire damage, for had he not hit the plaintiff, the plaintiff would probably not have been hit by the second driver.

2. The Doctrinal Solutions

Problems arising in this category of cases can be resolved in several ways. First, courts may simply apply the preponderance-of-the-evidence standard. The plaintiff's lawsuit would thus either be dismissed or else allowed with regard to the specified fraction of the damage that can be attributed to each individual defendant. A number of American courts have adopted this solution. They tend to do so, however, in a special type of case: where a single wrongdoer could be held causally responsible for the entire damage on the 'but-for' causation grounds, while an indeterminable fraction of that damage had been inflicted by another wrongdoer. In these cases, the courts' inability to differentiate between the two fractions of the damage created a liability scheme under which the indeterminate wrongdoer is totally absolved from liability towards the victim, while the determinate wrongdoer—the 'but-for' cause of the entire damage—is forced to compensate the plaintiff for that damage.[77]

Other courts, American and non-American alike, have preferred other doctrinal solutions. Under one of those solutions, each wrongdoer will be deemed liable for a fraction of the plaintiff's damage. The relative size of that fraction will be determined by the risk of sustaining the damage to which each respective wrongdoer exposed the plaintiff. If there is no evidence that can apportion the relevant risks, liability for the plaintiff's damage will then be divided equally between the wrongdoers. Congruent to the probabilistic 'principle of insufficient reason',[78] the wrongdoers will thus be deemed to have exposed the plaintiff to equal amounts of risk. In the *Dogs Case*, for example, the relative physical strength of each dog could be used as indication of the risk externalized by each dog-owner.[79] In the *Cattle Invasion Case*, several variables can be used. These include the size of each herd, its genus, and the periods of trespass on the plaintiff's fields by each herd.[80] This solution has some support in

[77] See *Huddell v Levin*, 537 F 2d 726, 737–9 (3d Cir 1976). This case involved a person killed in a car accident. His estate sued both the negligent driver who had hit the car of the deceased and the manufacturer of the car driven by the deceased. It was argued that if the car's headrest had not been defective, the deceased would not have been killed. The court required the plaintiff to prove the distinct fraction of the damage sustained by the deceased as a result of the defective headrest; otherwise, the suit against the manufacturer would be dismissed. The negligent driver, on the other hand, would have to compensate the plaintiff fully, regardless. The ruling was not unanimous: ibid. at 744–7. For an analogous application of the burden-of-proof doctrine, see *Ryan v Mackolin*, 237 NE 2d 377 (Ohio 1968), where two accidents occurred within 5 months of each other.

[78] See J. M. Keynes, *A Treatise on Probability* (1921), ch. 4.

[79] In *Cornhauser v Melech*, 42 (2) Piskey Din 573 (1988) (Hebrew), the Israeli Supreme Court followed the same technique. In a further hearing of the same case (*Melech v Cornhauser,* n. 73 above), the decision was reversed and the majority held each of the wrongdoers liable for the plaintiff's entire damage.

[80] In *Genosar v Dchabra* (n. 74 above), upon which the *Cattle Invasion Case* is based, the defendant's liability was determined according to the number of days his herd remained in the plaintiff's fields, as opposed to the other herds. It seems that the Court did not have any other relevant information to base its ruling on.

Israeli case law, but is probably limited to property damage.[81] In the United States, this solution was held applicable to cases involving plaintiffs who sustained multiple injuries from different wrongdoers, with *relatively lengthy intervals* between each injury.[82] In England, the Court of Appeal has recently adopted this solution in a case in which the plaintiff was wrongfully exposed to asbestos dust during his consecutive employment by several employers and sued one of them. Each of the exposures contributed to the plaintiff's damage that was indivisible. The Court held that the correct approach to the problem at hand is to divide the liability for the plaintiff's injury on a time-exposure basis.[83]

Imposition of liability for the plaintiff's entire damage on both wrongdoers is yet another way of resolving the problem at hand. This approach can be justified from different angles. First, since the damage resulting from the wrongdoers' actions is indivisible, each wrongdoer should, arguably, assume responsibility for the entire damage: the indivisibility of the plaintiff's damage must not harm the innocent plaintiff to the benefit of a blameworthy wrongdoer.[84] The second line of argument emphasizes the *simultaneous* effect of the wrongdoers' actions: this effect entails that the magnitude and nature of the plaintiff's damage are attributed to the synergetic operation of the two wrongful forces. Analogously to the joint-tortfeasor doctrine, this doctrinal approach deems each wrongdoer an indispensable cause of the entire damage. This approach would not necessarily result in an imposition of full liability in every case. In the *Dogs Case*, for example, full liability might be justified. In that case, damage engendered by the simultaneous attack that was launched by the two dogs was not a simple aggregate of two individual assaults. This proposition certainly holds true for the emotional damage sustained by the plaintiff and is likely to be correct with regard to his physical damage as well. By contrast, the damage suffered by the plaintiff in the *Cattle Invasion Case* was the simple sum of the two damages separately inflicted by the two herds.

[81] On physical injuries, see discussion below. See also A. Porat, 'Relaxation of Cause-In-Fact Rules for Broadening the Scope of Tort Liability' 1 *Ybk Israeli Law* 240 (A. Rozen-Zvi (ed.), 1991) (Hebrew).

[82] See *Loui v Oakley*, 438 P 2d 393 (Haw 1968). The court emphasized that it was a matter of public policy whether to impose full liability on the defendant who caused the first accident in which the plaintiff was injured, whether to relieve him of any liability, or whether to hold him partially liable. Choosing the third solution, according to a rough estimation of the defendant's part in the infliction of the damage, seemed preferable to the court. The court further maintained that if such an estimation were not possible, liability would be divided equally between the various defendants. Cf. *Ryan v Mackolin* (n. 77 above).

[83] *Holtby v Brigham & Cowan (Hull) Ltd.* [2000] 3 All ER 421 (CA). Ultimately, the plaintiff received a more generous amount of compensation for reasons that belong to the appellate procedure. Ibid. 431. See also *Thompson v Smith Shiprepairs (North Shields) Ltd* [1984] 1 All ER 881, 909–10.

[84] For different doctrinal solutions of the problem at hand, see H. L. A. Hart and T. Honoré, *Causation in the Law* (2nd edn., Oxford, 1985) 227–9.

In that case, the simultaneous operation of the two wrongdoers did not magnify the plaintiff's damage.[85]

The full-liability solution is commonly employed by the Israeli case law in instances involving physical damage. Israeli courts have held that when the litigated injury is indivisible and physical, rather than merely proprietary,[86] in nature, none of the blameworthy defendants should be allowed to absolve himself or herself from liability for that damage. Presumably, these holdings rest on a twofold rationale: first, physical injuries, as opposed to proprietary damages, are largely indivisible; second, the effect of the simultaneous operation of the defendants' wrongful forces must necessarily have magnified the plaintiff's overall injury. The defendants were therefore held liable for the entire damage sustained by the plaintiff, jointly and severally.[87]

English and American courts have occasionally adopted a similar approach, but on different grounds. In the eyes of these Anglo-American courts, the defendants' blameworthiness—as contrasted with the innocence of the injured plaintiff—is the dominant reason for imposing liability for the plaintiff's entire damage upon each defendant. This rationale does not distinguish between physical injury and proprietary damage. For example, when a plaintiff is injured in a car accident involving two wrongdoers and his ensuing damage is indivisible, liability for the entire damage would normally be imposed on both wrongdoers. In English case law, this outcome is premised on the risks created by the wrongdoers: since either of the two risks could have equally materialized into the litigated damage, each wrongdoer ought to assume liability for the entire damage. Such a wrongdoer can escape full liability only by providing evidence that preponderantly disassociates him from the damage. Alternatively, such a wrongdoer is allowed to adduce evidence that would limit his liability to a specific fraction of the damage.[88] American courts have adopted the same solution in a variety of circumstances, for example, in cases involving consecutive car accidents that ended up in an indivisible damage.[89] This solution also was applied by the courts in nuisance cases where the plaintiff suffered an indivisible damage from more than one

[85] Arguably, imposition of liability for the entire damage on each wrongdoer is too harsh a solution for the problem. This solution is as harsh towards the defendant as the no-liability solution towards the plaintiff. The proportionate-liability solution therefore seems to be the best one, for it sensibly balances between the wrongdoer's and the victim's interests.

[86] See above 79.

[87] Cf. *Melech v Cornhauser* (n. 73 above) with *Genosar v Dchabra* (n. 74 above).

[88] *Fitzgerald v Lane* (n. 76 above); *Dingle v Associated Newspapers Ltd.* [1961] 2 QB 162 (CA). See also discussion above.

[89] For American cases akin to *Fitzgerald v Lane*, ibid., and in which courts reached a similar conclusion, see *Micelli v Hirsch*, 83 NE 2d 240 (Ohio 1948); *Maddux v Donaldson*, 108 NW 2d 33 (Mich 1961). See also *Chrysler Corp. v Todorovich*, 580 P 2d 1123 (Wyo 1978), a case whose facts resemble those in *Huddell v Levin* (n. 77 above), but which was decided differently by the court. Cf. the dissenting opinion in *Huddell v Levin*, ibid. 744–7.

nuisance created by different wrongdoers,[90] and there are other representative examples.[91]

The different solutions adopted by different courts in relation to cases falling under the present category reflect an incremental case-by-case approach. Although not devoid of all merit, this approach lacks an underlying backbone of unifying principles that could provide a coherent and comprehensive solution to the problem at hand. These principles will be laid out in Chapters VI and VII.

E. CASES OF DAMAGE ORIGINATING BOTH FROM A WRONGDOER AND A NON-WRONGFUL CAUSE

1. Cases Comprising the Category

We now turn to our last category of cases. In these cases, part of the plaintiff's damage is established to have been wrongfully caused by the defendant, with the remaining part originating in a non-wrongful cause. The damage is indivisible, so the fraction of the damage that must be attributed to the defendant is impossible to prove. The following are paradigmatic examples for this category of cases.

> *The Appendix Case.* The plaintiff underwent a simple operation that threw him into emotional depression. Because the operation had been essential for the plaintiff's health, the ensuing emotional damage was not actionable. During the plaintiff's pre-surgical treatment, negligence had occurred, which led to further surgery, aggravating the plaintiff's depression. This actionable damage merged with the plaintiff's non-actionable damage.[92]

[90] *Town of Sentinel v Riley*, 43 P 2d 742, 746 (Okl 1935). In this case, a nuisance-creator was held liable for the plaintiff's entire damage, although other nuisance-creators also contributed to the damage. The court treated each of the nuisances as a *sufficient cause* of the entire damage (although each nuisance arguably caused an indeterminate part of that damage). For other nuisance cases in which courts have reached the same conclusion, see *Landers v East Texas Salt Water Disposal Co.*, 248 SW 2d 731 (Tex 1952); *Velsicol Chemical Corp. v Rowe*, 543 SW 337 (Tenn 1976).

[91] For a case where liability was imposed jointly and severally on two physicians whose separate, successive malpractice caused the plaintiff damage that could not be individually attributed to either one, see *Gilson v Mitchell*, 205 SE 421 (Ga 1974).

See also *Azure v City of Billings*, 596 P 2d 460 (Mont 1979). In this case, the plaintiff was assaulted and his injuries were aggravated by the police's wrongful omission in failing to permit him to receive medical care following his arrest. It could not be ascertained which part of the plaintiff's damage resulted from the assault and which from the negligent omission. The court imposed full liability on the municipality that employed the police force. The Court's main line of reasoning was that overcompensation is preferable to undercompensation.

[92] An adaptation of *Nagar v Vilensky*, 43(3) Piskey Din 284 (1989) (Hebrew).

> *The Fire Case*. A fire broke out in the plaintiff's library. The fire department did not act with due diligence, so many books were burned and became damaged beyond repair. It cannot, however, be determined which books were burned as a result of the fire department's negligence and which were doomed to burn regardless of that negligence.[93]

This category of cases appears to be very close to the fourth category. There is, however, an important difference between the two categories: in cases falling into the present category, part of the litigated damage is positively known to have originated in a non-wrongful cause. There is also a certain similarity between this and the second category of cases: in cases falling under either of the two categories, the claim that the plaintiff's entire damage was wrongfully inflicted by the defendant is positively known to be ungrounded. This similarity would become evident if we were to decompose the plaintiff's damage into fractions (as could possibly be done in the *Library Case*). Each fraction of the damage would then pose the very same question that arises in connection with the entire damage in cases belonging to our second category: Was it inflicted *solely* by the wrongdoer or did it originate *solely* in the non-wrongful cause? In any such case, holding the defendant liable for the entire damage would produce both excessive deterrence and excessive compensation.

2. The Doctrinal Solutions

The doctrinal solutions for cases falling under the present category are essentially identical to those provided by judges for our fourth category of cases. Imposition of full liability on the defendant is one of the most recurrent solutions adopted by the courts. As just noted, this solution is problematic since it results in both overdeterrence and overcompensation. When applied to the present category of cases, this solution is especially harsh towards the defendants: in a fourth-category case, the defendant can, in principle, recover indemnification from another wrongdoer, a possibility not available to defendants in the present category of cases. This solution is also especially generous to the plaintiffs, since they would recover compensation for damage unrelated to any wrongful cause. Despite these problems, which are both obvious and serious, courts have failed to draw any distinction between the two categories of cases when they opted for the full-recovery solution.[94] In Chapters VI and VII, we

[93] An adaptation of *City of Oakland v Pacific Gas & Electric Co.*, 118 P 2d 328 (Cal 1941). The fire services in this case were held liable for the entire damage.

[94] See *Nagar v Vilensky* (n. 92 above); *Melech v Cornhauser* (n. 73 above). See also *City of Oakland v Pacific Gas & Electric Co.* (n. 93 above); Hart and Honoré (n. 84 above) 231. The Court's approach would seemingly be different if the non-actionable causal factor partially responsible for the damage were the plaintiff's own negligent behaviour. See *Deutsch v Connecticut Co.*, 119 A 891 (Conn 1923).

offer a different solution to this category of cases. Under our solution, plaintiffs would generally receive partial compensation for their damages. This principled solution is justified on the grounds of deterrence and corrective justice.

III

Res Ipsa Loquitur

A. *RES IPSA LOQUITUR* AND STATISTICAL NEGLIGENCE

LIKE everything else in the law, the *res ipsa loquitur* presumption is prescriptive in character. The Latin phrase '*res ipsa loquitur*' refers to 'a thing that speaks for itself', which is not the case with the 'things' that, under the presumption, tell the court that the litigated damage is likely to have resulted from the defendant's negligence. In its typical form, as adopted in virtually all Anglo-American jurisdictions, the presumption allows judges[1] to draw an inference of negligence on the part of the defendant from the following set of cumulative basic conditions:

(1) the occurrence that resulted in the plaintiff's damage could not normally take place without the defendant's negligence;
(2) the occurrence must have been caused by an agency or instrumentality over which the defendant exercised exclusive control;[2]
(3) the occurrence did not take place due to a contribution or voluntary action of the plaintiff;
(4) other evidence that could shed light on the course of the events is unavailable.

Under these conditions, each of which must be established by a preponderance of the evidence, the defendant may or may not have been negligent. The defendant's negligence is only one of the possibilities that offer an explanation for the damage sustained by the plaintiff. Another possibility is that of *damnum sine injuria*, a misfortune that entails no injustice to the plaintiff, and one can also think of more remote scenarios under which the damage was caused by an unknown tortfeasor rather than by the defendant. Damage litigated in a *res ipsa loquitur* case thus could have occurred through the defendant's negligence, in which case the defendant must make good the damage and thereby rectify the injustice. This possibility, however, is uncertain

[1] As elsewhere in the book, the term 'judges' is used here generically, thus extending also to jurors.

[2] In medical malpractice cases, courts often ignore this condition or explicitly assume its fulfilment. See, e.g., *Ratcliffe v Plymouth & Torbay Health Authority* [1998] PIQR 170, 178–86 (CA). See also the Israeli Supreme Court's decision in *Raz v Elisha Hospital*, 47 (3) Piskey Din 805 (1993) (Hebrew) (observing that the instrumentality condition can be satisfied by any item of medical equipment, including gloves worn by nurses and doctors and, indeed, the hospital building's walls).

because the damage could also have resulted from some misfortune for which the defendant bears no blame. Yet, despite the existence of an innocent explanation for the damage, the law tells the judge that she or he may prefer the injustice scenario over that of misfortune and hold the defendant negligent and liable. This, indeed, is the gist of the *res ipsa loquitur* presumption: it allows judges to infer negligence under uncertainty even when that inference is unwarranted from an epistemological point of view. The presumption thus allows judges to assume risk of error in their final verdict and to shift that risk to the defendant.

From an epistemological viewpoint, by allowing judges to procreate knowledge out of ignorance, the presumption is bound to produce distortions. But the presumption must not be examined only through the epistemological lens. Its real goal is normative rather than epistemological. The presumption is not a tool by which past events can be reconstructed with accuracy. Rather, it is a rule of decision that allocates risk of error between plaintiffs and defendants. This rule was designed for cases where judges have run out of facts, that is, for settings where none of the factual scenarios that are put on trial is epistemologically warranted. By marking the defendant as a permissible bearer of the risk of error, this decisional rule allows judges to allocate that risk in a way that favours the plaintiff. Here, the term 'allows' emphasizes that judges have a licence to infer negligence whenever the basic conditions of the presumption are adequately established.

The presumption's licence to infer negligence is merely an authorization bestowed upon judges, and authorization is not a directive. Even when the basic facts have been adequately established by the plaintiff, the judge may still prefer the misfortune scenario over that of injustice. The presumption's 'things' therefore have no voice of their own and thus do not really speak 'for themselves': it is the judge who may give them a voice if she or he so decides, and her or his decision as to whether to do so crucially depends upon *other things*. These other things are the relevant normative considerations upon which the judge may decide to activate the presumption in the plaintiff's favour.

When viewed from this angle, the presumption appears to be vacuous and redundant. If a negligence inference totally depends upon factors other than the presumption's basic conditions—so that a finding that the defendant acted negligently is entirely a matter of those extrinsic factors—the presumption is then manifestly redundant and can safely be erased from the book of laws. Alternatively, if a negligence inference only partially depends upon those extrinsic factors—so that a finding that the defendant acted negligently is a matter of synergy between those factors and the presumption's basic conditions—then the presumption also appears redundant, but for an altogether different reason. Under this latter interpretation—which is, in fact, the presumption's official understanding in virtually all Anglo-American jurisdictions—the defendant would be held negligent only when the synergy between the presumption's basic conditions and other relevant factors were to yield preponderance of the evidence in favour of the negligence scenario. If so, this is no innovation for the general law: in law, *any* combination of evidence that produces the same probabilistic effect arguably leads to a similar verdict. The *res ipsa loquitur* presumption would consequently make no independent point, thus producing no added value for the law.

On each of these two interpretations, the presumption might also produce anomalies. Recall the first basic condition that needs to be proved preponderantly by the plaintiff: the litigated occurrence must normally coincide with *a* negligence scenario. The presumption thus appears to be telling judges that they may *not* hold the defendant negligent even when the allegation that he acted negligently in one way or another is more probable than not. This is so because three additional requirements need to be satisfied in order to activate the presumption and because the negligence inference is not mandatory under the presumption itself. Under the general 'balance of probabilities' proof standard, such an outcome appears anomalous.

These two objections will be labelled, respectively, 'the argument from redundancy' and 'the argument from anomaly'. Understanding the *res ipsa loquitur* presumption crucially depends on the fate of these objections. In light of these objections, it may well be the case that the presumption should be understood and applied differently. The Israel Supreme Court, for example, has interpreted the presumption in a way that sidesteps these objections. Consequently, the Israeli *res ipsa loquitur* arrangement has branched away from its common law origins. In Israel, the *res ipsa loquitur* presumption is not merely a permissive inference. Rather, it is a mandatory requirement that leaves judges no discretion whatsoever. Under that requirement, the defendant *must* be held negligent whenever the presumption's basic conditions are adequately established at the end of the trial and the defendant has failed to prove, on a balance of probabilities, that there was no negligence on his part. The defendant thus is not allowed to seek refuge in the uncertainty of the case by furnishing a factual scenario that is merely as plausible as that of the plaintiff.[3] In any such case, the statistically preponderant probability of negligence would yield victory for the plaintiff.[4]

[3] English courts once adopted the same interpretation of the presumption. See *Barkway v South Wales Transport Co. Ltd.* [1948] 2 All ER 460, 471; *Moore v R. Fox & Sons Ltd.* [1956] 1 QB 596. This interpretation, however, was rejected by the Privy Council in *Ng Chun Pui v Lee Chuen Tat* [1988] 1 RTR 298, a case in which the Law Lords unanimously held that the presumption entailed no shift in the formal burdens of proof. Furthermore, in *Ratcliffe v Plymouth & Torbay Health Authority* [1998] PIQR 170, the Court of Appeal held that the sole function of the *res ipsa loquitur* presumption was to furnish a *prima facie* proof of negligence. There is, however, an authoritative view that the presumption shifts the burden of adducing evidence to the defendant: see *Henderson v Henry E. Jenkins & Sons* [1970] AC 282, 301–2.

[4] See *Neumann v Cohen*, 24 (2) Piskey Din 229 (1969) (Hebrew), and the discussion below.

That interpretation of the presumption adequately responds to the argument from redundancy. The argument from anomaly, however, still retains much of its force by focusing on the second, third, and fourth components of the presumption.[5] Under the general 'balance of probabilities' proof standard, a defendant should be held negligent whenever his negligence is more probable than not. Hence, a plaintiff should succeed in establishing the defendant's negligence by establishing only the first component of the presumption. The requirement that the plaintiff must also establish the remaining components places an extra burden upon him. This overburdening of the plaintiff seems to have no justifiable purpose and therefore appears anomalous.

One can, however, avoid this anomaly by distinguishing between the two ways—one statistical and the other individualized—in which negligence can be established. Normally, a plaintiff is required to establish the defendant's negligence by case-specific evidence, that is, by evidence that points to a concrete act or omission committed by the defendant. If such an act or omission amounts to negligence and if it is causally responsible for the plaintiff's damage, then the defendant should be held liable. This normal proof requirement is individualized in nature.[6] But there are cases in which there is no evidence that could point to a specific act or omission by which the defendant negligently damaged the plaintiff; at the same time, general experience instructs the judges that in the given type of cases, the defendant's negligence is predominantly responsible for the plaintiff's respective damage. Statistical inference of negligence consequently becomes available. Normally, no such inference may be drawn against the defendant even when it is sound from a probabilistic point of view. A person should be held responsible only for what *he or she* did individually rather than for being affiliated by the judge to some statistically significant group of people, in which the wrongdoers form the majority. As the famous saying goes, 'For statistics there are no individuals, and for individuals no statistics.'

Under the *res ipsa loquitur* presumption, however, one can make a justifiable exception to this theory. We identify this exception as 'the statistical negligence principle'. Under this principle, naked statistical evidence that merely typifies the case at hand as belonging to a general negligence category will not open the defendant's pockets to the plaintiff; however, it might do so when the *res ipsa loquitur* presumption enters the scene. There are two versions of

[5] In Israel, there is an additional requirement for activating the presumption: the plaintiff must demonstrate that *at the time that his damage was inflicted*, he did not know and could not have reasonably known how it was inflicted: Torts Ordinance [New Version], s. 41. At the same time, it was held that the presumption would be activated against the defendant only when the actual course of events remained uncertain at the end of the trial. The presumption would not apply if a specified factual scenario pointing either to the negligence or faultlessness of the defendant were more probable than not. See *Neumann v Cohen*, Ibid.; *Naim v Ministry of Education and Culture*, 42 (1) Piskey Din 153 (1985) (Hebrew).

[6] This point is discussed above in Ch. I.

this presumption, one weak and the other strong. Under the strong version, when the presumption's conditions are adequately established by the plaintiff, the defendant will be held negligent on statistical grounds alone. In such cases, the presumption's statistical base (Condition 1) is supplemented by two individualized liability grounds (Conditions 2 and 3). If the defendant fails to provide countervailing evidence that proves, on a balance of probabilities, that he was not negligent, the court will rule against him. The defendant would thus be deemed to have acted in *some* negligent way causally associated with the plaintiff's damage.

Examples of statistical negligence, taken from the common experience of mankind, are abundant. A proposition that in the presence of due diligence, a barrel will not fall from an upstairs window on to a passer-by in the street is part of that experience.[7] The same experience also tells us that in the absence of negligence, bales of sugar do not fall from hoists;[8] cranes do not collapse;[9] trains do not collide;[10] aircraft do not crash on taking off[11] or disappear on flights in good weather;[12] commercial airliners do not crash;[13] stones are not found in bread[14] and glass in spinach;[15] livestock does not wander loose on highways;[16] gas and water do not escape from mains[17] and electricity from wires and appliances;[18] structures do not collapse;[19] construction panels do not fall on workmen;[20] pieces of ceiling plaster do not fall on hotel guests;[21] elevators do not fall;[22] vehicles do not veer on to pavements and hit pedestrians[23] or to the wrong side of the road into the path of oncoming traffic;[24] wheels do not detach from moving vehicles;[25] surgical instruments are not left in a patient's body after an operation;[26] simple medical treatments

[7] *Byrne v Boadle* (1863) 159 Eng Rep 299; *Hake v George Wiedemann Brewing Co.*, 262 NE 2d 703 (1970).

[8] *Scott v London & St. Katherine Docks* (1865) 3 H&C 596.

[9] *Swan v Salisbury Constructions* [1966] 1 WLR 204.

[10] *Skinner v L.B. & S.C. Railway* (1850) 5 Exch 787.

[11] *Street on Torts* (10th edn., 1999) 259.

[12] *Restatement (Second) of Torts* (1965) 160.

[13] *Cox v Northwest Airlines Inc.*, 379 F 2d 893, 895; *Brecker v American Airlines Inc.*, 200 F Supp 839, 840 (SDNY 1961).

[14] *Chapronière v Mason* (1905) 21 TLR 633.

[15] *Restatement (Second) of Torts* (1965) 159.

[16] *Watzig v Tobin*, 642 P 2d 651 (1981).

[17] *Hollywood Shop Inc. v Pennsylvania Gas & Water Co.*, 411 A 2d 509 (1979).

[18] *Humphrey v Twin State Gas & Electronic Co.*, 139 A 440 (1927); *Cain v Southern Massachusetts Telephone Co.*, 107 NE 380 (1914).

[19] *Lynden Transport Inc. v Haragan, Alaska*, 623 P 2d 789 (1981); *Boyer v Iowa High School Athletic Association*, 152 NW 2d 293 (1967); *Emerick v Raleigh Hills Hospital*, 184 Cal Rptr 92 (1982).

[20] *Bennett v Chemical Construction (GB) Ltd.* [1971] 1 WLR 1571.

[21] *Restatement (Second) of Torts* (1965) 160.

[22] *Griffen v Manice*, 59 NE 925 (1901); *Kunzie v Leeds Inc.*, 34 NE 2d 448 (1941).

[23] *Ellor v Selfridge & Co. Ltd.* (1930) 46 TLR 236; *Watson v Thomas S. Whitney & Co. Ltd.* [1966] 1 WLR 57.

[24] *Richley (Henderson) v Faull* [1965] 1 WLR 1454.

[25] *Swiney v Malone Freight Lines*, 545 SW 2d 112 (1976).

[26] *Mahon v Osborne* [1939] 1 All ER 535 (CA).

with a solid record of success do not fail;[27] hospitals do not become infected with bacteria;[28] owned dogs do not wander on streets unaccompanied by their owners and bite pedestrians;[29] and there are plenty of other useful examples.[30] Each of these examples involves statistical negligence. Under the strong version of *res ipsa*, this negligence would be attributed to a defendant who falls into the relevant statistical category and fails to exclude himself from the typicality by proving, by a preponderance of the evidence, that he was faultless.

As already indicated, this strong version of the presumption has not been endorsed in Anglo-American jurisdictions. These jurisdictions prefer the weak version. In these jurisdictions, the presumption does not shift the burden of persuasion and the consequent risk of non-persuasion to the statistically negligent defendant. Consequently, in cases of irreducible uncertainty, where the defendant's case-specific negligence is merely as probable as not, the defendant must be held not liable even when he falls within one of the statistical negligence categories. His falling within one of those categories as a matter of generalized frequency of events has been held to be insufficient for imposing liability in torts.[31] Subject to a few exceptions, such as market-share liability,[32] liability in torts has been held to be attributable only on individualized grounds. The defendant's action may be classified as negligent only by virtue of its specific properties and not by its statistical categorization. The famous criminal law precept 'Judge the act, not the actor' thus seems to be at work also in torts. Under the prevalent view of the *res ipsa loquitur* presumption, it does not even shift on to the defendant the production burden, that is, the formal (as contrasted with merely tactical) burden of bringing forth evidence. According to this view, the presumption identifies the defendant's negligence as a mere possibility, so it only allows judges and jurors to infer negligence from the circumstances of the case.

In a number of exceptional cases, such as the famous medical malpractice decision *Ybarra v Spangard*,[33] courts shifted the production burden to the defendants. *Cassidy v Ministry of Health*[34] is one of the prominent English examples of this approach. This approach places the production burden on the defendants in the sense that it is for them 'to show that the accident was just as consistent with their having exercised due diligence as with their having been

27 *Saunders v Leeds Western Health Authority* (1984) 129 SJ 225; *Amar v The* Histadrut *General Patients' Health Care Association*, 46 (1) Piskey Din 712 (1989) (Hebrew).

28 *Raz v Elisha Hospital*, (n. 2 above).

29 W. L. Prosser and W. P. Keeton, *Prosser and Keeton on the Law of Torts* (5th edn., 1984) 244–5.

30 See J. G. Fleming, *The Law of Torts* (9th edn., 1998) 360–4; W. V. H. Rogers, *Winfield and Jolowicz on Torts* (15th edn., 1998) 191–3; J. W. Salmond and R. F. V. Heuston, *Salmond and Heuston on The Law of Torts* (21st edn., 1996) 360–4.

31 See Chapter I above.

32 See Chapter V below.

33 *Ybarra v Spangard*, 154 P 2d 687 (1944).

34 *Cassidy v Ministry of Health* [1951] 2 KB 343, 365.

negligent'.[35] 'In that way'—so it was explained—'the scales which had been tipped [by the presumption] in the plaintiff's favour . . . would be once more in the balance, and the plaintiff would have to begin again and prove negligence in the usual way'.[36] However, in cases representing the presently dominant trend, courts have held that the presumption merely allows the plaintiff to surpass the no-evidence barrier and thus avoid direct dismissal of his lawsuit.[37] Under this view, statistical inference of negligence furnished by the presumption simply amounts to a piece of circumstantial evidence from which case-specific negligence may be inferred in conditions of uncertainty.[38] This interpretation is unequivocally supported by all contemporary treatises on the law of torts, including the Second Restatement.[39]

The presumption's effect thus reduces to establishing trialworthiness of the plaintiff's case, which shifts to the defendant only a tactical burden. In other words, absence of case-specific evidence pointing to the defendant's negligence would not be fatal to the plaintiff's case. Once the presumption is put to work, it requires the defendant to come forth with exonerating evidence. Failure to do so allows the court to impose the risk of error on the defendant by holding him negligent. This risk is not negligible. Non-production of exonerating evidence by the defendant would allow the court to infer that such evidence does not exist; in certain cases, it would also indicate that the defendant has withheld some important evidence, unfavourable to his case, in order to seek refuge in the shadows of uncertainty. The defendant would consequently be held negligent and liable. Defendants facing those prospects would thus ordinarily attempt to rebut the inference of negligence allowed by the presumption.[40] There is, therefore, no substantial difference between the accepted doctrine and the competing interpretation of the presumption that shifts the burden of adducing evidence to the defendant. The traditional 'bursting bubble' metaphor clearly downplays the presumption's importance by focusing on the consequences of a case in which the defendant comes forth with self-exonerating counter-proof that bursts the *res ipsa* bubble. Although technically correct, this description fails to emphasize that providing the required counter-proof that would satisfy the judges that no evidence is being concealed is often a formidable task. By making the plaintiff's case, the presumption increases the defendant's risk of losing the case.

On this understanding of the presumption, risk of error that would inevitably accompany any final verdict is allowed to be placed on the defendant. This consequence is entailed in the principle under which the presumption

[35] *Henderson v Henry E. Jenkins & Sons* (n. 3 above). [36] Ibid.

[37] Prosser and Keeton (n. 29 above) 257–9. [38] Ibid.

[39] *Restatement (Second) of Torts* (1965) 165.

[40] With the advent of all-encompassing pre-trial disclosure requirements, the formal production burden has also lost much of its practical significance in civil litigation. See R. J. Allen, 'Presumptions in Civil Actions Reconsidered' (1981) 66 *Iowa L Rev* 843, 860. Trialworthiness is a far more significant consequence of the presumption.

makes the plaintiff's otherwise unsubstantiated case trialworthy. The presumption prescribes that a verdict for the plaintiff *must be considered* as a possibility even if no further evidence is adduced, so that the defendant may be held negligent solely for falling into the relevant statistical negligence category. This possibility would, of course, depend on the relative frequency of negligence incidents within the relevant statistical category and on the case-specific evidence lain out before the court. The mere existence of this possibility would, however, always place some risk of error on the defendant. This risk may not always materialize, but it is not trivial either: some of the defendants held negligent under the presumption may be genuinely negligent, but some of them may be faultless. The crucial factor is that the defendant can claim no immunity from this risk by saying: 'Naked statistical negligence will not do.'

This understanding of the *res ipsa loquitur* presumption adequately responds to the argument from anomaly. On this understanding, a defendant cannot normally be held liable on statistical evidence alone, but he can be held liable when the presumption applies. It would therefore not be enough for the plaintiff to establish only the first pillar of the presumption. If he could make his case trialworthy by virtue of this pillar alone, the defendant could then be held liable on the basis of naked statistics. The plaintiff is therefore required to individualize the potential negligence inference against the defendant by establishing Conditions 2 and 3. To justify his reliance on the presumption, the plaintiff must also demonstrate the unavailability of individualized evidence that could point to the defendant's negligence or faultlessness (Condition 4).

This understanding of the presumption also adequately responds to the argument from redundancy. The presumption is not redundant because it establishes trialworthiness of the plaintiff's case that could otherwise be dismissed on no-suit grounds. When the law prescribes that naked statistical evidence will not do, an exception to this general prescription cannot be an otiose component in the justice machinery. When the law says that statistical negligence might do whenever the fundamentals of *res ipsa loquitur* are established, this statement is neither redundant nor trivial. For that reason, a recent announcement by the Canadian Supreme Court that *res ipsa loquitur* is dead[41] is rather akin to the first newspaper obituary on Mark Twain, which he famously described as premature. According to the Court itself, once the *res ipsa loquitur* conditions are established, there is a basis upon which the trial court may draw appropriate inferences that ascribe negligence to the defendant.[42] Because courts are generally reluctant to rely on naked statistical evidence,[43] this point is not trivial. By making this point, the Canadian

[41] *Fontaine v Loewen Estate* [1997] 156 DLR (4th) 581, 585. For a discussion of this case, celebrating the death of *res ipsa loquitur*, see M. McInnes, 'The Death of Res Ipsa Loquitur in Canada' (1998) 114 *LQR* 547.

[42] *Fontaine v Loewen Estate* (n. 41 above); McInnes (n. 41 above).

[43] Chapter I of this book discusses critically this reluctance.

Supreme Court has effectively acknowledged that a naked statistical case, made out by a tort plaintiff in a Canadian court, is trialworthy (even though the plaintiff might not be declared the winner at the end of the day). The Court held that this accepted consequence need not be termed '*res ipsa loquitur*', and we have every reason to believe that no tort plaintiff would be upset by this purely conceptual holding. From a tort plaintiff's perspective, as long as his naked statistical case is deemed trialworthy, so that he retains the chance of winning his case, the formal origin of this trial advantage—*res ipsa* or *Fontaine v Loewen Estate*—makes no difference. We equally suspect that a faultless defendant who was nevertheless found liable with the help of *res ipsa* would be equally upset if his liability were grounded upon *Fontaine v Loewen Estate*. To paraphrase: the *res ipsa loquitur* doctrine has been pronounced dead by the Canadian Supreme Court, but it seems to be still alive and well in Canada under a different name.

B. STRONG PRESUMPTION OR WEAK PRESUMPTION?

At this juncture, we can compare the strong and weak versions of the *res ipsa* presumption. Under the strong version of the presumption, once its basic conditions (Conditions 1–4) have been adequately established by the plaintiff, the burden of persuasion shifts to the defendant, so that the latter must preponderantly prove that he was faultless. In other words, the defendant's exonerating account must be evidentially better—that is, more probable—than the plaintiff's version of the case. Under the weak version of *res ipsa*, the defendant need only neutralize the negligence inference allowed by the presumption. In other words, it would be sufficient for the defendant to provide an exonerating account that is as good as the plaintiff's version of the case. If the defendant fails to provide such an account, he would normally be held negligent. The qualifier 'normally' is doctrinally necessary here: under one of the two variants of the weak presumption version of *res ipsa*, the presumption shifts to the defendant only a tactical, as opposed to evidential, burden, so that in theory, the defendant may be exonerated even when his account is not as good as that of the plaintiff. This possible outcome is predicated on the discretionary, rather than mandatory, nature of the negligence inference that this variant of *res ipsa* prefers. Under the second weak variant of *res ipsa*, the presumption shifts to the defendant the formal production burden, and the negligence inference, activated by the defendant's failure to discharge that burden, is mandatory rather than discretionary. Consequently, the defendant must be held negligent if he fails to neutralize the presumption's effect by providing an exonerating account of the events that is at least as good as the plaintiff's theory of the case. As already indicated, the difference between the two weak variants is insignificant: it is highly unlikely that a defendant would escape liability under the discretionary variant of the presumption, if his evidence has failed to neutralize the negligence inference. Under the mandatory variant, such an outcome is altogether impossible, and the difference between 'impossible' and 'highly unlikely' does not merit much discussion. The difference that really matters is the one that exists between the strong and the weak versions of the presumption. This difference tells judges how to resolve balanced cases in which no preference can be accorded to one of the competing accounts of the events. Because in tort litigation, factual impasse is not a rarity, the difference between the weak and the strong versions of *res ipsa* can really make a difference: if the persuasion burden and the corresponding risk of non-persuasion are not shifted from the plaintiff to the defendant, as prescribed by the presumption's weak version, then the plaintiff will lose the case; if the strong version of the presumption is at work, the plaintiff will win.

Which version of the presumption—strong or weak—is preferable as a matter of policy? An important probabilistic factor, first pointed to four decades ago by Vaughn Ball,[44] strongly favours the weak version of the presumption. For reasons that will soon become apparent, we will label this factor 'double-counting'. As Vaughn Ball observed:

> The risk of non-persuasion is allocated (a great part of the time, at least) upon the basis of the probability of the existence of the fact in the run of cases of the particular kind, absent any specific evidence. Since the evidence and the jury's consideration of it have come to naught, we will make the fewest mistakes if we let the case fall back into the general class, to be decided on those original probabilities. But the jury, unless it lacks the common knowledge we ascribe to it by definition, has begun its own deliberation with those probabilities in mind, and it is the combination of both those and the probability drawn from the specific evidence, that the jury says are at balance. If we then use the initial probabilities to remove the balance, we are in some sense counting them twice.[45]

This observation holds true in the present context, similarly to other comparable contexts that involve legal presumptions. Factual impasse settings, in which the *res ipsa loquitur* presumption becomes operative, are formed by the combination of two factors: (1) evidence produced at the trial; and (2) general experience by which this evidence and its probative impact are evaluated. The general experience factor accommodates the relevant background probabilities, including the findings necessary for the application of *res ipsa*, namely:

(1) the probabilistic fact that the occurrence that ended up in the plaintiff's damage does not normally take place without negligence;

[44] See Vaughn C. Ball, 'The Moment of Truth: Probability Theory and Standards of Proof' (1961) 14 *Vanderbilt L Rev* 807.

[45] Ibid. 817–18. An example of the fallacy spotted by Professor Ball can be found in Julius Stone, 'Burden of Proof and the Judicial Process' (1944) 60 *LQR* 262, 278.

(2) the fact that the occurrence must have been caused by an agency or instrumentality over which the defendant exercised exclusive control; and
(3) the fact that the occurrence did not take place due to a contribution or voluntary action by the plaintiff.

A judicial final decision that attests to factual impasse must therefore already accommodate each of these factors. These factors must have already added the appropriate strength to the evidence adduced by the plaintiff. They must have allowed the plaintiff to even the score in his evidentiary competition against the defendant. Presumably, in the absence of these factors, the plaintiff's account of the events would have been held less probable than the defendant's account. If any of these factors were now to be allowed to break the impasse by tilting the scales of justice in the plaintiff's favour, this factor would then be counted twice, so the plaintiff would receive a double credit for his evidence. Under any rational theory of fact-finding, this outcome would be anomalous. In the absence of offsetting policy considerations, the strong presumption version of *res ipsa* must consequently be rejected.

The required policy considerations cannot be easily identified. From the fairness perspective (which can be associated with corrective justice), the law's remedial machinery should be put in motion only when there are preponderantly good reasons for doing so. As explained in Chapter I, when the reasons for doing so are just as good as the reasons for keeping the machinery dormant, there is no justification for interfering with the status quo. From the optimal deterrence perspective (which also accommodates the relevant adjudicative constraints), there must be some special reason for holding the defendant liable when the probability of the plaintiff's case does not exceed 0.5. In the absence of such a reason, the defendant should prevail. This point has also been explained in Chapter I. Things seem to be no different in the realm of distributive justice, for there seems to be no reason for according preference to the plaintiff's welfare over that of the defendant when the competing contentions of the two are equally probable. Indeed, the *res ipsa* conditions are a poor proxy for identifying wealth and power relationships that are relevant for distributive purposes. A poor bicycle rider may hit a rich pedestrian who has just disembarked from her Rolls Royce; so when the rider's negligence is as probable as not, it would clearly be an affront to common sense if he were to be held liable by virtue of distributive justice. The case against the strong version of *res ipsa* thus appears to be overwhelming.

We will, nonetheless, postpone our final conclusion on that issue until our analysis of the presumption's conditions is complete. This analysis reveals that the presumption correctly identifies the defendant as a *typically* cheapest cost-avoider of the damage. This status justifies imposition of liability for the damage on the defendant. Moreover, the presumption correctly identifies the defendant as *typically* responsible for the uncertainty of the case. In other words, it correctly identifies the defendant as typically the cheapest cost avoider of the evidential damage. This factor also marks the defendant as liable in torts. The strong version of *res ipsa*, consequently becomes justified.

C. *RES IPSA LOQUITUR* AND THE CHEAPEST COST-AVOIDER

The strong version of *res ipsa loquitur* does have a plausible rationale. This rationale is economic in character. Under this rationale, the presumption identifies the cheapest cost-avoider of the litigated damage at the lowest adjudication cost and imposes on him liability for that damage. In this theory, the 'cheapest cost-avoider' status—as Calabresi and Hirschoff propose to understand it[46]—derives from a person's position in relation to the damage. Specifically, it depends on a person's comparative ability properly to consider if and how to dispense resources in order to avoid the damage (but not necessarily on his actual ability to prevent the damage cost-efficiently[47]). A person best positioned to perform this calculation is the cheapest cost-avoider. The holder of this status can thus be described more accurately as the 'best assessor' of the situation at hand. As such, he will internalize either the cost of preventing the damage or the damage itself (in the form of liability in torts and the consequent compensation duty). This person will decide whether to avoid the damage by accounting both for the probability of the damage and for its magnitude. He will thus compare the expected, rather than

[46] See G. Calabresi, *The Costs of Accidents* (1970) 68–94, 135–73, 244–65; G. Calabresi and J. T. Hirschoff, 'Toward a Test for Strict Liability in Torts' (1972) 81 *Yale LJ* 1055. For critical discussion of this approach, see I. Englard, *The Philosophy of Tort Law* (1993) 31–5 (arguing that the instrumentalist objectives favoured by this approach are likely to be thwarted by their complexity and lack of necessary information).

[47] Another approach links the 'cheapest cost-avoider' status to a person's actual ability to prevent the damage cost-efficiently. This approach invokes the famous Learned Hand formula, according to which negligence will occur if B<PL. In that formula:

> B is the burden of precautions that represents the costs that need to be spent on taking the adequate precautions;
> L is the loss that can be avoided by taking these precautions; and
> P is the probability of L, as determined before the event.

See *Conway v O'Brian*, 111 F 2d 611, 612 (2d Cir 1940), *rev'd on other grounds*, 312 US 492 (1941); *United States v Carroll Towing Co.*, 159 F 2d 169 (2d Cir 1947). This formulation of tort liability was adopted and refined by Judge Richard Posner. See R. A. Posner, 'A Theory of Negligence' (1972) 1 *J Legal Studies* 29; R. A. Posner, 'Strict Liability: A Comment' (1973) 2 *J Legal Studies* 205; W. M. Landes and R. A. Posner, *The Economic Structure of Tort Law* (1987) 54–84. For critique of this approach, see I. Englard, 'The System Builders: A Critical Appraisal of Modern American Tort Theory' (1980) 9 *J Legal Studies* 27, 33–55 (arguing that Posner's principle is inherently ambiguous, which makes it operationally insignificant, and that a reductionist attempt at making it operative would oversimplify the efficiency problem and generate distortions). For a general appraisal of the economic approach to tort liability, see G. T. Schwartz, 'Reality in the Economic Analysis of Tort Law: Does Tort Law Really Deter?' (1994) 42 *University of California Los Angeles L Rev* 377.

full, value of the damage with the cost of avoiding it. This self-interested choice of the cheapest cost-avoider will augment social utility.

To understand this point, one must revisit the foundational conditions for *res ipsa*. Specifically, one should juxtapose the first pair of these conditions with their second pair. The second pair of these conditions—absence of fault on the part of the plaintiff and absence of evidence highlighting the actual course of the events—identifies the victim of the damage as a person with a relatively limited opportunity to foresee the damage and to calculate the means and costs of its prevention. These conditions imply that information necessary for foreseeing the damage and for calculating its prevention was not reasonably available to the victim. The first pair of *res ipsa* conditions—the preponderance of the general probability of negligence, coupled with the damaging instrumentality over which the defendant exercised exclusive control—identifies the defendant as the person best situated to foresee the damage and to calculate its prevention. There is, in other words, a strong likelihood, if not virtual certainty, that the defendant was the cheapest cost-avoider—that is, the best assessor—of the litigated damage. Under the *res ipsa* conditions, the defendant's ability to foresee and calculate the prevention of the damage was not only better than that of the plaintiff; typically, it would also be better than that of any other person who could be associated with the infliction of the damage. This factor marks the defendant as the economically optimal bearer of liability for that damage. The prospect of being held liable in torts under the strong version of *res ipsa* would discourage many such defendants from causing damage. Note that the defendant would assume this comparative situational superiority over others because of his exclusive control over the instrumentality that caused the damage. He would not assume the cheapest cost-avoider status when the instrumentality conditions were not satisfied.

Arguably, judges should determine the cheapest cost-avoider status without resorting to presumptions. Although generally correct, this argument underestimates the importance of inferential shortcuts that save adjudication costs. Such shortcuts would be justified when they produce a preponderant rate of correct decisions in the long run of cases. The strong version of the *res ipsa loquitur* presumption is one of such shortcuts. Ascertaining the cheapest cost-avoider status and its underlying features may be costly. Costs involved in this endeavour may well exceed the gains that the resulting enhancement of adjudicative accuracy would produce. The *res ipsa loquitur* presumption saves those costs without seriously undermining adjudicative accuracy. This presumption enables judges to identify properly the cheapest cost-avoiders of tort damages in a preponderantly large number of cases. At the same time, it exempts both judges and litigants from conducting inquiries into this status in circumstances in which such inquiries would be more expensive than productive. Indeed, under the presumption's basic conditions, it would be activated only in those instances in which case-specific evidence is notoriously scarce, if not altogether unavailable.

D. *RES IPSA LOQUITUR* AND LIABILITY FOR UNCERTAINTY

For reasons that single out the defendant as the best assessor of the situation and, consequently, the cheapest cost-avoider of the litigated damage, the *res ipsa loquitur* presumption also identifies him as the person who could substantially reduce the factual uncertainty of the case. The fact that *res ipsa* cases are evidentially deficient presents an impediment to the efficient allocation of liability in torts. This impediment, identified by this book as evidential damage,[48] constitutes a serious problem for law enforcement that a typical *res ipsa* defendant could cost-efficiently prevent. The liability threat that such defendants would face under the strong version of *res ipsa* would, therefore, induce them to reduce the incidence of evidential damage.

Typically, a *res ipsa* defendant would be the cheapest cost-avoider of the evidential damage not only before the occurrence of that damage, but also after its occurrence. The *res ipsa* conditions place the defendant under both undispellable and unverifiable suspicion of negligence. The judge's inability to dispel or to verify that suspicion results from the way in which the defendant employed the relevant agency or instrumentality. In these circumstances, the defendant's inability to disassociate his possible fault from the plaintiff's damage raises yet another suspicion. The missing evidence might be missing because it is objectively unavailable, but it might also be missing because either the plaintiff or the defendant decided to suppress it. In the light of the defendant's superior access to that evidence, the probability of its suppression by the defendant is higher than that of the alternative possibilities. This factor lends yet another support to the idea of holding such defendants responsible for the uncertainty of the case. Consequently, the evidentially damaged plaintiff should be allowed to recover an evidential addition to his case at the defendant's expense. Since the case is balanced—as it always is under the *res ipsa* conditions—and because *any* evidential addition to the plaintiff's case would yield victory for him, the plaintiff should win the case. The strong version of the *res ipsa* presumption would achieve this outcome by shifting the persuasion burden to the defendant.[49]

This understanding of *res ipsa* turns the presumption into a restricted variant of the evidential damage doctrine that we develop in Chapter VI. Because

[48] See Chapter VI below.

[49] In applying this version of *res ipsa*, one should, however, be aware of the danger of double-counting. If the judges arrived at a factual impasse after considering the probability of evidence-suppression by the defendant, they should not use it against him for the second time. See nn. 44–5 above and accompanying text.

the evidential damage doctrine is general in scope, its application would provide a more adequate solution to the uncertainty problem. We will now exemplify this point by discussing *Rabena v City of New York*,[50] a relatively recent case that emphasizes the limits of *res ipsa*. In that case, a severely handicapped and mentally retarded infant was taken unharmed to a special school, but returned home with a thigh injury. The infant sustained the injury between the time he was put on a special bus that took him to the school and the time he returned home with the same bus. His mother and natural guardian brought a negligence action to recover money damages for his injury. This action was brought against the school's operator, the bus company, and the Municipality (on the theory that the latter was responsible for the operation of both the school and the bus).

At trial, the defendants' employees testified that 'the infant plaintiff was well secured and strapped in the bus, did not whine or cry, and that there were no unusual occurrences or accidents'.[51] They also testified that the plaintiff 'was delivered to his mother in front of his residence in the same condition he was received by them'.[52] At the end of the trial, the defendants moved for a direct dismissal of the action, and the court ruled in their favour. The court ruled in favour of the defendants because the plaintiff had adduced no evidence identifying the specific act of negligence that had resulted in the injury and the specific wrongdoer responsible for that act.

To avoid dismissal of the case, the plaintiff contended that the court should activate the *res ipsa loquitur* presumption in his favour. He claimed the presumption to be applicable because of the circumstances and nature of his injury and because of his inability to communicate. However, based on an oft-quoted passage from *Prosser*,[53] the court declined to accept this claim. It held that the plaintiff had failed to identify the instrumentality from which his injury had resulted. As noted by the court:

> Res ipsa loquitur by its term means 'the thing speaks for itself' and that means the thing or the instrumentality that caused the injury to speak for itself. *It clearly does not mean the injury speaks for itself.* It means that when the initial fact, namely, what thing or instrumentality caused the injury has been shown then and not before, an inference

[50] *Rabena v City of New York*, 556 NYS 2d 807 (1990). [51] Ibid. 808. [52] Ibid.

[53] Prosser stated that: 'it is never enough for the plaintiff to prove merely that he has been injured by the negligence of someone unidentified. Even though there is beyond all possible doubt negligence in the air, it is still necessary to bring it home to the defendant. On this too the plaintiff has the burden of proof by a preponderance of the evidence; and in any case where it is clear that it is at least equally probable that the negligence was that of another, the court must direct the jury that the plaintiff has not proved his case. The injury must either be traced to a specific instrumentality or cause for which the defendant was responsible, or it must be shown that he was responsible for all reasonably probable causes to which the accident could be attributed. Accordingly, res ipsa loquitur is held not to apply where a chair is thrown from an unidentified window in the defendant's hotel, or where the presence of such an object as a bolt on a railway platform might easily have been due to the act of a third party, or where gas or water or electricity escape from fixtures controlled in part by another' (Prosser and Keeton (n. 29 above) 248–9).

arises that the injury occurred by reason of the negligence of the party or parties who had it under exclusive control.[54]

Therefore, 'while the Court is sympathetic to the plaintiff's plight, that does not exempt him from the law'.[55]

In this case, the probability of the allegations identifying the school's operator and the bus company[56] as the wrongful origin of the plaintiff's injury equalled 50 per cent, respectively. Moreover, it was practically certain that a wrongful act or omission committed by one of those defendants had caused the plaintiff's injury. Therefore, any reduction in one of the two probabilities of fault would increase the other probability, thus identifying one of the defendants as the most likely origin of the injury. Arguably, under these circumstances, the case should have gone to the jury. Thus, if the jury were to accept the school operator's account of the events, it would have found the bus company responsible for the plaintiff's injury. Alternatively, if the jury were to accept the bus company's account, it would have placed the responsibility for the injury on the school's operator. However, there is also a third possibility: the jury could have found the two accounts equally probable, in which case it would have to dismiss the action. Arguably, because this third possibility is the only scenario in which the action could be dismissed, the court should have allowed the case to be decided on the merits instead of dismissing it directly.

The court's decision rested on the implicit, but unequivocal, assumption that *none* of the possibilities could benefit the plaintiff because these possibilities were purely statistical. In the court's view, the jury could not rule for the plaintiff even if it were to accept the self-exonerating account of one of the two defendants as preponderantly probable. This acceptance could not adequately identify the other defendant as the wrongful origin of the plaintiff's injury. Negligence that a plaintiff attributes to a defendant must be established by case-specific evidence. This evidence must identify the specific act or omission that constitutes negligence. Naked statistics do not establish the plaintiff's case. Indeed, this point is well-entrenched in positive law and we have discussed it in Chapter I.

The *Rabena* court, however, did not address two additional possibilities, which have a common denominator: liability *for* uncertainty. First, by adopting this perspective, the court could have held the school's operator responsible for the plaintiff's evidential damage. As determined by the court, during the plaintiff's school hours, the school's operator exercised exclusive custody and control over the plaintiff and was responsible for the plaintiff's safety.

[54] *Rabena v City of New York*, (n. 50 above), 810 (1990) (emphasis added).

[55] Ibid. 811.

[56] We exclude the Municipality from this analysis because its liability derived from that of the other defendants. The Municipality could be found liable for the plaintiff's damage only if any of these defendants were to assume liability.

This responsibility involved 'reasonable inspection and repair' and 'personal supervision of and safety of the children' entrusted in the operator's care.[57] If so, the school's operator had borne the auxiliary duty to provide both full and credible information about the plaintiff's day at school. The operator owed this duty to the plaintiff's mother. This duty seems to have been violated. The only information that the operator could provide to the plaintiff's mother was the standard incantation 'nothing unusual'. Moreover, this uninformative incantation was merely as probable as its factual contradiction that came from the bus company. Arguably, the plaintiff's mother—and, consequently, the plaintiff—were thus wrongfully deprived of valuable information that reflected the plaintiff's legal rights. This evidential damage equals the total value of the plaintiff's right to recover for his injury. On this theory, the school's operator could have been forced to fully compensate the plaintiff. Furthermore, if the same argument were to apply to the bus company,[58] then it could have equally been held responsible.

Second, the Municipality that stood behind both the school's operator and the bus company should certainly have been held responsible for the plaintiff's evidential damage. Because this damage was not self-inflicted, one of these agents for the Municipality must have inflicted it on the plaintiff. Furthermore, under a broader interpretation of the *res ipsa* presumption, both the school and the bus, with all their facilities, could have been treated as instruments over which the Municipality exercised exclusive control by its agents. This interpretation of the instrumentality condition would have activated the presumption in the plaintiff's favour.[59]

E. CONCLUSION

The *res ipsa loquitur* presumption is neither redundant nor anomalous. This chapter has justified both the weak and the strong versions of this presumption. From an economic perspective, the strong version of the presumption is preferable to its weak version. As demonstrated above, the *res ipsa* presumption is closely related to two legal doctrines: one that disfavours naked statistical evidence and one that imposes liability for uncertainty. The presumption constitutes an important exception to the former doctrine and an important—albeit imperfect—variant of the latter doctrine.[60]

[57] See *Rabena v City of New York* (n. 50 above), 810.

[58] This possibility emerges from the court's statement ibid. 810–11.

[59] Former Israeli Chief Justice Meir Shamgar developed a similar interpretation in *Raz v Elisha Hospital* (n. 2 above). Arguably, the municipality could be held liable under the theory that one of its agents must have caused the plaintiff's damage.

[60] The evidential damage doctrine, however, is yet to gain general recognition by the positive law. In Chapter VI, we argue that it deserves such recognition.

IV

Risk as Damage

A. THE NATURE OF THE PROBLEM

EVERY tort begins with the creation of a risk of inflicting damage. However, unlike criminal law, which imposes liability for attempts, tort law does not impose liability for creation of bare risk. Tort law imposes liability for damage, and risk, in itself, is not regarded as damage. If a person drives at a very high speed and exposes a pedestrian to a substantial risk of injury that ultimately does not materialize, the driver will not be liable towards the pedestrian.[1] The pedestrian's luck amounts to luck for the driver as well: since the former was lucky enough to escape injury, the latter is lucky enough to escape liability in torts.

Although risk in itself is not a ground for imposing liability in torts, its creation is included on the list of factors that determine tort liability. The way in which risk is created and imposed on others bears strongly upon liability in torts. Under the prevalent tort law doctrine, risk-creation generally needs to be accounted for by judges in determining whether a person who inflicted the litigated damage did so wrongfully. In our example above, if the pedestrian were actually injured by the driver and the legal regime were that of negligence, then the magnitude of the risk to which the driver exposed the pedestrian would affect the resolution of the question of whether to impose liability on the driver. Creation of risk also has significant bearing in determining the scope of the wrongdoer's liability. Thus, if the pedestrian injured in the accident were contributorily negligent, then the magnitude of the risk created by the negligent driver would influence the apportionment of the damage between the parties.

The way in which the risk of inflicting damage was created is also of significance in cases involving risks that might materialize in the future. In such cases, although the plaintiff remains as yet undamaged, the risk of sustaining damage to which the defendant exposed the plaintiff is likely to materialize in the future. Thus, when a court considers an injunction to prevent the defendant from engaging in an activity that might become a nuisance for the plaintiff, the nature of the risk that the defendant's activity involves would

[1] Provided the incident has not created fear or anxiety for the pedestrian, in which case, the legal result may be different. See discussion below.

certainly be an important factor in the court's decision.[2] A rather more difficult question is whether such a plaintiff also is entitled to damages. Presumably, she is entitled to recover compensation from the defendant: the defendant wrongfully forced her to live in the shadow of the risk, so he must compensate her for this detraction from her well-being.

Let us take another example, one that involves a physician who negligently treated a patient and thereby reduced her chances of recovery. There is a chance that the patient will recover, as well as a chance that she will not recover. If she ultimately does not recover, her failure to recover might be either related or unrelated to her negligent treatment by the physician. Each of these two scenarios would have a positive probability. For such cases, a legal system could adopt a rule that would force defendants to compensate plaintiffs for their reduced chances to recover.[3] Under such a system, risk-creation would be significant even when no damage is presently incurred, as long as there is uncertainty as to whether it will be incurred in the future.

Let us take now a case that belongs to a different category of risk-related cases. In this category of cases, the plaintiff was injured, but whether the injury resulted from the defendant's wrongdoing is impossible to determine. This category can be well exemplified by our negligent physician case if we assume that, ultimately, the patient did not recover. Let us also assume that the plaintiff had only a 40 per cent chance of recovery in the absence of negligence. This implies that the probability that the plaintiff would have sustained her damage even if negligence were not to occur equals 60 per cent. If so, the plaintiff would then fail to prove her case under the preponderance-of-the-evidence standard. Yet, as in the previous example, the legal system may well recognize the plaintiff's right to compensation for the loss of chances. As demonstrated below, despite the similarity between these last two examples, the doctrinal solutions offered for the two types of cases have not always been identical.

This issue is discussed at a later point in this chapter. At the present stage, we would like to identify two basic principles that we employ in our subsequent discussion. First, *risk matters*: the fact that the defendant exposed the plaintiff to a risk of sustaining harm is generally relevant to the defendant's liability. Second, *there is no liability for bare risk*: if the defendant's wrongful action could not have inflicted the litigated damage or the perilous event is over, so there is no chance of future damage, there is no ground for holding the defendant liable in torts. No liability would thus be imposed in our

[2] An injunction issued before the tort materializes is known as a *quia timet* injunction. See R. F. V. Heuston and R. A. Buckley, *Salmond and Heuston on The Law of Torts* (21st edn., London, 1996) 555.

[3] This rule would not be necessary in cases where the plaintiff's condition will become certain within a short period of time.

driver-pedestrian example. In that example, the pedestrian was wrongfully exposed to a serious risk; however, the event is over, the risk did not materialize, and it therefore no longer exists. If the pedestrian was lucky, the driver will be lucky too.

In Part B of this chapter, we examine the possibility of imposing tort liability for bare risk. We first clarify this notion. Subsequently, we examine the normative arguments that tilt the scales both in favour and against liability for bare risk. This is done from three perspectives: that of retributive justice; that of corrective justice; and, finally, that of deterrence. The traditional doctrinal proposition that both an undamaged person's good luck and a damaged person's bad luck must go to the wrongdoer is not trivial. Indeed, why should tort liability be premised on luck? Nevertheless, we demonstrate that risk-based liability in torts is normatively unfounded and that tort liability must rest on the existence of actual damage. This discussion will clarify and support the prevalent legal doctrine. In Part C, we examine the possibility of imposing tort liability for lost chances. The notion 'lost chances' is used here in a very broad sense: it is predicated on the existence of uncertainty with regard to the relevant damage. Lost chances are, thus, detected in cases where the defendant created a wrongful risk and there is uncertainty as to whether this risk materialized as damage or will materialize as damage in the future. Different legal systems differ in their approaches to this type of cases,[4] and in what follows we examine these various approaches. We demonstrate that liability for lost chances will often be justified by deterrence. At the same time, imposition of that liability will often violate the principles of corrective justice. We also demonstrate that the 'evidential damage' doctrine advocated in Chapters VI and VII would provide the best solution to the problem at hand. This doctrine also would obviate the various doctrinal ramifications of the 'lost chance' doctrine.

B. LIABILITY FOR BARE RISK

1. Risk-Based Liability versus Damage-Based Liability

Under the prevalent legal doctrine, liability in torts can only be imposed when the plaintiff has sustained damage that was wrongfully inflicted by the defendant. It is, however, not inconceivable to imagine a legal system that imposes liability for bare risk. The amount of compensation to be awarded under such a system would equal the *expected damage* causally associated with the wrongful conduct. If this conduct were to involve a 50 per cent probability of inflicting damage equal to £1,000, then the defendant would have to

[4] See above 74–6.

pay £500 in liability damages. This compensation would not be dependent on whether any damage was actually incurred in the past or might be incurred in the future. Thus, a driver who drove her car at an unreasonable speed would be liable to the amount equivalent to the multiplication of the damage that could have occurred and the probability of its occurrence. This calculation would be made from an *ex ante* perspective, and (once again) regardless of whether any damage actually occurred. Compensation recovered from the driver, together with the damages paid by other wrongdoers, could be used to compensate victims of torts (for example, through establishment of a compensation fund or another appropriate scheme, such as social insurance).[5]

This substitution of the traditional damage-based liability with risk-based liability might provide the solution for a number of problems that remain unresolved under the prevalent tort law doctrine. Under the latter doctrine, imposition of tort liability depends, to a great extent, on sheer luck. The occurrence of damage depends on numerous factors, which are never fully controlled by the wrongdoer. The latter can exercise control over only some of those factors. Consequently, a lucky wrongdoer, whose actions did not ultimately end up in a damage, would escape liability, while a less fortunate wrongdoer, whose actions ended up in a damage, would be held liable. In many cases, the lucky wrongdoer might even be more blameworthy than the unlucky one. In addition, the extent of tort liability presently imposed on wrongdoers does not reflect the degree of their blameworthiness. The extent of that liability is determined solely by the outcome of the relevant conduct: the moral gravity of the wrongdoer's transgression is brushed aside. Damage-based liability therefore appears to be at odds with *retributive justice* principles. These principles prescribe that punishment must fit the moral gravity of the wrongdoing, and damage-based liability systematically violates this prescription. For example, if Bill's very dangerous and irresponsible conduct caused a £100 damage, he would have to pay only this amount. At the same time, Heather—whose conduct was wrongful, but far less dangerous and not as irresponsible as that of Bill—would have to pay £1,000,000 in damages, if that was the actual extent of the damage that she happened to inflict.[6] Arguably, the element of chance embedded in damage-based liability violates not only the principles of retributive justice, but also those of individual

[5] C. H. Schroeder, 'Corrective Justice and Liability for Increasing Risks' (1990) 37 *University of California Los Angeles L Rev* 439; C. H. Schroeder, 'Corrective Justice, Liability for Risks, and Tort Law' (1990) 38 *University of California Los Angeles L Rev* 143. For a critical discussion, see K. W. Simons, 'Corrective Justice and Liability for Risk-Creation: A Comment' (1990) 38 *University of California Los Angeles L Rev* 113; I. Englard, *The Philosophy of Tort Law* (Aldershot, 1993) 221–3. See also A. Porat, 'Compensation for Risk-Creating and Loss of Chances' (2000) 23 *Iyunei Mishpat* 605 (Hebrew).

[6] Cf. G. T. Schwartz, 'The Vitality of Negligence and the Ethics of Strict Liability' (1981) 15 *Georgia L Rev* 963.

moral responsibility.[7] Adoption of a general principle that would impose liability for bare risk, and thereby force risk-creators to pay for their expected damages, would eliminate this problem. Under that principle, it is not the outcome that determines liability in torts but, rather, the magnitude of the risk generated by the defendant's wrongful conduct. Materialization of the risk into actual damage is beyond the wrongdoer's control and should, therefore, not affect his liability.

Upon closer scrutiny, however, imposition of liability for bare risk would not necessarily be consistent with retributive justice. This is so because there is no necessary relationship between the magnitude of the risk created by a wrongdoer and his moral blameworthiness. A person who negligently embarks on a highly risky course of action is not necessarily detestable from the moral point of view. Driver Bill, for example, may decide to drive his car at 110 mph in order to bring his sick neighbour rapidly to the hospital. Driver Heather, in contrast, may decide to speed at 90 mph for sheer fun. The risk attendant upon Bill's driving was certainly greater than the risk created by Heather. Yet, the relative blameworthiness of these two presumably negligent drivers is a more complex issue. If liability in torts were to be derived from the blameworthiness of the wrongdoer's conduct, the extent of the risk engendered by the wrongdoer would never be decisive. This factor should only be one of the parameters that would ultimately determine the wrongdoer's liability and its extent. If a legal system were to be shaped in this way, then it would certainly promote retributive justice. However, as demonstrated below, this would be done at the expense of optimal deterrence.

From the perspective of *corrective justice*, is there a difference between damage-based liability and risk-based liability? Either way, the plaintiff would be compensated only if she had actually suffered damages as a result of the wrongful conduct. From her point of view, there is, therefore, no difference between the two legal regimes. The principal difference between the two regimes pertains only to the wrongdoer. Under the damage-based regime, it is only the wrongdoer who compensates the victim for the actual damage he caused to the victim. Under the risk-based regime, the wrongdoer, along with other wrongful creators of risks (those who did cause damage and those who did not alike), participate in a comprehensive compensation scheme that aims at compensating all victims of torts. Each wrongdoer would participate in the scheme by paying to the appropriate compensation fund the amount equivalent to the expected damage associated with his wrongful conduct. None of

[7] Schroeder (n. 5 above). For a similar argument based on Kant, see G. O. Robinson, 'Probabilistic Causation and Compensation for Tortious Risk' (1985) 14 *J Legal Studies* 779, 789–90. For illuminating attempts to reconcile damage-based liability with morality, see T. Honoré, 'Responsibility and Luck: The Moral Basis of Strict Liability' (1988) 104 *LQR* 530; J. Waldron, 'Moments of Carelessness and Massive Loss', in D. G. Owen (ed.), *Philosophical Foundations of Tort Law* (Oxford, 1995) 387.

the wrongdoers would, consequently, be forced to pay for the entire damage that he inflicted. His participation in the compensation of tort victims would be limited to the expected value of the damage, as estimated prior to its actual infliction. Note that individuals who wrongfully created risks that ultimately did not materialize into damages would bear similar liability.

Arguably, this risk-based liability scheme is inconsistent with corrective justice precisely because it decouples the 'doer' from the 'sufferer' and thereby eliminates the bilateral relationship between the two. Under an influential corrective justice theory advocated by Ernest Weinrib, this bilateral relationship is essential for implementing corrective justice in torts.[8] We, however, hold a different view of corrective justice. Our concept of corrective justice is less demanding. In our opinion, corrective justice would be maintained when the wrongdoer is made liable for the damage he inflicted; the victim is compensated for the wrongful damage she suffered; and the wrongdoer participates in financing the mechanism that facilitates compensation for his victim.[9] This conception is similar, although not identical, to that of George Fletcher. According to Fletcher, the right to compensation and the duty to compensate must not be strictly correlative. A victim may well be entitled to compensation for her wrongful loss, while the wrongdoer may be exempt from the duty to compensate the victim. Such victims might have rightful compensation claims against an appropriate state agency, but not against their wrongdoers.[10] Our conception of corrective justice does not do away with the correlativity criterion. Under our conception, the wrongdoer's liability for the damage he caused correlates with the victim's right to receive compensation for the damage she suffered. We thus believe that even if the victim obtains her redress through a compensation scheme, rather than directly from her wrongdoer, corrective justice would equally be attained as long as the wrongdoer equitably participates in the financing of the scheme.[11]

This conception of corrective justice is inconsistent with Christopher Schroeder's theory. According to Schroeder, corrective justice requires that the wrongdoer be held liable for the risk he created, irrespective of whether he actually caused any damage.[12] In our view, this unadulterated risk-based approach is at odds with corrective justice: if no damage was inflicted, then there is nothing to be corrected. Schroeder's approach suits better the retributive justice principles. Our conception of corrective justice insists on the actual infliction of damage. In our scheme, damage-infliction is, indeed, a

[8] E. Weinrib, 'Understanding Tort Law' (1989) 23 *Valpariso U L Rev* 485; E. Weinrib, *The Idea of Private Law* (Cambridge, Mass, 1995).

[9] See below 132–8.

[10] G. P. Fletcher, 'Fairness and Utility in Tort Theory' (1972) 85 *Harvard L Rev* 537. According to Fletcher, the cases in which corrective justice dictates that the victim is entitled to damages but the injurer is not liable are those in which the injurer is entitled to an excusatory defence.

[11] See below 132–8.

[12] Schroeder (n. 5 above).

precondition both for holding the wrongdoer liable and for compensating the victim. Bare risk, therefore, does not warrant compensation. However, our scheme justifies compensation in a number of instances that have been erroneously classified as cases of mere risk-creation. Those instances have the following defining characteristics:

(1) there is an identifiable group of wrongdoers and an identifiable group of victims, and it is apparent that one or more victims have been damaged by one or more wrongdoers;
(2) it cannot adequately be determined which specific wrongdoer damaged any of the victims; and
(3) damages inflicted by the wrongdoers and suffered by the victims can be adequately estimated.

This category of cases is discussed in Part C of this chapter.[13]

At first glance, imposition of liability for creating risk is consistent with the *deterrence* objective of the law of torts. For the sake of simplicity, let us assume that tort liability under the given legal regime is based on negligence. Under the economic interpretation of the negligence doctrine, as represented by the famous Learned Hand Formula, tort liability should be imposed on the defendant whenever $B<PL$. B denotes the costs of discharging the burden of precaution; P is the *ex ante* probability of inflicting the relevant damage due to the lack of the required precautions; and L represents the magnitude of that damage.[14] Under the best interpretation, these variables refer to marginal values. Consequently, the defendant will be held negligent when his marginal costs of avoiding the damage are lower than the marginal reduction in the expected damage.[15] The threat of liability in torts thus provides an incentive for potential wrongdoers to take efficient precautions. It induces them to compare the costs and benefits of avoiding the damage. Under this framework, a potential wrongdoer will compare the reduction in the expected damage with the cost of taking precautions; and he will then choose to take precautions if, and only if, this cost is lower than the corresponding reduction in the expected damage and the corresponding liability in torts. Operation of the negligence doctrine would consequently minimize the aggregate cost of accidents and of their prevention and, thereby, would promote optimal deterrence.[16]

The same outcome would be attained also by a legal regime that imposes liability for creating risk. Under that regime, a potential wrongdoer also would find himself required to compare the reduction in the expected damage with the cost of taking precautions. He would find himself in this position because any wrongful imposition of risk upon another person would entail liability in the amount of the expected damages.

[13] See below 125–9. [14] *US v Carroll Towing Co.*, 159 F 2d 169 (2d Cir 1947).
[15] R. Cooter and T. Ulen, *Law and Economics* (2nd edn., Reading, Mass, 1997) 276–7.
[16] R. A. Posner, 'A Theory of Negligence' (1972) 1 *J Legal Studies* 29.

This point can be usefully illustrated by the following example. A potential wrongdoer is considering whether or not to take precautions that cost £10 and, thereby, reduce to zero the 10 per cent probability of causing damage in the amount of £150. Under the controlling legal regime, tort liability is imposed only for infliction of actual damage. For the sake of simplicity, we also assume that there are no errors in the detection of wrongdoers and in trial fact-finding. Thus, if the damage occurs as a result of the wrongdoer's failure to take adequate precautions, he will then have to compensate the victim in the amount of £150. As there is a 10 per cent probability that the damage will actually occur, the potential wrongdoer will estimate his risk as amounting to £15 in liability damages (assuming he is neutral towards risk). He will then consider the cost of precautions (£10) that would enable him to avoid that liability and, thereby, save £5. This will induce him to eliminate the risk, and optimal deterrence will be attained. Exactly the same effect could, however, be attained in a legal regime that imposes liability for creating risk irrespective of whether the damage actually occurs. Under that regime, a potential wrongdoer would estimate that if he does not prevent the risk (already determined as amounting to £15), he will *certainly* have to pay £15 in liability damages (we assume once again that there are no errors in the detection of wrongdoers and in trial fact-finding). The potential wrongdoer will thus be induced to prevent the risk. Incidentally, this example also demonstrates that a legal system that imposes liability in accord with the blameworthiness of the defendant's conduct—rather than in proportion to the risk generated by the defendant's wrongful conduct—is a system that maintains sub-optimal deterrence in order to promote retributive justice.[17] To attain optimal deterrence it is essential that a potential wrongdoer be induced to consider only the reduction in the expected damage attendant upon taking precautions, as compared with the cost of those precautions. All other factors are extraneous to deterrence and, therefore, must not be taken into account. If a potential wrongdoer were to consider his prospective liability as a payment that would be either higher or lower than the expected damage, this would produce either excessive or insufficient deterrence, respectively.

Liability for bare risk has a further economic advantage. Many potential wrongdoers are risk-averse and, as such, tend to spread the liability risk by insuring themselves. The risk-spreading mechanism created by insurance is socially advantageous, but costly. A regime that imposes liability for bare risk would introduce a substantial saving in the risk-spreading costs since it spreads the accident risks directly. Under that regime, many potential wrongdoers would simply prefer liability to insurance.

A legal regime that imposes liability for creating risks therefore appears to possess a number of normatively attractive features: it sets incentives for

[17] See above 105.

efficient conduct; it spreads the costs of accidents; and it also facilitates compensation of victims who have sustained damage after being wrongfully exposed to risk. From the retributive justice perspective, risk-based liability is imperfect, but still better than the current damage-based system. The prevalent tort law doctrine nevertheless declines to accept the idea of imposing liability for bare risk. Under this doctrine, tort liability can be imposed only for actual damages. Why is this so? Is it only because risk-based liability is at odds with corrective justice?

This question has a number of plausible answers, all taken from the domain of pragmatism. Generally speaking, it is hard to see how a regime of risk-based liability could be enforced. In order to achieve optimal deterrence and ensure that victims of torts are properly compensated, it is essential that at least most (if not all) risk-creators, actually be found liable for the expected damage that originates from their wrongful conduct. Consequently, it would become necessary to detect wrongful impositions of risk, to identify the risk-creators and subsequently prosecute them for imposing the risks. However, unlike actual damage, imposition of bare risk is largely non-observable by potential plaintiffs. Moreover, even when risk-imposition is observable by plaintiffs, it often remains unverifiable at trial. These problems are aggravated by the costs that would be incurred by the need to initiate and prosecute lawsuits against risk-creators. Note that people who were wrongfully exposed to risk but ultimately sustained no damage would not be entitled to compensation. Therefore, they would have no incentive to facilitate enforcement of the law. To make things concrete, imagine a legal system where every single driver who exceeds the speed limit for a minute or two is apprehended and subsequently brought to trial in order to be forced to pay for the expected damage. This system would obviously be dysfunctional (and would also produce gross incursions into individual freedoms). As explained in Chapter I, these and related problems would distort the adjudication system.[18]

These difficulties call for alternative ways of enforcing risk-based liability in torts. One such way is to impose liability only on those defendants who created especially serious risks (in terms of both the probability and the magnitude of the associated damage). This would undoubtedly reduce the relevant enforcement costs. None the less, this seemingly improved system of risk-based liability would hardly produce satisfactory results. There is no reason to believe that severe risks dominate the cluster of risks faced by society. The multitude of small risks, as an aggregate, constitute at least a substantial part of that cluster. If so, the exemption from liability bestowed upon creators of small risks would reduce the general compensation level to below the expected damage value. Consequently, risk-creators would not be sufficiently

[18] See above 29–34.

deterred. Money collected from them as liability damages would also not be sufficient for compensating all victims of torts.

Another alternative is to account for the existing enforcement difficulties in determining the extent of liability to impose on wrongful risk-creators. In this system, any defendant found liable would have to pay liability damages that would reflect not only the risk itself, but also his or her chances of being apprehended, prosecuted, and found liable. This increased liability would offset the underdeterrence effect engendered by the low probability of law enforcement. For example, if a negligent driver occasionally creates a risk estimated at £10—a sum that reflects the expected damage associated with his negligence—but is caught only one in ten times, a rule that would force him to pay £100 would induce him to anticipate £10 in liability damages. His deterrence would consequently be optimal.

This alternative has obvious disadvantages. First, it would eliminate the enforcement problem only partially. Second, it would induce risk-creators to devise ways of avoiding apprehension instead of developing methods of decreasing risks. Third, by amplifying the liability only of those risk-creators who are detected and successfully prosecuted, this alternative would be tainted with the same problems of luck and injustice that the risk-based liability system seeks to resolve.

Despite its drawbacks, the prevalent damage-based liability system is, therefore, preferable to any system that grounds tort liability upon creation of risks. If the two systems are adequately enforced, their impact on deterrence will be essentially the same. However, adequate enforcement of a risk-based system of liability is an unlikely scenario. In contrast, damage-based liability rules would be much easier to enforce. First, actual damages are both observable and verifiable, and their producers can be identified more easily. Second, actual damages are much easier to measure than the magnitude of a non-materialized risk. Third, victims of torts who have sustained actual damages, and who therefore expect compensation, have a strong incentive to initiate the prosecution of wrongdoers. The non-victims of bare risks have no such incentive.

From the corrective justice perspective, damage-based liability is obviously preferable to risk-based liability: in cases involving bare risk but no actual damage, there is no injustice to be rectified. From the retributive justice viewpoint, actual damage constitutes a fairly good (albeit imperfect) indication of the magnitude of the risk created by the wrongdoer and of the blameworthiness of his conduct. Wrongful damage largely originates in blameworthy conduct that involves serious risk. Actual damage can, consequently, serve as an adequate proxy for reprehensibility.[19]

[19] Cf. G. Calabresi, 'Concerning Cause and the Law of Torts: An Essay for Harry Kalven, Jr.' (1975) 43 *University of Chicago L Rev* 69; G. O. Robinson, 'Multiple Causation in Tort Law: Reflections on the DES Cases' (1982) 68 *Virginia L Rev* 713, 737–8.

2. Liability for Bare Risk as Supplementing Damage-Based Liability

In this section, we consider the possibility of imposing liability for creating risk as a supplement to traditional liability for actual damage. This idea has to contend with a threshold objection: the combined system of liability would produce excessive deterrence. Take John, who creates a 10 per cent risk of inflicting damage of £150, so that the expected damage equals £15. This risk could be eliminated at a cost of £10. If John does not take precautions and the damage occurs, he will be liable for that damage (£150). Consequently, John's liability risk—estimated prior to taking precautions—is £15. John would therefore prefer to expend £10 on precautions, rather than risk paying £15 in liability damages. Under a combined legal regime that imposes liability for both risks and actual damage, if John does not take precautions, he will face a liability risk worth roughly £30. Specifically, he will face a 10 per cent risk of paying £150 for the actual damage, in addition to his certain £15 liability for the bare risk (for the sake of simplicity, we ignore here the enforcement difficulties).[20] John therefore faces greater liability risk than the risk to which he wrongfully exposes others. As a result, he might take socially wasteful precautions.

Facially, this scenario seems to present no difficulties, since a £30 liability would strengthen John's willingness to expend £10 on precautions, which would be efficient.[21] However, if we modify the example by increasing the cost of precautions to £20, the problem of excessive deterrence becomes apparent. John would then consider the possibility of being found negligent, even though there is no negligence in a decision not to invest £20 in order to eliminate a risk worth £15. He would consider that possibility because one can never be sure of the court's decision.[22] If so, then John might be willing to spend £20 in order to avoid a £30 liability.[23] This would not happen if John's liability risk were only £15.

Therefore, in order to justify liability for bare risk on grounds of deterrence as supplementing liability for actual damage, it must be demonstrated that the risk constitutes special damage to society and is not merely a potential for actual damage. In what follows, risks having this special feature will be

[20] The risk equals £28.50, since in cases where actual damage has occurred, the wrongdoer compensates the victim for the actual damages and is exempt from additional liability for the amount of the expected damage (£150 × 10% + £15 × 90% = £28.50).

[21] In this case, too, making the potential injurer pay compensation above the expected damages of his behaviour could produce inefficiencies. Thus, the potential injurer might invest more than necessary in precautions due to his fear of being held liable for a large amount of damages.

[22] For the effect of mistakes made by the courts on injurers' incentives in a legal regime of negligence, see G. Calabresi, 'Optimal Deterrence and Accidents' (1975) 84 *Yale LJ* 656, 656–62; G. Calabresi and A. K. Klevorick, 'Four Tests for Liability in Torts' (1985) 14 *J Legal Studies* 585, 618 *et seq*.

[23] In this example, the risk-creator will expend £20 on precautions if the probability of the court finding of negligence is higher than 66% (£30 × 66% = £20).

referred to as damaging *per se*. Liability for creating risk can also be justified by showing that the risk-creator would escape liability for the actual damage if the risk were to materialize.

Is a special 'damaging-*per-se*' feature of the risk necessary for imposing liability under retributive justice? Retributive justice does not entail any such requirement: it can justify liability for any risk, regardless of whether it has this special feature and irrespective of whether the risk has materialized into actual damage. As clarified above, retributive justice supports liability for bare risk as an alternative to damage-based liability. This support rests on two different grounds. First, a person who created a wrongful risk that only due to good fortune did not result in damage is blameworthy: good luck is not a normatively sound ground for treating one's otherwise blameworthy conduct as unblameworthy. Second, a person whose moral guilt was relatively minor, but who, nevertheless, caused substantial damage, ought to be held liable in proportion to his blameworthiness, rather than to the extent of the damage. Bad luck is not a ground for aggravating one's liability under the principles of retributive justice.

For these reasons, a mixed legal regime where wrongdoers are held liable for both bare risk and full-fledged damage would be only partially embraced by retributive justice. Such a regime would refrain from treating a wrongdoer's good luck as grounds for an exemption from tort liability, an outcome that retributive justice would welcome. However, this regime also would undermine retributive justice in refusing to give any liability discount for bad luck.

Is a special 'damaging-*per-se*' feature of the risk necessary for imposing tort liability under corrective justice? The answer to this question should be in the affirmative. Corrective justice is founded upon *restitutio ad integrum*. Under this principle, the duty to make good the damage wrongfully sustained by the plaintiff is at the very core of liability in torts. Corrective justice is equally founded on the non-interference principle: if the demand to activate the justice machinery goes beyond damage-rectification, the machinery should remain dormant. If the plaintiff sustained no actual damage, there is nothing to correct. Therefore, bare risk would not be actionable under corrective justice; but if a risk wrongfully generated by the defendant was damaging *per se*, then the risk was not bare. By definition, any such risk is regarded as damage that merits rectification. Outcomes reached in such 'special risk' cases under the corrective justice regime would, thus, be similar to the outcomes necessitated by deterrence. There would, however, still be an important difference between the outcomes reached under these two regimes. Under the deterrence regime, any 'special risk' would be actionable in torts, irrespective of whether it was inflicted upon an individual plaintiff, upon a third party, or upon society at large. In contrast, corrective justice would still insist that the 'special risk' be directed against the plaintiff, so that the damage ascribed to that risk was actually sustained by the plaintiff.

But are there any real cases where risk can be treated as damaging *per se*? At first glance, such cases not only exist, but are also important paradigms of torts. Creation of risk can instil fear in people. Thus, exposing people to environmental pollution might cause not only physical injuries, but also leave many uninjured people in a state of undispellable fear of becoming injured in the future. Compensation for causing fear would be justified by both deterrence and corrective justice (let alone retributive justice). Deterrence would be achieved because the wrongdoer becomes liable for damage that he actually caused to society.[24] Because fear actually detracts from the plaintiff's well-being, awarding compensation to the plaintiff would also make good the individual damage, as required by corrective justice. Such compensation has, indeed, been awarded to plaintiffs by a number of courts in the United States.[25] However, this has been only in cases where it was unclear whether the plaintiff would sustain physical injury in the future. Furthermore, judges and juries who awarded that compensation must have implicitly accounted for the possibility that the plaintiffs' fear would be realized. Compensation awarded to those plaintiffs therefore must have been affected by their unarticulated chances of becoming physically damaged.

Despite their surface appearance, these cases do not truly manifest compensation for bare risk. Rather, they represent an acknowledgement that a person's well-being is determined not only by his physical and proprietary conditions, but also by his mental condition. There is an emotional facet to a person's well-being, so that a wrongful infliction of emotional harm—for example, by instilling fear and anxiety—may well be and, indeed, should be treated as actionable damage. For this reason, it might be objectionable to award damages to a person who was exposed to a risk without actually experiencing fear or anxiety.

In other cases, the deterrence objective would justify imposition of liability for creating bare risk. These would be cases where wrongdoers might escape liability for an unidentifiable damage, usually inflicted on society at large. Consider once again the environmental pollution example. Some of the damages originating from pollution are tangible and, as such, do not pose any special problems of compensation. Yet, pollution often causes an additional, distinct type of damage, which the traditional doctrine of torts leaves without redress. Pollution often results in injuries of which their victims are unaware. These victims would not sue for damages. Some of the damage caused by pollution is latent. This damage develops and becomes apparent many years after its perpetration. Victims of such damage would, consequently, find it difficult, if not altogether impossible, to identify the causes of their damage and to prove

[24] Compensation is usually not awarded for fear, because proving its existence would usually be costly. Generally speaking, tort law is reluctant to award compensation for non-pecuniary losses. See Salmond and Heuston (n. 2 above) 214–18.

[25] See J. B. Weinstein, *Individual Justice in Mass Tort Litigations* (Evanston, Ill, 1995) 152–4; *Werner v Blankfort*, 42 Cal Rptr 2d 229 (1995).

those causes in court. Pollution also harms subsequent generations and the environment itself, and waiting for these victims to bring lawsuits would be inefficiently unwise. Hence, liability currently faced by wrongful polluters requires enhancement. Adequate enhancement could be provided by holding the polluters liable for the risks they create. This form of liability might resolve the insufficient deterrence problem. It also would be consistent with retributive justice, but not with corrective justice.[26] Although perfectly justifiable, this form of compensation would not amount to genuine compensation for special risks that are damaging *per se*. Compensation awards that exceed proven damage might, indeed, be efficient from the deterrence perspective and might also be justified on grounds of retribution. However, none of these instrumental and moral justifications would be based on recognition of the damage as actually embedded in the risk. Rather, they would be grounded in recognition of factual uncertainty and evidentiary limitations that would unduly benefit wrongdoers. Because wrongdoers would exploit these drawbacks by taking privately profitable, but socially damaging, actions, they ought to be appropriately deterred and must not be left unpunished. Holding a wrongdoer liable for the risks he has created would force him to internalize all the damage that originated from his conduct, including damage that cannot be identified, but is known to exist. Such liability would also mean that the wrongdoer receives his just desert. Both deterrence and retributive justice would, therefore, justify this liability principle.[27]

Risk can also be perceived as damage when it affects the value of a person's property. Take John, for example, a person who lives in an area wrongfully exposed to a high risk of flooding. This risk would wrongfully reduce the value of John's property. Thus, if John were previously able to collect £X in rentals, he would now be able to collect only £(X–Y). And if he were previously able to sell the property for £X, presently he would be able to sell it for only £(X–Y). Under each of these scenarios, damage suffered by John (£Y) is real. This damage might remain real even when it transpires that the risk has faded away. Thus, if John had actually sold the property for £(X–Y) at the time when its price was still affected by the risk of flooding, John's loss of £Y would be his damage. If left uncompensated, this damage does not fade away.[28] Furthermore, John might have insured his property against wrongful

[26] Corrective justice requires that the wrongdoer compensate the victim for neither more nor less than the damage she suffered.

[27] Cf. R. D. Cooter, 'Punitive Damages, Social Norms and Economic Analysis' (1997) 60 *Law & Contemporary Problems* 73.

[28] On the possibility of awarding damages for the diminution in property value due to its exposure to risk, see C. E. Miller 'Law and Uncertainty—Risks and Legal Processes', in R. Baldwin (ed.) *Radiological Risk and Civil Liability: A Review of Recent Developments in the United Kingdom,* (London, 1997) 273, 277–8. The author describes a case, *Merlin v British Nuclear Fuels PLC* [1990] 2 QB 557, in which a family sued for diminution in the value of the house in which they lived due to its exposure to radiation from a nuclear reactor. The lawsuit was dismissed, since it was established that the statute breached by the defendants and on which the lawsuit was based does not constitute grounds for awarding economic damages for diminution in property value.

risks associated with flooding. He also might have incurred other expenses related to his efforts to prevent or mitigate flooding damage. Together with the relevant increment in the insurance premiums, these expenses also constitute damage sustained by John, which is both tangible and recoverable.

A person's exposure to the risk of sustaining physical injury can be conceived of in a similar way. Any such person can be described as having his worth diminished by the exposure. For example, such a person may plausibly be taken as being more vulnerable than in the past.[29] Indeed, should he now wish to take out life insurance or purchase a health insurance policy, he would be required to pay a higher premium. For any such person, the increase in the insurance premium would constitute a loss that results from his exposure to the relevant risk. This loss would not evaporate even if the risk were to cease to exist at some later point in time.[30] Similarly, if a person who was killed in a road accident had, until then, lived with a risk that had reduced his life expectancy, his dependants would recover an appropriately decreased amount of compensation from the wrongdoer in the road accident.[31] Moreover, it is often reasonable for a person living under such risk to expend substantial amounts of money and resources on preventive measures. These measures would include consumption of special food, special medical treatment and equipment, and even change in residence.[32] Money and efforts expended on these measures would constitute a loss. This and similar losses might be incurred regardless of whether the risk ultimately materializes into actual injury.[33] They should, therefore, be treated as actionable damage on the grounds of deterrence, retribution, and corrective justice alike.

However, this type of damage, too, cannot be regarded as a special risk that is damaging *per se*. Rather, it is a traditional type of damage shaped by people's reasonable practices and valuations, as affected by their perceptions of risks. There seem to be no special bare risks that merit compensation in torts.

[29] This type of reasoning was used by some American courts in awarding damages in cases where the victim was exposed to risk but there was no way of knowing if he would suffer any actual damage in the future. Weinstein (n. 25 above) 152–4.

[30] For a similar argument, see Robinson (n. 7 above) 787–8; D. Rosenberg, 'The Causal Connection in Mass Exposure Cases: A "Public Law" Vision of the Tort System' (1984) 97 *Harvard L Rev* 849, 885–7.

[31] On the use of this argument to justify compensation for a victim when it was not clear whether his life expectancy had indeed been reduced due to exposure to risk, see Rosenberg, ibid. 885–7.

[32] Rosenberg (n. 30 above) 885–7; S. R. Perry, 'Protected Interests and Undertakings in the Law of Negligence' (1992) 42 *U Toronto LJ* 247, 267–9.

[33] This approach was taken by some American courts, which led them to award damages to victims who were exposed to wrongful risks. Weinstein (n. 25 above) 152–4; *Werner v Blankfort* (n. 25 above).

C. LIABILITY FOR LOST CHANCES

Thus far, our discussion has been based on the premise that the defendant exposed the plaintiff to a risk that left no tangible impact on the plaintiff's person or property. We now turn to cases where the existence of this impact is uncertain. Specifically, we focus on cases where the defendant wrongfully exposed the plaintiff to a risk that may or may not have materialized into damage; consequently, the occurrence and/or extent of the plaintiff's damage remain uncertain. In such cases, a demand is often made that the plaintiff be compensated for her or his 'lost chances', that is, for her or his current or prospective damage multiplied by the probability of the proposition that causally attributes the damage to the defendant's wrongdoing.

This part of the chapter therefore does not deal with cases where wrongfulness of the defendant's conduct is unproven. In a legal regime based upon fault, if a defendant cannot be held to have acted wrongfully, there is obviously no scope for liability in torts. We thus deal only with cases that involve uncertainty with regard to the causal relationship between the risk wrongfully created by the defendant and the litigated damage (that might have already been suffered by the plaintiff or might be sustained by her or him in the future). These cases are divided into three categories. In the first category of cases, it is established that the defendant's wrongdoing caused damage to the plaintiff, but the extent of the damage is uncertain. In the second category, it is established that the defendant committed a wrongdoing against the plaintiff, but it is uncertain whether the plaintiff sustained any damage. In cases belonging to the third category, it is established that the defendant wrongfully created risk, but it is uncertain whether the defendant violated any protected interest of the plaintiff. In all of these categories of cases, the uncertainty may relate either to the past or to the future: it may relate to the occurrence of the damage, to its magnitude, or to the question whether the defendant's wrongdoing actually infringed on the plaintiff's protected interests.

An epistemological argument can be made against recognizing lost chance as damage in relation to each of the categories. The notion of damage signifies an event: in reality, things either happen or do not. Lost chance is an inherently epistemic concept: it signifies the degree of the fact-finder's knowledge about the events, and the fact-finder's balance of knowledge versus ignorance is, arguably, not damage.

In what follows, we consider this difficulty as affecting each category of cases. The key question that arises here is whether in light of the two principal objectives of the law of torts—deterrence and corrective justice[34]—lost

[34] In this context, we are not discussing retributive justice, since a system that imposes liability for actual damage, whether it is certain or not, does not aim at meeting the requirements of retributive justice.

chances should be treated as actionable damage, despite this difficulty. Intuitively, the most obvious case in which damages must be awarded is when only the magnitude of the litigated damage is uncertain (Category 1). A more complicated case is one that involves uncertainty with regard to the actual occurrence of the damage (Category 2). The most difficult case is one that involves uncertainty as to whether the defendant infringed any protected interest of the plaintiff (Category 3). This intuitive ordering reflects the existing doctrinal arrangements. However, as demonstrated below, this intuition is not invariably correct and is, therefore, bound to produce distortions.

1. Uncertainty with Regard to the Extent of the Damage

The following example is paradigmatic of this category of cases.

> *The Loss of Income Case.* Jim was injured in a car accident caused by Tony's negligence. As a result of that accident, Jim suffers from a disability that reduces his ability to work. He therefore sues Tony for his loss of income. Presently, as well as before the accident, Jim worked as a clerk and his income was very low. In assessing Jim's loss of income, the court must determine whether he could have secured a more profitable job had he not been injured in the accident. There is a 30% chance that had Jim remained uninjured, he would have worked as a seaman in the merchant marine and earned a much higher income. Jim's injury made it impossible for him to perform this kind of work. There is, however, also a 70% chance that even had the accident not occurred, Jim would have continued to work as a clerk. Under this scenario, Jim's complaint as to lost income would be unwarranted.[35]

There are two different approaches that can be taken by a judge with regard to the problem at hand. Under the one approach, Jim's lawsuit must be dismissed because he cannot establish any loss of income by a preponderance of the evidence. The second approach (adopted by the Israeli Supreme Court[36]) favours compensation. Under this approach, Jim must be allowed to recover from Tony 30 per cent of the difference between a seaman's earnings and a clerk's earnings. Holding Tony liable for Jim's lost chances is consistent with deterrence. As noted earlier, optimal deterrence requires that a wrongdoer be exposed to a risk of liability in the amount of the expected damage caused by his wrongdoing. This objective would, indeed, be attained by forcing Tony to compensate Jim in such a way. Suppose that Tony's negligent driving had exposed ten pedestrians to a 10 per cent risk of injury, so that one out of the ten pedestrians would be injured. In other words, Tony's driving created the

[35] An adaptation of *Hayu v Ventura*, 38(4) Piskey Din 393 (1984) (Hebrew).

[36] *Hayu v Ventura*, ibid.

risk of injuring one person out of ten. In addition, seven out of these ten people would not lose any income, should any of them become injured, as opposed to the remaining three people, who would suffer such a loss. Should any of the latter three people become injured, he would sustain a loss in income in the amount of £10. Furthermore, there is no way of establishing after the event the group to which each person belongs. Risk imposed by Tony's wrongdoing would thus amount to £3 in terms of lost income (£10 × 10% × 3). From the optimal deterrence perspective, it is therefore imperative that Tony assume a liability risk in the amount of £3. Compensation for lost chances would force him to assume this liability risk. In contrast, under the preponderance-of-the-evidence standard (the P>0.5 rule), Tony would assume no liability risk whatsoever (since the probability that he inflicted the litigated damage falls below 50 per cent). Along with similarly situated drivers, Tony would, consequently, remain insufficiently deterred: the P>0.5 rule would allow him to take precautions below the optimal level without paying the price.

In our example, compensation for lost chances would promote deterrence better than the P>0.5 rule would. This observation, however, is not unqualified. As just demonstrated, application of the P>0.5 rule in cases where the chance wrongfully taken away from the plaintiff amounts to 50 per cent or less would result in underdeterrence. There are, however, many cases where the relevant chances are higher than 50 per cent. In such cases, application of the P>0.5 rule would allow plaintiffs to recover for their entire damage. This possibility might offset the insufficient deterrence problem. However, the P>0.5 rule and the lost chance rule would both produce optimal levels of deterrence only when the total amounts of the awards recovered by plaintiffs under each rule are equal and when each of those amounts reflects the losses actually sustained by the plaintiffs. This would happen only when the average loss suffered by plaintiffs who did not surpass the 50 per cent probability threshold is roughly equal to the average loss suffered by plaintiffs whose cases are more probable than not. When this is not the case, the lost chance rule would lead to more efficient outcomes than the P>0.5 rule would produce. A full analysis of the P>0.5 rule, as affecting the deterrence and corrective justice objectives of the law of torts, has already been undertaken in Chapter I. We therefore will not return to the issues raised by that analysis. Indeed, the above discussion has assumed that the relevant rules of evidence and procedure set adequate incentives for the parties to come forth with evidence with respect to the litigated damage, its magnitude, and its underlying cause. We also disregard the administrative costs under the two rules. Those costs include judicial error, litigation expenses, and impediments to settlements.

Facially, compensation for lost chances is inconsistent with corrective justice. Corrective justice demands *restitutio ad integrum* in the sense that a wrongdoer must restore the victim's original position. To make things concrete, let us return to our example. Had Tony not injured Jim, Jim would have been either a 100 per cent clerk or a 100 per cent seaman. In the real world, there is no factual scenario in which Jim could be a 70 per cent clerk and a 30 per cent seaman. Jim's compensation for his lost chances would therefore be either excessive or insufficient and would never reflect the damage that he actually sustained. To be sure, application of the P>0.5 rule and the corresponding 'winner-takes-all' principle involve risk of error. Yet, this is not a problem for corrective justice: corrective justice sets forth the law's substantive goals, rather than the means for attaining those goals. Apart from that, as explained in Chapter I, the justice machinery should only be activated against the defendant when the evidential reasons for doing so are stronger than the reasons for leaving the machinery dormant. Arguably, this idea is also in line with corrective justice principles.

An appropriate re-conceptualization of 'damage' might be able to reconcile compensation for lost chances with the principles of corrective justice. In our example, the wrongful injury has deprived the victim of a valuable asset: his ability to make a free and autonomous choice between different careers. The victim has thus been wrongfully deprived of an opportunity to increase his earnings. Admittedly, neither the court nor anyone else (including the victim himself) could provide a satisfactory answer to the counterfactual question: What use would the victim have made of that opportunity, had he not been injured? This question has no determinate answer. Yet, the earning opportunity itself has clearly been diluted by the victim's injury, so his asset had lost some of its value. This loss can be determined by considering the victim's earning possibilities before and after the accident. In our example, Jim was deprived of an opportunity of becoming a seaman. For him, that opportunity was a valuable asset that he would not have given up for free. The value of that opportunity is roughly equal to 30 per cent of the difference between the clerk's and the seaman's respective earnings.

Similar problems may arise in cases involving uncertain events that occurred in the past. The following example is paradigmatic of this type of case.

> *The Dogs Case.* Two dogs, each of which belongs to a different wrongdoer, simultaneously attack Jill. The ensuing damage is evidentially indivisible, for it is impossible to establish which dog did what.[37]

Different legal systems provide different solutions for this type of case. Under the prevalent doctrine, plaintiffs situated similarly to Jill would be either fully or partially compensated.[38] Compensating Jill for lost chances—for example, by forcing each wrongdoer to pay her 50 per cent of her damage, if the ferocity

[37] This example is based on *Melech v Cornhauser*, 44(2) Piskey Din 89 (1990) (Hebrew).

[38] See above 76–81.

of the two dogs and other relevant factors are unknown—would be entirely consistent with deterrence. Holding the wrongdoers both jointly and separately liable for Jill's entire damage would also promote the deterrence objectives of the law of torts. But would it be consistent with *corrective justice* if the defendants were to compensate Jill for her lost chances? This issue presents a difficulty: any attempt to divide Jill's damage between the two wrongdoers would force one of them to pay for a greater damage than he actually inflicted, while the other wrongdoer would pay for a lesser damage than he inflicted.[39] In the absence of evidence, the factual accuracy of the required division of the damage would be a matter of pure luck. Yet, the court's inability to divide the damage truthfully does not exclude the possibility of dividing it equitably. Forcing each wrongdoer to compensate Jill for the chances he took away from her would minimize the discrepancy between the compensation paid and the damage inflicted. This solution could thus be considered second-best; accordingly, it should be opted for whenever the first-best solution is unavailable.

Arguably, this second-best solution would still be inconsistent with corrective justice principles, which mandate that a person cannot be held liable for unproven damages. Moreover, the re-conceptualization of 'damage' made in the *Loss of Income* example is inapplicable here. In the present case, there is no plausible concept of damage (save for the new concept offered by the evidential damage doctrine[40]) that could accommodate the opportunity asset that was taken away from Jill by each of her wrongdoers. The difference between the two cases has to do with the type of uncertainty that exists in each of them. In the *Loss of Income Case*, uncertainty is attached to events that are hypothetical and yet to unfold; in the *Dogs Case*, it relates to events that occurred in the past. Future events can be perceived as non-exhausted opportunities, which enables their accommodation under the re-conceptualized notion of 'damage' whenever a valuable opportunity is wrongfully taken away from the plaintiff. Past events cannot undergo this re-conceptualization because the opportunities they relate to have already been exhausted.

2. Uncertainty with Regard to the Occurrence of the Damage

In cases falling into this second category, the wrongdoer's risky conduct may or may not have damaged the plaintiff. The following case illustrates this type of uncertainty.

[39] If the fact that both dogs injured Jill *simultaneously* is significant with regard to the magnitude of her damage, in the sense that the total amount of the overall damage is greater than the sum of each of the damages caused separately by each dog, corrective justice would justify imposing liability on each of the two dog-owners for the full amount of the damage, since each of them caused all the damage. See above 79–80.

[40] See below chapters VI and VII.

Medical Malpractice (Future Injury) Case. Ruth is a physician who negligently provided medical treatment to Helen. Before Ruth's intervention, Helen's chances of recovery from her illness had been 25%. As a result of the negligent treatment, Helen's chances of recovery decreased to 10%. What the future holds for Helen is as yet unknown.

In this case, Ruth deprived Helen of her entitlement to receive adequate medical treatment. Because this entitlement was violated, Helen's well-being has been reduced, an event that certainly can be perceived as the erosion of one of her valuable assets. Helen's loss thus equals her final damage, which is yet to evolve, multiplied by the probability that the damage will arise in the future due to Ruth's fault. The fact that Helen's health may ultimately remain undamaged is immaterial: what the future holds for Helen is, admittedly, impossible to tell, but it is certain that her future *now appears* much bleaker than previously was the case. Since Helen's future became bleaker due to Ruth's wrongdoing, Ruth should compensate Helen for the reduction of her chances of recovery.

Under the deterministic approach to causation, this outcome would be unacceptable. Arguably, the range of scenarios pertaining to Helen's health is strictly dichotomous: in reality, Helen would either be injured or not, so there is no third scenario under which she would be inchoately injured (that is, fluctuate between factual health and factual sickness).[41] Our response to this deterministic objection points to its temporal arbitrariness: Helen's lawsuit against Ruth must be decided now, rather than in the future, so her well-being ought to be evaluated in a way that reflects its present conditions. These conditions include Helen's increased vulnerability to certain occupational and leisure activities that might accelerate the sickness yet to develop. Helen might consequently refrain from those activities, a restriction she would not have confined herself to, had Ruth treated her properly. These conditions also include an increase in health and life insurance premiums that Helen may now be required to sustain. Helen would obviously have not incurred these additional expenses had Ruth treated her properly. For these reasons, Helen's compensation may well exceed the multiplication of her final damage by the probability that she will become damaged in the future due to Ruth's fault. Compensation for this expected final damage would cover only the increase in Helen's insurance premiums, but not her additional types of damage. Supporters of the deterministic approach have correctly observed that the problem at hand is uncertainty; that this kind of problem is epistemological; and, consequently, that Helen's real complaint is about the fact-finders' state of knowledge, rather than about her state of health. These supporters have, however, overlooked the fact that uncertainty often moves from the epistemological to the real domain when it

[41] S. R. Perry, 'Risk, Harm, and Responsibility', in D. G. Owen (ed.), *Philosophical Foundations of Tort Law* (Oxford, 1995) 321. See also M. Stauch, 'Causation, Risk, and Loss of Chance in Medical Negligence' (1997) 17 *OJLS* 205, 223.

affects people's decisions, and many of those decisions detrimentally affect people's well-being.

We now move to discussing a similar case, but one in which the plaintiff has already sustained the litigated injury.

> *Medical Malpractice (Past Injury) Case.* Ruth is a physician who negligently provided medical treatment to Helen. Before Ruth's intervention, Helen's chances of recovery from her illness had been 25%. As a result of the negligent treatment, Helen's chances of recovery decreased to 10%. Ultimately, Helen did not recover, and it is unknown whether she would have recovered had Ruth treated her properly.

In cases similar to this, American and Israeli courts tend to award plaintiffs damages for their lost chances of recovery. English courts exhibit adherence to the P>0.5 rule, so that the plaintiff recovers the full amount of her damage if her lost chances are above 50 per cent and goes uncompensated if those chances do not surpass that threshold.[42] Academic writers are similarly divided over the right solution: some favour compensation for lost chances,[43] while others call for a more restrictive approach.[44]

Would it be appropriate to award Helen compensation for her lost chances? Is there any material difference between the two *Medical Malpractice* examples? From the perspective of deterrence, the two cases are similar; accordingly, Helen must be compensated for her lost chances (and attendant losses) in both. From the corrective justice viewpoint, the two cases are different. In the *Past Injury Case*, Ruth's negligence either damaged or did not damage Helen: there is no intermediate possibility.[45] As in the *Two Dogs Case*, re-conceptualization of 'damage' would not help Helen (subject to the evidential damage doctrine[46]). An attempt to redefine Helen's damage in terms of lost opportunities to recover is doomed to failure. This attempt

[42] For references, see above 74–6.

[43] J. H. King, 'Causation, Valuation, and Chance in Personal Injury Torts Involving Preexisting Conditions and Future Consequences' (1981) 90 *Yale LJ* 1353; Robinson (n. 7 above); Rosenberg (n. 30 above); Stauch (n. 41 above). Stauch (ibid. 219) argues that ruling according to chances is preferable to an all-or-nothing ruling in cases for which statistical data with regard to the relevant probabilities are available. See also S. Levmore, 'Probabilistic Recoveries, Restitution and Recurring Wrongs' (1990) 19 *J Legal Studies* 691, who claims that ruling according to chances has become particularly common in medical malpractice cases for two reasons: first, such cases are recurring events for which statistical data exist; second, in such cases, restitutionary damages cannot be awarded, since the injurers are not enriched by their wrongdoings.

[44] See Stauch (n. 41 above) 223, who seems to support the view that ruling according to chances in cases in which there is a risk of future damage (the *Medical Malpractice (Future Injury) Case*) violates deterministic causation principle.

[45] See Stauch, ibid. 217–18, for the claim that ruling according to chances in such cases is not contrary to the deterministic causation approach, since such a ruling does not make any claim about the state of the world, but, rather, about the state of our knowledge about the world. For a different view, see H. Reece, 'Losses of Chances in the Law' (1996) 59 *MLR* 188.

[46] See below Chapters VI and VII.

would not withstand a counterargument that since Helen's fate as a patient was predetermined by factors unrelated to her treatment by Ruth, her chances of recovery were unaffected by Ruth's negligence. Because this scenario is more probable than the 'lost chance' theory of the case, it should prevail.

Arguments available to Helen in the *Future Injury Case* would be unavailable in the case of *Past Injury*. In the *Past Injury Case*, Helen's well-being did not become more vulnerable than it had been before treatment: she actually did not recover from her illness; so the only issue is that of competition between Ruth's negligence and other potential causes of Helen's damage. There is no intermediate possibility that could benefit Helen. The insurance argument, available to Helen in the *Future Injury Case,* also would be problematic here. According to this argument, artificially adapted to the circumstances of the *Past Injury Case*, Ruth should be liable at least for the insurance premium that Helen would have been required to pay to insure herself against the relevant type of medical malpractice. Helen, however, did not actually pay any insurance premium for the increased risk created by Ruth (if she had paid such a premium, then compensation for the premium would not be unreasonable). Therefore, Helen did not and will not incur the expenses that the insurance argument points to. Under another version of the insurance argument, Helen had been unaware of Ruth's negligence and was correspondingly unaware of the risk to which she would be exposed. This non-awareness had prevented Helen from taking out the appropriate insurance policy. Arguably, if Helen had taken out such insurance—which she no longer can do—she would now have been entitled to full indemnification for her losses. We believe that this argument is unpersuasive. Even if Helen had insured herself against Ruth's negligence, then all the arguments we have offered as available to Ruth would also be available to Helen's underwriter. Consequently, since the scenario in which Helen was actually injured by Ruth is not preponderantly probable, Helen would not be able to make a warranted indemnification claim to her underwriter.[47]

We now turn to evaluating the lost chances in our *Medical Malpractice* examples (assuming that courts would be prepared to award plaintiffs compensation for 'lost chances' also in the *Past Injury* type of cases). In the *Future Injury Case*, Helen should recover 15 per cent of her final damage, as it might evolve. This is so because seventy-five out of a hundred patients situated similarly to Helen are doomed not to recover; so only twenty-five patients out of a hundred would actually be affected by malpractice that brings the

[47] Under a different line of argument Helen lost the chance of seeking alternative treatment. Arguably Helen relied on Ruth's competence and, therefore, did not approach another physician, who might have given her better treatment, in which case Helen's damage would have been prevented. This lost chance is equivalent to the actual damage suffered by Helen multiplied by the probability that it was a result of Ruth's wrongdoing. Perry (n. 41 above) 339.

patient's chances of recovery down to 10 per cent. This group of twenty-five malpractice-affected patients thus includes ten patients who do manage to recover (so their good luck translates into good luck for their physicians) and fifteen patients who do not recover. Helen's chances of being one of those fifteen patients therefore equal 15/100.

In the *Past Injury Case*, Helen's compensation should be about 17 per cent of her entire damage. In this case, Ruth's malpractice placed Helen amongst a hundred patients of whom only ten will recover. However, we already know that Helen is not one of those ten lucky patients: her non-recovery is an accomplished fact. This places Helen amongst the ninety patients who did not recover. This group comprises seventy-five patients who were doomed not to recover irrespective of malpractice (since each of these patients' original chances of recovery equalled 25 per cent) and fifteen patients who did not recover because of malpractice. Hence, the chances that Helen is one of those fifteen patients equal 15/90, that is, about 17 per cent.

This section's final example is a case that involves a violation of the patient's right to informed consent. This type of case involves uncertainty as to whether the patient would have consented to the medical treatment if he or she had been fully informed of the relevant risk.

> *The Informed Consent Case.* Rachel undergoes surgery. Her doctors did not inform her of the risk involved in that surgery prior to the procedure. Although the surgery is performed impeccably, Rachel ends up with severe physical damage that has resulted from complications. Antecedently, these complications were unlikely, but not unexpected. Rachel therefore sues the doctors for her damage. She claims that she would not have undergone the surgery had she been adequately informed of the risk involved. The doctors contend that Rachel would have undergone the surgery in any event.[48]

Would Rachel be entitled to recover compensation for violation of her right to informed consent, and if yes, in what amount? In Israel, the Supreme Court ruled that a plaintiff in Rachel's position is entitled to compensation because her autonomy was infringed. The majority justices, however, also inferred from the facts of the case that the plaintiff would have consented to the surgery even if she had been properly informed of its risk, so her physical damage was not caused by violation of her autonomy. The Court therefore awarded the plaintiff only a modest amount of compensation for her non-pecuniary damage.[49]

Difficulties involved in awarding compensation to plaintiffs like Rachel are similar to those that arise in the *Past Injury* type of cases: in both types of

[48] For a discussion of the causation problems in cases like this, see Englard (n. 5 above) 161–73. For a similar case decided in Canada, see *Hollis v Dow Corning Corp.*, 129 DLR 4th 609 (1995).

[49] *Daaka v Carmel Hospital, Haifa*, 53(4) Piskey Din 526 (1999).

cases, physical damage sustained by the plaintiff either did result or did not result from the defendant's wrongdoing, and there is no intermediate possibility. We cannot, therefore, offer a re-conceptualization of the notion of 'damage' for these cases so that Rachel, along with similarly situated plaintiffs, be regarded as damaged by the defendant's wrongdoing. Rachel and similar plaintiffs can surely be awarded compensation for the non-pecuniary damage to their autonomy. This form of compensation, however, is unrelated to any physical injury that might have resulted from the surgery.[50] Another means of compensating such plaintiffs is provided by the evidential damage doctrine, as we explain in Chapters VI and VII.

3. Uncertainty as to whether the Defendant Violated the Plaintiff's Protected Interest

In the cases examined thus far, violation of the plaintiff's protected interest by the defendant's wrongdoing was properly established; so the only problem was uncertainty with regard to the damage. In this section, we deal with cases where the violation issue is uncertain. Specifically, we deal with cases that have the following features:

(1) the defendant's wrongdoing has been established;
(2) the plaintiff sustained a damage that might have been caused by that wrongdoing ('might'—because the damage could have equally been caused by a factor unrelated to the defendant); and
(3) it is uncertain whether the defendant's wrongdoing actually violated any of the plaintiff's protected interests.

The following are two representative examples.

> *The Radiation Case.* Glenn's factory emits carcinogenic radiation. In the area affected by the radiation, the incidence of cancer rises by 25%: while prior to the factory's operation, only 80 people contracted cancer each year, 100 people now become afflicted each year. There is, however, no evidence that could preponderantly identify those people who actually contracted cancer as a result of exposure to the radiation, as opposed to those who are simply victims of misfortune. All 100 people file lawsuits against Glenn. Jacob is one of those 100 plaintiffs, and we focus on his lawsuit.

> *The Tobacco Case.* Philip is the only cigarette manufacturer in the country. He is responsible for wrongful advertising of his cigarettes, which

[50] Even if the surgery had been successful, the mere act of performing it without Rachel's consent constitutes a violation of her autonomy.

turned many people into smokers at a time when smoking hazards were largely unknown or underappreciated. Years later, many of those smokers, including Jacob, have developed lung cancer. This illness could have also originated from other causes, unrelated to Philip's wrongdoing. The probability that Jacob's illness did result from smoking cigarettes manufactured by Philip equals 20%.

In the *Radiation Case*, Jacob seems to have a strong compensation claim based on his lost chances: arguably, Glenn's wrongdoing increased Jacob's chances of contracting the illness or, conversely, decreased his chances of remaining healthy. There seems to be a basic similarity between this case and the *Medical Malpractice (Past Injury)* example, so the two cases should, arguably, be treated in a similar way. In both cases, the plaintiff was injured and there is a probability of less than 50 per cent that this injury was caused by the defendant's wrongdoing. However, the two cases also differ in a number of important respects. Damage inflicted by the wrongdoer in the *Radiation Case* is systematically inflicted on a large number of people. This 'recurrent wrong' feature does not exist in the *Past Injury Case*. Apart from this point, in cases similar to our *Radiation* example, the probability that the wrongdoing was directed against and consequently injured the particular plaintiff would typically be less than 50 per cent. This would not necessarily be so in cases represented by the *Past Injury* example. Most importantly, in the *Past Injury Case* the wrongdoer had clearly infringed one of the plaintiff's protected interests. In the *Radiation Case*, the plaintiff failed to establish such an infringement.

Do these differences have any legal significance?

(a) Systematic Infliction of Damage

This factor is relevant to corrective justice. As such, it points in favour of imposing liability on Glenn in accordance with the chance that his wrongdoing damaged Jacob. From the corrective justice viewpoint, holding Glenn systematically liable in this and similar cases would both compensate the victims and force Glenn to make an adequate payment for his wrongdoing. (Incidentally, this solution would also be justified by retributive justice, as the payment extracted from the wrongdoer equals the expected damage.[51]) Admittedly, most of the plaintiffs who have developed cancer were actually not injured by the radiation, so they would receive compensation to which they are not entitled. Moreover, the plaintiffs who were actually injured by the radiation, the minority of the group, would be undercompensated. These outcomes are at odds with the *restitutio ad integrum* principle. However, if Jacob and similarly situated plaintiffs are denied remedy altogether, the

[51] See above 101–10.

affront to corrective justice would be even greater. The partial compensation solution would, therefore, be the best corrective justice alternative for this and similar cases. In the *Past Injury Case*, this alternative would not be available: imposing liability on the physician according to the chances that the plaintiff's damage was caused by the former's wrongdoing would force the physician to pay compensation for damage she did not inflict. Note that the two examples would have been similar had the malpractice incident established against the physician (or, more realistically, against her hospital) been recurrent.

(b) Probability below 50 Per Cent

This factor is relevant to deterrence. Under the doctrine that imposes liability for lost chances, Glenn would pay 20 per cent of Jacob's damage. Under the $P>0.5$ rule, Glenn would be released from liability. However, since Glenn's wrongdoing is recurrent and since his typical probability of inflicting the damage is below 0.5, release from tort liability in this and similar cases would severely undermine deterrence. This would not always happen in the *Past* and *Future Injury* types of cases. In such cases, the lost chances occasionally exceed 50 per cent, so that under the $P>0.5$ rule, the plaintiffs become entitled to full recovery. This may offset the underdeterrence effect that would be generated by the release from liability granted to defendants in $P\leq0.5$ cases.[52]

(c) Unproven Infringement

Unproven infringement of a protected interest of the plaintiff is the main argument against imposing liability on the *Radiation Case* defendant. Arguably, this factor crucially distinguishes the *Radiation Case* from the *Past Injury* example. To be more accurate, in the *Radiation Case*, the wrongdoer created a very low *a priori* risk (a 0.02 per cent annual rate, assuming that 100,000 people were exposed to the radiation) for potential victims, including Jacob. The risk to which Ruth exposed Helen in the *Past Injury Case* was much higher. The difference between the *Past Injury* and the *Radiation* examples would become transparent if we were to use the wrongdoer's *a priori* risk as a criterion for evaluating the extent to which the plaintiff's protected interest was infringed. Indeed, the prevalent tort law doctrine is more reluctant to impose liability in the *Radiation* type of cases than in cases such as the *Past Injury*.

The *Tobacco Case* is seemingly closer to the *Past Injury Case* than to the *Radiation Case*: the plaintiff in the *Tobacco Case* was wrongfully exposed to

[52] See above 118.

a much higher risk of cancer than his *Radiation Case* counterpart. This difference, however, is real only *ex ante*, that is, before we know that each of the plaintiffs actually sustained the litigated damage. After the event—once it becomes known that each of the plaintiffs sustained that damage—the *ex post* probabilities associating the defendants' wrongful actions with the plaintiffs' respective damages should be taken into account. Each of those probabilities is quite high. Consequently, the *Tobacco Case* should, indeed, be treated similarly to the *Radiation Case*. Both cases warrant compensation from the deterrence and the corrective justice perspectives, since both entail systematic infliction of damage and a probability below 50 per cent. Therefore, imposition of liability on the defendants in the *Radiation* and *Tobacco* cases is of greater necessity than in the *Past Injury Case*.[53]

Our final example illustrates yet another type of case that falls under the presently examined category. In this type of case, although there is a general probability that the plaintiff's damage has resulted from the defendant's wrongdoing, the plaintiff fails to establish that the defendant actually exposed her even to the slightest risk or infringed any of her protected interests. Nevertheless, there are good reasons for holding the defendant liable in proportion to his chances of having caused the plaintiff's damage.

> *The DES Case.* DES, a drug designed to prevent miscarriages and wrongfully manufactured by hundreds of companies, turns out to be latently carcinogenic to female foetuses. Twenty-five years later, many of the women whose mothers took the drug have contracted uterine cancer. None of the plaintiffs can evidentially link the specific pills her mother took to a specific manufacturer. Lisa contracted uterine cancer because her mother took DES. She sues XYZ Pharmaceutical Company for her damages. At the time relevant to Lisa's lawsuit, XYZ controlled 10% of the DES market.

Full analysis of this type of case is provided in Chapters II and V. Courts in the United States held DES defendants liable in proportion to their respective shares in the market. The doctrine they applied in so doing is known as Market Share Liability ('MSL'). Liability imposed on wrongdoers under MSL is similar in its extent to liability for lost chances.

Lisa's case against XYZ is manifestly difficult to establish, as she cannot prove even *prima facie* that XYZ infringed any one of her protected interests. The probability that one of Lisa's protected interests was infringed by XYZ corresponds with the 10 per cent probability that XYZ caused the litigated damage. None the less, Lisa's case warrants compensation more than any of our previous examples do. Imposition of liability on XYZ and similar

[53] See J. D. Hanson and K. D. Logue, 'The Costs of Cigarettes: The Economic Case for Ex Post Incentive-Based Regulation' (1998) 107 *Yale LJ* 1163; A. Porat, 'The Tobacco Litigation and the New Challenge of Tort Law' *Mishpatim* (forthcoming 2002) (Hebrew).

manufacturers would create a regime in which the wrongdoer pays for the damage that he inflicted; the victim is compensated for the wrongful damage she has suffered; and the wrongdoer participates in financing the mechanism that facilitates the compensation of the victim. MSL is, therefore, entirely consistent with corrective justice. Furthermore, this liability is necessitated by deterrence concerns: under MSL, the wrongdoers ultimately pay for the losses they actually inflicted.[54]

D. CONCLUSION

In this chapter, we have ruled out tort liability for bare risk. We have also demonstrated that liability for lost chances is both conceptually and functionally problematic. Nevertheless, we do not believe that adherence to 'all-or-nothing' solutions, as furnished by the P>0.5 rule, is normatively appropriate in lost-chance cases. In Chapters VI and VII, we examine such cases under a partial liability regime founded on the evidential damage doctrine. Grounded on both deterrence and corrective justice, this new doctrine will provide a principled solution to the problem at hand. Under this doctrine, defendants would be held liable in all types of cases examined in Part C above. Consequently, the wrongdoer would *always* pay for a fraction of the damage that was sustained or is expected to be sustained by the plaintiff. This fraction would be determined by the probability of the allegation that the damage was caused by the wrongdoer.

[54] See below Chapter V.

V

Collective Liability

A. THE NATURE OF THE PROBLEM

TORT law sets two prerequisites necessary, although not always sufficient, for imposing liability on a defendant for an injury sustained by the plaintiff: first, the defendant must have behaved in a wrongful way; second, the defendant's wrongful behaviour must be the factual cause of the plaintiff's injury. Naturally, the plaintiff bears the burden of proof with regard to these two conditions. The plaintiff will succeed in her or his lawsuit only if she or he persuades the court on a balance of probabilities that these two conditions have, indeed, been met.

This chapter deals with a distinct category of cases where the plaintiff is unable to prove one of these two conditions (or both), but can adequately identify a group of individuals to which her or his wrongdoer belongs. In a legal system that adheres to strictly individual liability in torts, such plaintiffs would have no cause of action.[1] Consequently, they would be left uncompensated for their injuries. However, an entirely different outcome would be attained in a legal system that is prepared to relax the individual liability requirement and to allow collective liability in torts. Under such a system, every member of the identified group that includes the unidentifiable wrongdoer would be required to pay for all or some of the plaintiff's damage.[2] The

[1] A. Porat, 'Collective Liability in Tort Law' (1994) 23 *Mishpatim* 311 (Hebrew). We assume throughout this discussion that the group to which the wrongdoer belongs cannot be regarded as a group of joint tortfeasors, aiders, or abettors, in which case holding the wrongdoer responsible for the plaintiff's damage would not constitute a deviation from the principle of individual liability. We also assume that the persons comprising the group are not vicariously liable; vicarious liability is a well-known exception to the principle of individual liability, which will not be discussed here. Cf. R. A. B. Bush, 'Between Two Worlds: The Shift from Individual to Group Responsibility in the Law of Causation of Injury' (1986) 33 *University of California Los Angeles L Rev* 1473, 1476.

[2] In the typical case in which the question of collective liability arises, there is a less than 50% probability that each member of the wrongdoer's group caused the damage. However, the question of collective liability could also arise in a case where the probability is higher than 50%, but is based on naked statistical, rather than case-specific evidence. A well-known example illustrates this. Two different taxi companies operate in a given city, with one owning 60% of the taxis working in the city and the other owning 40%. A man is injured in a road accident, and he knows that he was hit by a taxi, but is unable to identify the company to which the taxi belongs. One possibility would be to release both taxi companies from all liability, for tort liability cannot be imposed on someone whose factual connection to the occurrence of the injury is based on naked statistics. Another possibility would be to impose liability on the taxi company that owns 60% of the city's taxis, for its liability can be established on the balance of probabilities. Finally, the third

concept of collective liability is as yet unrecognized under English and Israeli law. At the same time, as indicated in the preceding chapters, both English and Israeli courts have substantially relaxed the proof requirements that apply to causation issues, which has alleviated the task faced by the plaintiffs in proving their cases.[3] American courts, in contrast, began imposing collective liability many years ago, but they did so only in carefully delineated settings, especially identified for that purpose. Hence, there is no general collective liability doctrine in the United States either.[4] This chapter will demonstrate that collective liability in torts should be recognized as a general doctrine under the appropriate conditions.

B. IS COLLECTIVE LIABILITY JUSTIFIED?

The collective liability issue arises in three principal categories of cases. These are cases that exhibit (1) indeterminacy in causation; (2) indeterminacy in wrongfulness; or (3) indeterminacy in both causation and wrongfulness.

(a) Category I: Indeterminacy in Causation

In cases falling into this category, the defendant's wrongdoing has been established, but it cannot be adequately proved that it was the underlying cause of the plaintiff's damage. There is, however, a well-identified group of wrongdoers, to which the defendant belongs, and it has been established that one of the members of that group, who cannot be identified, actually inflicted the damage (as in the *Hunters' Case* and in the *DES Case*, discussed in Chapter II[5]).

(b) Category II: Indeterminacy in Wrongfulness

This category includes cases where it is established that the defendant caused the damage, but his wrongdoing is unproven. However, there is a well-identified group of individuals, to which the defendant belongs; each of these individuals was involved in causing the damage to the plaintiff; and it is established that

possibility would be to impose collective liability. See S. Shavell, *Economic Analysis of Accident Law* (Cambridge and London, 1987) 115–20; J. J. Thomson, 'Remarks on Causation and Liability' (1984) 13 *Philosophy & Public Affairs* 101, 127–33. We discuss this possibility later in this chapter. Problems involved in basing tort liability on naked statistical evidence are addressed in Chapters I and III.

[3] See above 78–81.

[4] The prevalent doctrinal attitude toward collective liability is presented in Chapter II. The mirror image of collective liability is 'collective entitlement'. Collective entitlement arises when the identity of the wrongdoer is known and there is an identifiable group to which the wrongfully injured individuals belong, but the exact identity of these individuals is unknown. See above 70–3, 125–9. See also below 174–9, 193–5.

[5] See above 58.

only one member of that group, who cannot be identified, is the actual wrongdoer (as in the *Two Cars Case*, discussed in Chapter II[6]).

(c) Category III: Indeterminacy in both Causation and Wrongfulness

In cases falling under this category, no wrongdoing on the part of the defendant can be proven; nor can it be established that the defendant caused the plaintiff's damage. There is, however, a well-identified group of individuals, to which the defendant belongs, and it is established that the plaintiff's damage originated from a wrongdoing committed by an unidentified member of that group (as in the *Injured Shoulder* and the *Cargo Cases*, discussed in Chapter II[7]).

The idea of collective liability has been developed as a means for resolving the evidential deficiency problem in adjudication. In reality, people are damaged individually and not collectively, and when they inflict damage on others, they do that individually as well. Reality, however, is not unfurled before judges as a non-convoluted picture that reveals all the workings of the relevant causal forces: litigated facts are intrinsically uncertain. Under the $P>0.5$ rule, this uncertainty should generally benefit defendants. Yet, in cases captured by each of the above categories, good reasons often exist for holding the defendants liable, which is especially true in recurrent-wrong situations. As we now explain, these reasons are grounded on both corrective justice and deterrence.

C. COLLECTIVE LIABILITY UNDER CORRECTIVE JUSTICE

1. The Bilateral Wrongdoer–Victim Relationship

Facially, collective liability and corrective justice are irreconcilable. Under corrective justice principles, tort liability is individual, rather than collective.[8]

The plaintiff's inability to prove causation or to establish wrongdoing is no reason for deviating from this basic requirement. Tort liability should,

[6] See above 59. [7] See above 59.

[8] See R. W. Wright, 'The Efficiency Theory of Causation and Responsibility: Unscientific Formalism and False Semantics' (1987) 63 *Chicago-Kent L Rev* 553. But see D. Rosenberg, 'The Causal Connection in Mass Exposure Cases: A "Public Law" Vision of the Tort System' (1984) 97 *Harvard L Rev* 849, 881–5; D. Rosenberg, 'Individual Justice and Collectivizing Risk-Based Claims in Mass-Exposure Cases' (1996) 71 *NYU L Rev* 210. For a thorough discussion, see Bush (n. 1 above). Bush argues that corrective justice and liberalism, two possible foundations of the concept of individual responsibility in torts, do not accommodate the concept of collective liability. None the less, Bush finds that collective liability is justified by communitarianism.

arguably, be imposed only within the bilateral wrongdoer–victim relationship,[9] as underscored by the three basic demands of corrective justice:

Demand 1: The wrongdoer should be liable only for the damage that he inflicted.

Demand 2: The victim should be compensated only for the wrongful damage that she suffered.

Demand 3: The wrongdoer should compensate his victim.

In many of the cases discussed in this chapter, collective liability does not violate Demands 1 and 2. Imposition of that liability in these cases might be at odds only with Demand 3. Yet, as already indicated, corrective justice would also be satisfied by forcing the wrongdoer to participate in financing the appropriate mechanism for compensating the wrongdoer's specific victim. In our view, it is not essential that the wrongdoer be forced to render compensation directly to the specific person he injured. Nor is it essential that the injured person receive compensation directly from her specific wrongdoer. Corrective justice would be satisfied so long as the payment made by the wrongdoer for his wrong facilitates his victim's reinstatement.[10]

Admittedly, our modification of Demand 3 does not conform with the traditional law of torts. Under the prevalent doctrine, the wrongdoer must compensate only the person he has injured.[11] Corrective justice, however, does not necessitate this restriction. It can be implemented without the restriction, making the latter normatively unnecessary. For example, one can devise a mechanism that collects compensation from all wrongdoers for damage they cause and compensates any person who sustains wrongful damage. This mechanism would be similar to social insurance, whereby speedy compensation is dispensed to all injured individuals, without requiring that they track down their particular wrongdoers and exact compensation directly from them. Corrective justice would be adequately attained as long as the wrongdoers pay their dues, the victims are compensated for their losses, and the payments made by the wrongdoers are used for compensating the victims. The direct payment requirement can, thus, only be understood as facilitating the attainment of corrective justice through adjudication. It seems to serve no substantive purpose.[12]

2. Category I: Indeterminacy in Causation

Corrective justice can, at times, justify imposition of collective liability in indeterminate causation cases belonging to this category. This, however, would not happen in every case. In the *Hunters' Case*, for example, imposition of collective liability would be unjustified. In that case, both defendants

[9] E. J. Weinrib, *The Idea of Private Law* (London, 1995) *passim*.

[10] See above 106–7. [11] Weinrib (n. 9 above). [12] See above 106–7.

wrongfully exposed the plaintiff to the risk of injury, but only one unidentified defendant inflicted the actual injury. Risk created by the other defendant did not materialize into any damage for the plaintiff, so its mere creation does not justify imposition of liability.[13] In this case, imposition of liability could therefore only be justified by the evidential damage doctrine, under which each of the defendants would be held responsible for the plaintiff's evidential damage. This justification is discussed in Chapters VI and VII.[14]

Imposition of collective liability in the *Hunters' Case* could, none the less, be advocated as a second-best alternative. Arguably, in a case like this, corrective justice mandates that it would be preferable to hold the defendants liable collectively than not to impose any liability at all. This argument compares two states of affairs:

1. The injured party receives full compensation, and one of the defendants—who, in actuality, did not inflict any portion of the damage—is held liable for half of that damage.
2. The injured plaintiff is left uncompensated for her damage and neither defendant is held liable.

Under this argument, the first state of affairs is preferable to the second because the deviation from corrective justice in the second state of affairs is more severe than in the first. This argument is rather problematic, for it suggests that corrective justice admits different degrees and that deviations from this type of justice are commensurable. But is it really possible to compare two distinct injustices from the corrective justice perspective? How can this be done without substituting corrective justice with a crude utilitarian calculus? There seems to be no satisfactory answer to these questions.[15]

In the *DES* and the *Blasting Caps* types of cases,[16] collective liability would be justified. In both of these cases, the defendants created a risk through their wrongdoing. This wrongful risk subsequently materialized into the plaintiffs' injuries. Arguably, this collective vision of the effect that was produced by the relevant causal forces is a form of *petitio principii*. Each individual defendant can, arguably, be perceived as creating its own individual risk. Therefore, if that risk did not factually contribute to the plaintiff's damage, there is no reason for holding the defendant liable. This individualized perception of the risk would, indeed, be justified, if the defendants had acted in isolation from one another. The actions taken by each defendant in both producing and marketing its products were, however, affected by other defendants' actions in the product market. The risk can therefore be perceived as collective, even though its materialization took different individual paths. In the *Blasting*

[13] See above 101–15.
[14] See below 162, 167, 174–5, 186–93.
[15] For a comprehensive discussion of this issue see Thomson (n. 2 above) 102–20.
[16] See above 64.

Caps type of case, an American court has adopted this reasoning by recognizing the doctrine of enterprise liability.[17]

Under the individualized perception of risk, as endorsed by most American courts in the *DES* type of cases, the problem arises in full force. American courts have largely resolved this problem in favour of plaintiffs by holding the defendants liable under the Market Share Liability doctrine ('MSL'). Under MSL, each defendant manufacturer is held responsible for the fraction of the total damage suffered by the plaintiff that is equal to the defendant's share of the relevant products market.[18] This share serves as a proxy for the probability that the litigated damage suffered by the plaintiff was inflicted by the defendant. We believe that this form of liability is also consistent with corrective justice. In behaving wrongfully, each defendant created a risk and thereby caused damage (although not necessarily to the specific plaintiff bringing suit against this specific defendant). It would consequently be justified to obligate the defendant to render compensation commensurate with the extent of the damage that he caused. As far as every specific plaintiff is concerned, the damage that she sustained was an outcome of her exposure to a wrongful risk. The relevant risk was certainly wrongful, although not attributable to any particular defendant. For this reason, the corrective justice principles recognize the plaintiff's entitlement to compensation. If the identity of the defendant who created the relevant risk could be determined, the duty to compensate the plaintiff would then be imposed on that defendant. However, this strictly bilateral doer–sufferer relationship is not an absolute prerequisite under corrective justice. This relationship ought to be a prerequisite for liability as long as the twosomes of doers and sufferers can be adequately identified. At the same time, the inability to make that identification, which characterizes the *DES* and similar cases, must not bring the plaintiff's story to a thoroughly unhappy end. Under MSL, each wrongdoer ultimately pays for the damage that he or she actually inflicted and each plaintiff ultimately receives compensation for the damage that he or she actually suffered. More importantly, under MSL, each wrongdoer effectively contributes to a general compensation mechanism that benefits the plaintiff who was actually damaged by that wrongdoer. The wrongdoer thus indirectly contributes to the compensation of *his or her* sufferer, which maintains the basic doer-sufferer relationship. This outcome is perfectly aligned with corrective justice. In reality, of course, each defendant may have compensated another wrongdoer's sufferer, with his or her sufferer being compensated by another wrongdoer belonging to the same group of wrongdoers. There is, however, nothing wrong in this 'liability exchange' system, so long as it produces corrective justice at the end of

[17] *Hall v E. I. Du Pont De Nemours & Co., Inc.*, 345 F Supp 353 (NY 1972).
[18] See above 61–7.

the day. An equally just possibility is to establish a statutory fund that would collect compensatory payments from all wrongdoers who created the relevant risk and subsequently compensate the relevant plaintiffs for their damage.

The relationship between corrective justice and collective liability raises several questions. First, must the imposed risk and the resulting damage be connected to each other? If they must, what is the nature of the required connection? Is this connection a prerequisite for imposing liability and awarding compensation under corrective justice? Does corrective justice require that all members of the group to which the wrongdoer belongs be proved to have created identical risks? This question focuses on the scope of the defendants' group: How, indeed, should this group be defined? Should it accommodate any person who is likely to be the wrongdoer or only a more specified class of defendants?

In our opinion, the demands of corrective justice would be satisfied if the wrongdoer were to contribute to the compensation of the victim actually injured by his actions by paying compensation not exceeding the damage he inflicted. The legal technique by which the compensation money is channelled from the wrongdoers to their victims is insignificant. Accordingly, under the collective liability technique, corrective justice will be achieved when the damaging event is recurrent for every member of the defendants' group and when the identity of the specific wrongdoer who actually damaged each individual victim is unknown. For that reason, the defendants' group must generally consist of wrongdoers who engage or engaged in similar activities (drug manufacturers, for example). When the wrongful action of a particular defendant is not recurrent and when this defendant cannot be linked to the damage suffered by any particular victim, holding that defendant liable in torts might force him to pay money damages even when he has caused no damage at all. In the absence of a long-run adjustment of compensation payments and awards, such distortions would be inevitable. For reasons already given, these distortions would violate the principles of corrective justice.

3. Category II: Indeterminacy in Wrongfulness

Under corrective justice, liability for inflicted damage can only be imposed when the infliction has been wrongful. In the *Two Cars Case*,[19] for example, none of the defendants would be held liable under corrective justice. The outcome would be different if the different instances of causally unattributable damage are recurrently created by a number of identified individuals and if the wrongful act is committed on each occasion by a different member of the group. This, of course, is not a very likely scenario. However, if this scenario were to unfold, imposition of collective liability would be compatible with corrective justice.

[19] See above 59.

This liability would be justified on grounds similar to those that justify imposing liability in the *DES* and *Blasting Caps Cases*. This system of liability would serve as a possible (although not necessarily the only) mechanism for transferring wealth from the wrongdoer to the victim. Under this system, each defendant's liability would be determined by the full value of the damage sustained by the plaintiff, multiplied by the probability of the claim that the defendant wrongfully inflicted that damage. Consequently, in the long run of cases, the amount of compensation paid by each defendant would reflect, as nearly as possible, the magnitude of the damage caused by his wrongdoing.

4. Category III: Indeterminacy in both Wrongfulness and Causation

As far as corrective justice is concerned, imposition of collective liability in cases falling under this category is profoundly problematic. This is so because the plaintiffs failed to establish two fundamental prerequisites for imposing tort liability: wrongfulness and causation. Yet, as we have just seen, under certain conditions, corrective justice justifies imposition of collective liability in indeterminate wrongfulness cases, which fall under Category II. We have also seen that corrective justice can justify collective liability in indeterminate causation cases (Category I). Would it, therefore, be possible to combine the relevant reasons and justify collective liability in cases featuring both types of problems?

The *Injured Shoulder Case*[20] is a clear example of indeterminacy in both wrongfulness and causation. In this case, imposition of liability cannot easily be aligned with corrective justice, for it would impose the compensation burden upon a number of people who are not wrongdoers and who did not cause any damage.[21] In the *Cargo Case*,[22] however, a different outcome can plausibly be reached. This case involves wrongfully inflicted damage that was a recurrent event for each of the defendants, rather than an isolated occurrence. In this and similar cases, damage was caused to containers belonging to people who used the shipping and storage services rendered by a shipping company and the port authority, respectively. The damage was inflicted wrongfully, but the wrongdoer's identity—the shipping company or the port authority—was unclear, as was the issue of causation. Similar to the *DES* type of cases, imposition of collective liability would create here a mechanism that, in the *long run*, would facilitate the transfer of compensation from the wrongdoer to the victim. Allocation of the compensation burden between the shipping company and the port authority should be in accordance with the probability that each defendant wrongfully inflicted the litigated damage. When this probability cannot be derived from the specific incident of the damage, it can be derived from past experience, for example,

[20] See above 59.
[21] But see the second-best argument in text accompanying n. 15 above.
[22] See above 59.

from the examination of similar incidents in which one of the two defendants was established to have wrongfully caused the damage.[23]

5. Collective Liability and the Extent of Compensation

Should collective liability be imposed on defendants both jointly and severally for the entire damage suffered by the plaintiff or should each defendant be responsible only for his fraction of the damage, as determined by the probability that he inflicted the damage on the plaintiff? Thus far, our discussion has rested on two assumptions. We have assumed that no difficulties are involved in identifying the defendants who form the group to which the actual wrongdoer belongs. We also have assumed that there is a realistic prospect of obtaining compensation and contribution payments from each of the group members. If these assumptions were uniformly valid, the above questions would have no significance: outcomes reached under the different liability rules would be identical, because each wrongdoer ultimately would pay for the damage he inflicted and each victim would receive full compensation for the damage she suffered. These assumptions, however, are far from being uniformly valid. Usually, they are not even realistic, hence the importance of the issue raised in this section.

A legal system that promotes corrective justice would impose collective liability in a way that would increase both the victims' chances of receiving full compensation for their damages and the wrongdoers' chances of paying full compensation for the damage they inflicted. Corrective justice may be best served by holding each defendant liable for the entire damage that the plaintiff sustained. This rule would be desirable as long as the defendants were in a better position than the plaintiff to collect contributory payments from other potential wrongdoers. Indeed, any such defendant would have an incentive to trace all the members of his group and collect their contributions if he is made liable for the entire damage.[24] If the plaintiff's ability to locate the members of this group and to collect damages were better than that of the defendants, imposition of partial, rather than full, liability on each individual defendant would be preferable. In any such case, the extent of the compensation duty to be imposed on each defendant should be determined by the probability that he inflicted the damage upon the plaintiff. In this way, the law would secure full (or nearly full) compensation for victims and full (or nearly full) liability for wrongdoers.[25]

[23] Also to be taken into account is the possibility that a connection exists between the inability to determine who caused the damage and the infliction of that damage by a particular defendant.

[24] This observation would hold true whenever the defendant's liability exceeds his relative share.

[25] This line of argument may appear problematic. Imposing liability on one member of the group for the entire damage can have the end result of his bearing the entire compensation burden if he fails to track down the rest of the members of the group and collect from them their

D. COLLECTIVE LIABILITY AND DETERRENCE

1. Causation and Deterrence

Is causation a prerequisite for optimal deterrence? Should liability in torts be conditioned on the existence of factual causation between the defendant's conduct and the plaintiff's damage? Why should the injurious consequence matter? Arguably, economic reasoning that adopts the optimal deterrence perspective favours a system that imposes liability for actions rather than for consequences. People scarcely, if ever, exercise full control over the consequences that attach to their actions. Consequences are frequently a matter of luck, while actions are not. An appropriate deterrence policy must, therefore, be directed at actions rather than consequences. According to that argument, tort liability should be imposed on a defendant if he acted wrongfully, even if he did not cause any damage to the plaintiff. This argument must still resolve the problem of standing and thereby identify the proper recipients of compensation. This argument must also account for the increase in the costs of adjudication that would inevitably arise if undamaged plaintiffs were given a licence to sue.[26] Yet, if these problems were somehow resolved,[27] the uneasy relationship between deterrence and causation would then become the critical issue.

There seems to be no difficulty in understanding why in a legal system under which liability is based on consequences, the extent of a wrongdoer's liability is determined by the magnitude of the inflicted damage, so that the wrongdoer is forced to pay neither less nor more than that damage. From the optimal deterrence perspective, the law of torts should be directed at minimizing the sum comprised of the total costs of accidents plus the total costs of their prevention. Therefore, it is imperative that a potential wrongdoer be forced to calculate his actions on the assumption that he will pay for any damage that his wrongdoing will cause. If his anticipated extent of liability were to fall below that amount, the deterrence would be insufficient. If the extent of liability anticipated by the wrongdoer were to exceed that amount, the deterrence would be excessive. Yet, why should a wrongdoer be liable for the damage he actually caused, rather than for the expected damage associated with his wrongdoing? What is the reason for conditioning his liability on the actual occurrence of the damage?

shares. This outcome thwarts corrective justice. Still, the victim will attain full compensation. But is this scenario preferable to one in which one wrongdoer bears part of the damage and the victim only receives partial compensation? As noted previously, comparing the two evils is deeply problematic. See text accompanying n. 15 above.

[26] This problem is examined above in Chapter I.

[27] See Chapter IV above.

In Chapter IV, we elaborate on this question and argue that liability for actual damage is preferable to liability for expected damage, which we call 'liability for creating risks'. We also argue in that chapter that making defendants *additionally* liable for expected damage when no damage actually occurred would produce overdeterrence. Finally, we identify situations in which optimal deterrence would be achieved by holding the defendant liable for the expected, rather than actual, damage. This solution is particularly suitable in cases in which the plaintiff's attempt to establish the defendant's liability for the actual damage is blocked by insurmountable evidentiary barriers.[28] Our subsequent discussion is, therefore, based on the assumption that underlying the given legal regime is the principle that wrongdoers should be liable for the entire damage that they cause.[29]

Does all this imply that collective liability cannot be imposed in the cases discussed in this chapter because causation cannot be proved? We believe that such a conclusion would be inaccurate. All that can be derived from our discussion here is that both overdeterrence and underdeterrence must be avoided. Therefore, a person should not be forced to pay compensation in excess of the amount necessary to cover the damage inflicted by his wrongful conduct. Nor should he be allowed to pay compensation below that amount. The required alignment between compensation and damage can, however, be maintained even when the issue of causation is indeterminate. Moreover, as will be demonstrated below, alignment of compensation and proven damage need not be an ironclad requirement. Rather, it should be treated as a rule that allows for exceptions.

2. Category I: Indeterminacy in Causation

We begin our discussion with the *DES* type of cases, which exhibit the indeterminacy-in-causation problem most vividly.[30] In any such case, making each defendant liable in proportion to its share of the relevant DES market would produce, in the long run, optimal deterrence. This result would be achieved because each defendant would eventually absorb the damage inflicted by its wrongful actions. Any such defendant would pay strictly for the damage it inflicted. It would never be forced to pay either more or less than that amount. This would provide an incentive for drug manufacturers to expend the appropriate amount of resources in order to test the safety of their drugs, to optimally neutralize the drugs' side-effects, to maintain research and

[28] Cf. G. Calabresi, 'Concerning Cause and the Law of Torts: An Essay for Harry Kalven, Jr.' (1975) 43 *U Chicago L Rev* 69, 86–7; Chapter IV above.

[29] This principle is subject to certain restrictions, primarily, the remoteness of the damage.

[30] See above 58.

[31] Although the manufacturers will pass on to consumers, through the product's price, the overall cost of their liability plus their damage prevention costs, this does not detract from their incentive to decrease this overall total. Such a decrease will enable them better to compete on the market.

development, and so forth.[31] By contrast, absolving DES defendants from tort liability would give a 'green light' to all drug manufacturers to expose their consumers to risk of injury without incurring any (except for some reputational) costs. Imposing MSL on each manufacturer could prevent this underdeterrence. Under MSL, each manufacturer would pay for the actual damage originating from its wrongdoing in the long run of cases.[32] As already indicated, the law of torts does not usually take this route; rather, it assigns liability only when causation with regard to the litigated damage is proven on a balance of probabilities. Yet, when proof of causation between the defendant's wrongful conduct and the ensuing damage is met with systematic obstacles, exposing the wrongdoer to a risk of liability that is equivalent to his expected damage would be the most appropriate solution to the problem. MSL in the *DES Case* and its like assigns liability to each defendant in the amount of his or her expected damage, which is also equal to the actual damage he or she inflicted on different plaintiffs in the long run.

Collective liability does not, however, unequivocally ensure optimal deterrence. There are cases in which optimal minimization of the damage would be secured only if the manufacturers were to work together toward this purpose, rather than independently of one another.[33] In the *DES* type of cases, for example, it is quite possible that prevention of the damage is very costly because it requires complicated, ongoing research. This cost may well be economically justified overall, since it is lower than the overall amount of damage caused by the drug. However, for an individual manufacturer this cost might be unaffordable. Even if the manufacturer were able to expend this cost, his savings in future compensation payments would rarely justify the expenditure. Furthermore, by making the required safety investment, the manufacturer would become exposed to free-riding by other manufacturers. Other manufacturers might capitalize on his research without bearing any of

For economic justifications of MSL, as well as a discussion of its drawbacks, see Rosenberg (n. 8 above) 861–77; N. Sheiner, 'DES and a Proposed Theory of Enterprise Liability' (1978) 46 *Fordham L Rev* 963, 1003–6. The latter article was published prior to the decision in *Sindell v Abbott Laboratories*, 607 P 2d 924 (Cal 1980), and in fact, envisioned the MSL before it was adopted by the courts.

[32] The market share does not always reflect the precise extent of the risk that each manufacturer created. Hence, some American courts have assessed the extent of risk by using the market share as a relevant, but not yet decisive, factor. See above 63, note 20. However, using market share as the sole determinant of the relevant risk would save administrative costs.

[33] Arguably, under a negligence regime, liability should not be ascribed to a person who could not have reasonably prevented the damage had he acted alone without the co-operation of others, even though co-operation was demanded by efficiency. The same argument is applicable to a strict product-liability regime, in which liability is imposed for design defects. Accordingly, it is arguable that the existence of a design defect should be measured according to the ability of each individual manufacturer, working *alone*, to prevent the defect. The following discussion takes the opposite course of argument.

its costs. This problem is likely to hinder damage-reducing co-operation between the manufacturers even when it is advantageous to each individual manufacturer.[34]

Another problem relates to a manufacturer who is willing to invest in reducing the damage, but is sceptical about his future ability to persuade the court that he succeeded in that endeavour even when the endeavour was actually successful. This manufacturer would estimate that his reduction of the damage would not appropriately reduce his liability. Because the identity of the manufacturer responsible for the reduction of the damage would be unverifiable, the damage reduction would benefit all manufacturers by reducing the extent of their liability. This anticipated outcome would dilute the incentive to minimize damage. Further on in this chapter, we discuss this problem in greater detail and offer a possible solution.[35]

The two problems discussed thus far are, admittedly, serious. None of them, however, refutes the claim that imposing collective liability in DES and similar cases is preferable, from the deferrence viewpoint, to not imposing liability at all.

There is yet another economic problem that presents a serious challenge to the idea of collective liability. This problem relates to the administrative costs that would be involved in operating a collective liability regime. Administration of this regime would be very costly because in each individual case, the court would have to ascertain the extent of the risk wrongfully externalized by the individual manufacturer. For example, a single defendant manufacturer who produced DES may have seriously endangered one of the plaintiffs (say, the plaintiff whose mother purchased the damaging drug from a drugstore that obtained most of its products from that manufacturer). Yet, it is clear that another plaintiff (say, the plaintiff whose mother resided in an area where none of the manufacturer's drugs were marketed) has no complaint against this particular defendant. This very plausible scenario divides the national DES market into a number of separate markets with different shares held by different manufacturers. Ascertaining the respective market shares of the various manufacturers would thus necessitate a complex investigation, which often would be economically unfeasible. In a landmark decision, the New York Supreme Court devised a solution to this problem. The Court decided that each defendant must compensate the various plaintiffs in proportion to that defendant's share of the national DES market, regardless of the extent of the risk it actually created toward each individual plaintiff. This liability

[34] Cf. S. Rose-Ackerman, 'Market-Share Allocations in Tort Law: Strengths and Weaknesses' (1990) 19 *J Legal Studies* 739. In many cases, an individual manufacturer would be able to act towards preventing damage, at least by providing an appropriate warning to drug consumers. See R. A. Bays, 'The Market Share Theory: Sindell's Contribution to Industry-Wide Liability' (1981) 19 *Houston L Rev* 107, 137.

[35] See below 151–5.

mechanism guarantees a substantial saving in administrative costs, since the market share of each defendant would have to be determined only once.[36] In the long run of cases, this mechanism would also properly allocate the compensation burden amongst different defendants. Furthermore, as held by the same court, a manufacturer would not be absolved from liability even if it could successfully prove that its product had caused no actual damage to any of the plaintiffs. Any such defendant would still be held liable in proportion to its share of the national market. It would be absolved from liability only upon showing that its drug was not marketed at all during the relevant points in time (in the DES context, during the time when one of the plaintiffs' mothers was pregnant and consumed the drug).[37]

Not all American courts have adopted the 'national market' system. Some courts have maintained that the relevant markets must be determined separately in each individual case. The uncertainty gaps created by this approach are filled by presumptions. For example, some courts have decided that in the absence of specific information, the defendants will be deemed to have had equal shares of the relevant market and to account for 100 per cent of that market. This presumption, however, has been held to be rebuttable: any defendant who successfully proves that it had a lower share of the market (or no share at all) would reduce (or eliminate) its liability accordingly.[38] This system is more expensive to administer than the mechanism devised by the New York Supreme Court.[39]

In sum, the administrative problem discussed in the above paragraphs can be overcome in a way less drastic than outright rejection of the MSL doctrine.

[36] We assume that this determination is applicable in other lawsuits.

[37] *Hymowitz v Eli Lilly & Co.*, 539 NE 2d 1069 (NY 1989). For support of this approach, see A. D. Twerski, 'Market Share—A Tale of Two Centuries' (1989) 55 *Brooklyn L Rev* 869, 872–3.

[38] *Martin v Abbott Laboratories*, 689 P 2d 368, 383 (Wash 1984).

[39] The refusal of some courts to impose collective liability on the basis of the national market, as well as their willingness to waive the liability of a manufacturer that proves that its product did not cause the damage in the given case, are the consequences of adherence to the traditional principle of factual causation, which, in effect, was discarded with the adoption of MSL. See Twerski (n. 37 above) 870–3. Imposing collective liability according to market share, regardless of which variation of this system is adopted, raises serious problems with respect to manufacturers that have ceased to exist. See P. D. Rheingold, 'The Hymowitz Decision—Practical Aspects of New York DES Litigation' (1989) 55 *Brooklyn L Rev* 883, 894.

Another argument that has been made against MSL is that applying this doctrine will result in a flood of lawsuits. G. O. Robinson, 'Multiple Causation in Tort Law: Reflections on the DES Cases' (1982) 68 *Virginia L Rev* 713, 732. For the drawbacks of this doctrine from the perspective of its administrative costs, see also K. M. Zitzer and M. D. Ginsberg, 'Illinois Rejects Market Share Liability: A Policy Based Analysis of *Smith v Eli Lilly & Co.*' (1990–1) 79 *Kentucky LJ* 617, 645–9; A. G. Celli, 'Toward a Risk Contribution Approach to Tortfeasor Identification and Multiple Causation Cases' (1990) 65 *NYU L Rev* 635. For suggestions on possible alternative solutions for cases like the DES cases, including first party insurance, see R. A. Epstein, 'The Legal and Insurance Dynamics of Mass Tort Litigation' (1984) 13 *J Legal Studies* 475, 494 *et seq.*; L. I. Boden, 'Comment on Epstein' (1984) 13 *J Legal Studies* 507, 514 *et seq.*; K. S. Abraham, 'Individual Action and Collective Responsibility: The Dilemma of Mass Tort Reform' (1987) 73 *Virginia L Rev* 845, 883 *et seq.*

Adoption of the 'national market' approach may well provide an adequate solution.[40]

Let us consider now the *Hunters' Case*,[41] which is slightly more problematic than the *DES Case*. In the *Hunters' Case*, holding both defendants liable (as actually decided by the California court) would facially produce excessive deterrence. This holding would force one of the defendants to internalize a fraction of the plaintiff's damage even though he caused no damage whatsoever. In this respect, the *Hunters' Case* stands in marked contrast to the *DES Case*. Although in both cases, defendants compensate plaintiffs for damages unaffiliated to those defendants, each DES defendant, as opposed to one unidentified hunter, is known to have damaged another similarly situated plaintiff.

In general the perspective is, considerations are almost indifferent with regard to the liability rule when the episode of damage is rare and unique, as in the *Hunters' Case*.[42] Still, collective liability is justifiable even in such cases, because its imposition will induce any potential wrongdoer to choose his course of action in light of its full expected damage.

Collective liability is more crucial, however, when the incidents of damage in which the wrongdoer is unidentifiable are recurrent in the framework of the activity. Let us assume that instead of exceptional events, we are dealing with a distinct and recurrent type of activity, such as hunting, in which, from time to time, damage is caused through wrongdoing and the identity of the wrongdoer cannot be proven. As opposed to the *DES Case* and its like, in which the recurrence of events relates to the infliction of damage by *each* defendant, here the recurrence of events relates to the infliction of damage in the framework of the activity in which the defendants partake. Let us also assume that a number of hunters wrongfully opened fire in the plaintiff's direction; that one of the shots injured the plaintiff; and that there is no way of identifying the specific hunter who fired that shot. We now consider two possible decisions:

1. None of the hunters is held liable for the plaintiff's damage (collective liability is not imposed).
2. Each hunter compensates the plaintiff in accordance with the probability that he caused the damage (collective liability is imposed).

Which decision is preferable? The first decision clearly leads to underdeterrence. Every hunter will know that he will pay compensation that falls below the damage he might actually cause. Therefore, instead of considering the

[40] Note that adopting different MSL systems in different jurisdictions may create additional problems. If, for example, a national market approach is adopted in New York and a more individualized approach is adopted in other states then, in the long run, firms that operated in New York will pay less than the damage they actually caused, while other firms will pay more.

[41] See above 58.

[42] But see *Cook v Lewis* [1952] 1 DLR 1 (the Canadian 'twin' of the *Hunters' Case*).

expected damage originating from his wrongdoing, the hunter will take into account a lower level of expected damage and, accordingly, will take sub-optimal precautions. The second decision produces optimal deterrence. Each hunter will be required to bear part of the unattributable damage and therefore will take into account beforehand his expected damage. This internalization of the damage will impel the hunter to take optimal precautions.[43] To sum up, deterrence considerations justify imposing collective liability in the present category of cases, especially when injurious incidents are recurrent in the activity in question.[44]

3. Category II: Indeterminacy in Wrongfulness

As with the previous category of cases, deterrence considerations would justify imposing collective liability in cases included in this second category, especially if the incidences of damage in which the wrongdoer is unidentified are recurrent either among the defendants or in the framework of the activity in question. The probabilistic compensation solution, applicable to the previous category of cases, would also be suitable here, subject to a few adjustments. These adjustments would be necessary because in cases included in the present category, there is not enough evidence to single out any one of the defendants as the wrongdoer. Each defendant is only suspected of being the wrongdoer due to his involvement in the event that ended up in the litigated damage. This suspicion, however, cannot be verified because we know that only one unidentifiable member of the defendants' group is actually the wrongdoer. Hence, although it is established that the damage was inflicted wrongfully, as in the *Two Cars Case*, attribution of the damage to a single defendant is problematic. Because the defendant may have been faultless, how can any kind of liability be attributed to his conduct? On the other hand, by absolving all defendants from liability in torts, the legal system would grant an exemption to the actual wrongdoer, who is known to be numbered amongst the defendants. What is preferable then—to hold the defendants collectively liable or not to impose any liability at all?

Let us examine this question from the optimal deterrence perspective in relation to the *Two Cars Case*. We assume throughout our discussion that the accident dealt with in that case is a recurrent event in the framework of the activity in question.[45] We further assume that liability is based on fault. Under these realistic assumptions, if cases falling into the present category

[43] This discussion assumes that each hunter's precautions are varifiable. Otherwise, the free-riding problem discussed in the DES context (above) will be present here as well.

[44] Note that under corrective justice, recurrence in the activity is not enough; it must be related to the specific defendants. See above 134–8.

[45] As opposed to a recurrent event among the defendants.

were to be resolved by imposing collective liability on the defendants—so that they would equitably share the compensation burden—then *reckless drivers* would be insufficiently deterred. In such a legal regime, compensation paid by reckless drivers would be lower than the damage they actually cause, and consequently they would act in the light of their liability risk, which is lower than the expected damage associated with their wrongdoing potential. The incentive of reckless drivers to take precautions would thus drop below its optimal level. In contrast, cautious drivers would be overdeterred. The compensation they would pay would be higher than the damage they actually cause, and they would act in the light of their liability risk, which would be higher than the expected damage associated with their wrongdoing potential. The pooling effect created by the wrongdoer-identification problem would thus concurrently produce underdeterrence and overdeterrence.

The underdeterrence problem would be further exacerbated under a legal regime that imposes no liability in the present category of cases. Under such a regime, reckless drivers would reap even greater benefit from the identification problem. The compensation paid by them would drop even further below the already-reduced rates under the equal-share collective liability regime described in the preceding paragraph. The no-liability regime would, however, be better from the deterrence perspective than the equal-share collective liability regime, as far as cautious drivers are concerned. These drivers would not be forced to pay for damage that they did not wrongfully inflict. The compensation paid by cautious drivers would thus better reflect the actual damage associated with their wrongdoing, so that they would be almost[46] optimally deterred.

If neither of these two regimes can produce optimal deterrence, how, then, can optimal deterrence be attained in the present category of cases? Is there a third, thus far unarticulated, legal regime, under which the optimal deterrence objective could be promoted more adequately? We believe that such a regime could, indeed, be devised. Under such a regime, every driver would pay damages in proportion to the risk of causing damage he created through his wrongful driving. This risk would be determined by the driver's probability of being the wrongdoer on the litigated occasion, which would be determined according to data relating to the specific accident, but not exclusively so. The courts would also take into account other statistically significant factors, such as the driver's driving history, age group, health conditions, the condition of his car, and the make of his car.[47] Information that the courts would consider would

[46] In effect, they would pay too little, since cautious drivers also sometimes cause accidents through negligence when the identity of the actual negligent driver is unknown.

[47] One can envision two possible forms of collective liability: one, advocated by us, in which the allocation of shares of the damage is determined according to probabilities; and the second, in which the allocation is determined according to the expected damage of each defendant. In the DES cases, both forms would have led to exactly the same outcomes. In the *Two Cars Case*, they could lead to different outcomes. This would be the case if one of the cars were small in size, while

thus be similar to the information processed by insurance companies in setting the premiums to be paid by car drivers for the appropriate insurance coverage. Note that the court would consider only information that may indicate the probability of the specific driver being the wrongdoer when he is involved in an accident. Consequently, information such as intensity of driving, which relates to the chances of his being involved in an accident, but not to the chances of his being the wrongdoer in an accident in which his involvement is an accomplished fact, is irrelevant for the purposes of imposing liability.

Under this liability regime, drivers would pay compensation that takes into account their wrongdoing potential. Low-risk drivers would pay relatively low compensation, while high-risk drivers would pay proportionately higher compensation. Consequently, each driver would act in the light of the real expected damage associated with his behaviour. Optimal deterrence would thereby be attained.

The only economic problem that can be envisioned in the application of this regime is the administrative costs involved. Information that courts would require for determining the relevant risks and the magnitude of the average damage would be costly both to obtain and process. This information, however, would facilitate the optimal deterrence of drivers, which would prevent heavier damage. The administrative costs expended in court would thus be offset by the social gains generated on the road.

4. Category III: Indeterminacy in Both Causation and Wrongfulness

In cases falling under this category, deterrence concerns weigh in favour of imposing collective liability. As in cases falling into one of the two previous categories, the damaging events in which the wrongdoer is unidentified—since they are recurrent either among the specific defendants or in the framework of the activity in question—is a factor that supports the imposition of collective liability.

In the present category of cases, the probability that the defendant inflicted the litigated damage on the plaintiff should be determined by data relating to the specific accident, but not exclusively by this factor. In this respect, cases falling under the present category are identical to those belonging to Category II. For the latter category of cases, we have proposed a special liability rule that aims at optimal deterrence. Under that rule, each defendant would have to compensate the plaintiff in the amount that correlates with the probability of that defendant wrongfully causing the litigated damage. This probability

the other were large in size. Even if the probabilities of each defendant being the wrongdoer in the specific accident were equal, the amounts of expected damage of each defendant would not be. However, from the deterrence perspective, this difference has hardly any relevance, since both forms of liability expose both drivers to an *ex ante* risk of liability that is equivalent to the amounts of their expected damage. Therefore, both forms are equally efficient.

would be determined on the basis of general statistical data that pertain to the litigated incident. These data would supplement the case-specific information.[48] However, as opposed to Category II cases, in which information relating to the defendant's probability of being involved in accidents in general would be excluded, this information is very much relevant for imposing liability in Category III cases. This is so because in the latter type of cases, the probability of a given defendant being the wrongdoer depends not only on his tendency to be the wrongdoer when his involvement in the accident is an accomplished fact, but also on his general chances of being involved in accidents.

This approach favours imposition of collective liability in the *Cargo Case*.[49] Each of the defendants should assume liability that equals the litigated damage, multiplied by the probability of the scenario in which the defendant inflicted the damage. This probability would be calculated, for example, on the basis of prior incidents in which similar damage was inflicted by identifiable wrongdoers.

We now turn to the *Injured Shoulder Case*,[50] in which an unidentified member of a hospital medical team that treated the plaintiff injured him. The plaintiff brought the action for money damages against all the team members, both jointly and severally. In many such cases, the plaintiff's inability to establish the wrongdoer's identity would not be crucial because the hospital would be vicariously liable for actions taken by any of its employees.[51] However, the vicarious liability option might not be available in all cases. Absent this alternative, imposition of collective liability may especially be justified from the deterrence perspective if the litigated incident is recurrent within the framework of the activity.

5. Collective Liability and the Extent of Compensation

The argument made on this issue in the context of corrective justice[52] applies with equal force to deterrence. There is no universally correct answer to the question: Is it preferable to hold each individual defendant liable toward the plaintiff for all the damage that was inflicted or only for an appropriate fraction of that damage? In collective liability cases, the extent of the compensation duty depends on each party's ability to locate and collect contribution payments from the potential wrongdoers that form the defendants' group. If the defendant is better situated than the plaintiff for collecting those payments, the defendant should then be held liable for the entire damage. If the opposite is the case, the defendant's liability should be limited to his fraction of the plaintiff's damage. In the long run, this method of determining the compensation duty would increase each defendant's chances of paying only for damage originating from his wrongdoing.

[48] See above 146–7. [49] See above 59. [50] See above 59.
[51] See above 68–9. [52] See above 138.

E. SPREADING THE DAMAGE

Another legitimate objective of the law of torts is spreading the damage amongst as many people as possible.[53] Increasing the number of people who bear the costs of a damage will decrease the economic burden imposed by the damage. From this perspective, it is generally preferable for a thousand people to sustain a £1 damage each than for one person to bear £1,000 in damages.[54] Consequently, liability in torts should be allocated in a way that best spreads the damage. One way of accomplishing this social objective is to impose liability on the cheapest spreader of the damage, that is, on the person who would spread the damage cheaply amongst the greatest number of people through insurance or self-insurance. For example, a product manufacturer would typically be the cheapest spreader of the damage associated with his products. Sometimes, he will take out an insurance policy that covers the damage. Alternatively—and subject to the market constraints—the manufacturer will incorporate into the price of his products the cost of his expected liability in torts; and, of course, he might also supplement this self-insurance with insurance. Both the insurance and the self-insuring price raising would thus serve as mechanisms for spreading the damage. A person's ability to spread the damage is measured not necessarily by the depth of her or his pockets or market power. This ability depends mainly on whether she or he can properly evaluate the expected magnitude of the damage and the probability of its occurrence.

Typically, the damage-spreading objective favours imposition of collective liability. Indeed, when an injured plaintiff sues a large number of defendants who are capable of spreading the damage, placing the burden of the damage upon all the defendants, as opposed to only one, would promote this objective. The outcome would only be different if the injured plaintiff were capable of spreading the damage—through either insurance or self-insurance—better than the defendants were. In the vast proportion of cases calling for imposition of collective liability, this latter scenario is unlikely to materialize. In such cases, illustrated by our *DES* and *Blasting Caps* examples,[55] each individual defendant can spread the damage far better than the injured plaintiff can. In such cases, therefore, the damage-spreading objective of the law of torts unequivocally justifies imposition of collective liability on all the defendants.[56]

[53] See Fleming James, 'Social Insurance and Tort Liability: The Problem of Alternative Remedies' (1952) 27 *NYU L Rev* 537. Usually, damage spreading is regarded as a secondary objective of tort law and not as its sole or primary objective; otherwise, the best legal regime would be social insurance.

[54] See G. Calabresi, 'Some Thoughts on Risk Distribution and the Law of Torts' (1961) 70 *Yale LJ* 499, 517–19 and see above 5–6.

[55] See above 64.

[56] An additional reason is the defendants' ability to insure against many incidents of damage in a concentrated fashion, which saves transaction costs. See Zitzer and Ginsberg (n. 39 above) 643–5.

The *Two Cars Case*[57] is no exception: it is more reasonable to place the damage-spreading requirement on car drivers than on passengers or pedestrians, so that each driver is required to purchase the appropriate insurance coverage for car accidents.[58] The same holds true in both the *Cargo* and the *Injured Shoulder* cases. In both of these cases, the defendants could anticipate and estimate the relevant damage better than the plaintiffs could. At times, the defendants were better able to spread the damage themselves by passing it on to consumers. Therefore, the defendants clearly were better spreaders of the damage than the plaintiffs were.

F. INCENTIVES FOR REVEALING THE TRUTH

1. The Search for the Truth: To What End?

From the discussion thus far, one can see that collective liability is justified by the absence of a better alternative. The only other available alternative—to absolve all the defendants completely—is more detrimental to the tort law objectives. Ideally, the court should determine the identity of the actual wrongdoer who inflicted the litigated damage and hold him liable for the entire damage. This, however, is similar to saying that certainty is better than uncertainty, an axiom that will not get the legal system very far because in cases dealt with by this book, uncertainty is a given condition.

As demonstrated above, corrective justice does not always support collective liability, since imposition of collective liability does not guarantee that the compensation duty imposed on an individual wrongdoer will correspond with the damage he actually inflicted. Moreover, even from the deterrence perspective, collective liability is merely the lesser of two evils. Indeed, imposing collective liability still does not eliminate the possibility that prospective wrongdoers will not have proper incentives to take precautions. Thus, in some cases, although every prospective wrongdoer can reduce damage by taking appropriate precautions, his savings of liability damages may not justify taking the precautions because he will share his investment with other collectively liable wrongdoers. In other cases, taking precautions is possible only if the prospective wrongdoers co-operate. Free-riding and related problems may hinder co-operation even when it is collectively beneficial to all parties involved.[59]

As explained in the preceding sections, the burden of compensation for damage should be allocated between members of the wrongdoers' group in

[57] See above 59.

[58] Since driving is an organized activity, it is both easy and relatively cheap for those engaging in the activity to insure against its risks, which cannot be said about those who engage in an activity such as walking.

[59] See below 141–2.

accordance with the probability criterion. Collective liability, which applies this criterion, aims at inducing the socially optimal investment in precautions by prospective wrongdoers. However, the uncertainty problem would often turn the determination of probabilities into a matter of guesswork. Admittedly, our methods for allocating the costs of damage under collective liability constitute no more than an attempt to cope with the unidentifiable wrongdoer problem. All of these methods aim at providing a second-best solution to the uncertainty problem because the first-best solution is unavailable.

Therefore, the law should aim at optimally minimizing the number of incidents in which the identity of the actual wrongdoer is unknown. We will now demonstrate that collective liability can contribute to the attainment of this goal by inducing prospective wrongdoers and victims of torts to alleviate the wrongdoer-identification problem. The relevant incentives for uncovering the truth can be divided into two categories: *ex ante* incentives and incentives that operate *ex post*. The *ex ante* incentives induce the prospective wrongdoers and victims of torts to take steps—*prior* to the occurrence of the damage—that will assist in revealing the actual wrongdoer's identity. The *ex post* incentives induce the prospective wrongdoers and victims of torts to take such steps *after* the occurrence of the damage. Generally, the *ex post* incentives combine into a single incentive to produce evidence capable of alleviating the wrongdoer-identification problem.

2. The *Ex Ante* Incentives

Precautions taken prior to an accident may often facilitate the wrongdoer's identification after the accident. Typically, it is the potential wrongdoers, not the potential victims of torts, who are able to take such precautions. Take a case in which a number of different manufacturers produce a similar drug (as in the *DES Case*[60]). Each manufacturer considers the probability of the drug producing damage for which he will be held liable. Each manufacturer also takes into account the wrongdoer-identification problem. Specifically, he considers the possibility that it will be impossible to determine which manufacturer's drug caused the damage that each victim sustains, and then ascribes an appropriate probability to that possibility. At the same time, it is possible that Manufacturer A can take steps to prevent the problem of identification. For example, he can make a precise and authenticated listing of each customer who purchases his drug. Any such customer will, of course, be free to purchase and consume similar drugs that other manufacturers produce and may well decide to do so. However, any customer whose name does not appear as a drug-buyer on A's list will have no claim against him. If all drug

[60] See above 58.

manufacturers were to take such measures, the problem of identification would be significantly alleviated.

The *Cargo Case* provides another example of *ex ante* incentives to minimize the extent of the identification problem. Let us assume that from time to time, damage is caused to containers that are shipped by sea and it is not possible to determine whether the shipping company or the port authorities caused the damage. Here as well, the prospective wrongdoers are able to prevent the identification problem almost completely by taking *ex ante* precautions: a meticulous examination of the goods when they 'pass hands' would solve the problem.

Our third example relates to exploding drink bottles. From time to time, a drink bottle explodes and causes damage, and there is no way of knowing who manufactured the bottle.[61] In this case, each bottle manufacturer can take measures in advance to facilitate identification of the actual manufacturer who caused the damage by marking the bottles he produces (for example, with inexpensive colour).

Although many potential wrongdoers are able to prevent in advance the identification problem, they are not always willing to do so. The decision whether or not to do so is economic in nature. Every potential wrongdoer takes into account two factors: the cost of eliminating or alleviating the identification problem and the benefits derived from doing so. The first factor is almost self-explanatory: at times, preventing the identification problem is exorbitantly expensive, so it is unreasonable to expect that anyone will take such measures. The second factor, however, is more complex. At times, prospective wrongdoers will prefer to perpetuate or even exacerbate the identification problem in order to prevent themselves from being identified as the actual wrongdoer. Consequently, they will not make even the slightest investment towards the subsequent proof of their identity and may even invest in making this more difficult.

If collective liability is not imposed, *the majority* of potential wrongdoers will benefit from the inability to identify the actual wrongdoer.[62] Even when collective liability is imposed, some wrongdoers will still prefer not to eliminate the identification problem. Naturally, these would be the prospective beneficiaries of the problem, namely, those wrongdoers who would pay less in liability damages than they would be required to pay if the problem did not exist. To exemplify this point, take a rule that allocates damage amongst potential wrongdoers on an equal basis rather than by applying the probability standard.

[61] Or it is not possible to determine the reason for the explosion: a defect in the product, negligence on the part of the retailer, or any other reason. See W. P. Keeton (ed.), *Prosser and Keeton on Torts* (5th edn., 1984) 253.

[62] The exception being, perhaps, those who do not cause any damage at all or cause minor damage and who are likely to be harmed from a bad reputation as damage-producers. For example, if a bottle company manufactures bottles that never explode, the company will want consumers to know this fact.

Under this rule, any wrongdoer with expected damage that exceeds the average would prefer that the identification problem persist.[63] In contrast, collective liability based on the probability criterion would reduce the number of potential wrongdoers who have an interest in maintaining this problem. Allocation of the damage by the probability standard, however, is still far from an all-encompassing solution to the problem. This criterion would intensify the indifference with regard to the identification problem amongst prospective wrongdoers. Under the probability criterion, each potential wrongdoer would expect to bear liability that is identical to his expected damage. Such a wrongdoer would have no incentive to eliminate the identification problem. Because elimination of the problem would not improve this potential wrongdoer's position, his investment in self-identification would be a waste of resources.[64] Hence, under a collective liability regime based on the probability criterion, only a few prospective wrongdoers would have an incentive to resolve (or alleviate) the identification problem. To be sure, the number of such wrongdoers would further decrease if collective liability were not recognized by the law of torts, but the gap between the two amounts does not appear to be particularly wide.

This gap, however, will not always be narrow. Thus far, our discussion has assumed that none of the prospective wrongdoers can prevent or minimize the damage by reasonable means. If we remove this assumption, a completely new picture emerges. Let us return to the *DES Case* and assume that one of the manufacturers could prevent or reduce the damage originating from his drug by taking certain precautions. If the expected damage associated with the manufacturer's drug were greater than the cost of the precautions, then deterrence would require that those precautions be taken. Unfortunately, for

[63] Note, however, that under the equal share standard, wrongdoers who expect to pay more than their actual share of the damage will have an incentive to solve the identification problem. After they do so, the equal share that each of the remaining wrongdoers in the group will have to pay will increase in amount; thus wrongdoers who can now, under the new situation, expect to pay more than their actual share of the damage will also try to eliminate the identification problem. This process will repeat itself time and time again, and it may end up eliminating the identification problem altogether. The question to what extent it will take place is contingent on the costs entailed in eliminating the problem.

[64] A numerical example can further explain this point. Defendant A produces expected damage of 10; Defendant B produces expected damage of 20; Defendant C produces expected damage of 30. Let us assume that in all occurrences of damage in which one of the three defendants caused the damage, it is impossible to identify which one actually did so; and let us further assume that each defendants' expected damage relates to activity over the period of a year. If collective liability is imposed for all the damage caused by the three defendants, and the damage is divided equally between them, each defendant will bear damage of 20 annually. Defendant A will prefer that the problem of identification be eliminated (for then he will bear damage of 10 annually); Defendant C will prefer that the problem persist (for otherwise, he will bear damage of 30 annually); and Defendant B will be indifferent to the matter (either way, he bears damage of 20 annually). If, on the other hand, the burden of damage is allocated between the three defendants according to the probability criterion, all three will be indifferent with regard to solving the problem of identification, since each one, in any event, will bear damage at a level equal to his expected damage.

reasons already given, the problems of wrongdoer identification and free-riding may discourage the manufacturer from taking these precautions. This disincentive would, however, disappear if the manufacturer were able to prevent the identification problem at a relatively low cost. In that case, the manufacturer alone would benefit from his investment in preventing or reducing the damage, which would provide him with an adequate incentive to invest in precautions.

Take, for example, a manufacturer (A) able to prevent a £20 damage by expending £10 on precautions. However, four additional manufacturers (B to E) produce products similar to A's product, and when one of those products causes damage, it is evidentially impossible to attribute that damage to any particular manufacturer. Prior to A's decision on whether to expend £10 on precautions, the damage associated with each product is £20. Manufacturer A knows that expending £10 on precautions may not convince the court that the damage associated with his product did in fact drop. How will he act?

Based on the above assumptions, A will not expend £10 to prevent a £20 damage: although socially desirable, this investment is privately unprofitable for A. This is so because A's liability in torts will be reduced only by £4. As long as the wrongdoer-identification problem remains unresolved, the court will estimate that the total amount of damage inflicted by manufacturers A to E equals £80 (the pre-precaution damage of £100 minus the £20 reduction following A's precautions). Because the court assumes that the manufacturers produce equal amounts of damage, each manufacturer will pay £16 in liability damages. This outcome will be good for B, C, D, and E, but clearly not for A.

Let us now assume that A can prevent the identification problem at a cost of £1. If so, then by making the total investment of £11 (in both precautions and his conclusive disassociation from the damage), A will eliminate a £20 damage. A's liability would consequently be reduced by £20 with the resulting £9 saving. Adequate deterrence would thus be attained in an economically efficient way.

A few lessons can be drawn from the preceding discussion. First, the absence of collective liability always provides an incentive for prospective wrongdoers not to take the socially desirable precautions and thus to exploit the identification problem instead of attempting to eliminate it.[65] Second, collective liability provides an incentive for *some* prospective wrongdoers to alleviate the identification problem. This affects any prospective wrongdoer who estimates his future liability damages as higher than the damage associated with his wrongdoing.[66] Third, under certain circumstances, collective liability induces prospective wrongdoers to resolve the identification problem as a necessary step in the process of preventing the damage itself.

[65] We assume that the probability of each defendant causing the damage to a specific plaintiff is typically below 50%. See above 130, note 2.

[66] The actual realization of this incentive will depend on the difference between the self-identification cost and the expected reduction of liability damages.

Note that collective liability raises the expected sanction for wrongful conduct: liability damages for prospective wrongdoers are higher in the presence of collective liability than in its absence. Because the identification problem substantially increases the costs of law enforcement (to the extent that the latter becomes economically unfeasible in a large number of cases), it is detrimental to deterrence. Hence, instead of making an exorbitant investment in the enforcement effort, society would be better off raising the sanction for wrongful conduct at zero cost by endorsing the collective liability doctrine.[67] From a general theoretical perspective, raising the amount of liability damages will produce the optimal outcome provided that the optimal liabilty amount can be determined. The collective liability doctrine does indeed determine the optimal amount of liability damages in applying the probability criterion (instead of setting arbitrary compensation figures, as often is the case with punitive damages).

3. The *Ex Post* Incentives

Incentives for revealing a wrongdoer's identity can also be set *ex post*, that is, after the occurrence of a damaging event. But who should be the target of those incentives: the defendants or the injured plaintiff?

In the *DES Case* and the *Blasting Caps Case* this question cannot be easily answered. On the one hand, the manufacturers possess information that may shed light on the identity of the actual wrongdoer. On the other hand, it is quite possible that no such information exists and it is in fact the plaintiffs who have better access to information that can alleviate the problem of identification. For example, despite the amount of time that has elapsed, the afflicted daughter of the woman who took DES may be able to reconstruct the relevant events and aid in identifying the manufacturer who produced the drug taken by her mother. A similar possibility may exist in the *Blasting Caps Case* and the like.[68]

In other examples that have been presented, the defendants have an obvious advantage over the plaintiffs with regard to the ability to produce relevant evidence. Thus, in the *Injured Shoulder Case*, the defendants have an unequivocal evidential advantage over the plaintiff, who was under anaesthetic at the time that the damage occurred. In that case, if any evidence

[67] Cf. L. Kaplow and S. Shavell, 'Accuracy in the Determination of Liability' (1994) 37 *J Law & Economics* 1 (demonstrating that law enforcement expenditures can be reduced by raising the legal sanction and by appropriately reducing the enforcement effort).

[68] In *Sindell* (n. 31 above) 929–30, the court maintained that neither the defendants nor the plaintiffs had any advantage in this context.

capable of identifying the wrongdoer does actually exist, it must be exclusively in the hands of the defendants, who have decided to withhold it. Indeed, this factor explains the decision reached by the court in the actual case. In the *Cargo Case*, the relevant circumstances are similar: the shipping company and the port authority usually have access to the evidence that could resolve the identification problem. In this and similar cases, a rule that absolves the defendants from liability (deriving from a doctrinal refusal to recognize collective liability) would provide them with incentive to withhold evidence. For such defendants, 'a conspiracy of silence' would usually be the best plan of action. It is quite possible, for example, that the members of the medical team in the *Injured Shoulder Case* are parties to just such a conspiracy: all of them share a vested interest in covering for one another.[69] In the *DES* and the *Blasting Caps Cases*, a conspiracy of silence could likely emerge in the form of a collusive agreement between the defendants. Under this agreement, which could be reached either explicitly or implicitly, each defendant would tell another defendant: 'If you refrain today from bringing evidence that will identify me as the actual wrongdoer who caused the damage, then tomorrow I will refrain from bringing evidence that will so identify you.' Because the defendant manufacturers are repeat players, against whom numerous lawsuits are brought on numerous occasions, it is unlikely that any one of those defendants will defect from the agreement and furnish evidence against another defendant. A unified class action against defendants may weaken the individual defendant's incentive not to defect, but this would hardly provide a panacea for evidentially incapacitated plaintiffs. Similar considerations would apply in cases analogous to our *Cargo Case* example, and the problem will persist as long as the inability to identify the actual wrongdoer absolves all defendants from liability in torts.

Under the collective liability regime, the identification problem can be adequately resolved. Under this regime, every defendant will know that the court will hold him liable unless he detaches himself from the collective. This prospect induces the defendant to produce evidence that disassociates him from the other potential wrongdoers. Therefore, all defendants, except for the one who knows that he is the actual wrongdoer, will produce evidence that might assist in resolving the problem of identification. To be sure, such efforts will not always meet with success, but they will certainly increase the probability of identifying the actual wrongdoer.

Arguably, collective liability weakens the incentive of plaintiffs to produce the wrongdoer-identifying evidence. Why should a plaintiff go to the trouble of producing such evidence if she is to be awarded full compensation in any event? A refusal to impose collective liability would ostensibly induce plaintiffs to

[69] *Prosser and Keeton* (n. 61 above) 253.

produce the required evidence.[70] Although facially appealing, this argument is ultimately unfounded. As already indicated, it is the defendants, not the plaintiffs, who have the best access to the relevant evidence in most cases. In not one of our examples, all paradigmatic, has the plaintiff had an evidential advantage over the defendants. Moreover, the incentive of defendants to withhold evidence when collective liability is not imposed is immeasurably stronger than the plaintiff's incentive to do the same when collective liability is imposed (as long as the liability imposed on each defendant amounts to only his fraction of the damage).

We should clarify why a plaintiff would have strong incentive to adduce evidence and identify her wrongdoer even when collective liability is imposed on each defendant on a fractional basis. First, a plaintiff is often motivated by a desire for retribution, which would encourage her to identify her particular wrongdoer and sue him personally even if she knows she will be fully compensated without identifying him. Second, a plaintiff knows that if she fails to prove the identity of her actual wrongdoer, she might not be awarded compensation for her entire damage. She may find herself unable to locate all the members of the group to which her actual wrongdoer belongs. Or she might discover that collecting compensation from every member of the group is either impossible or prohibitively expensive. Therefore, if any such plaintiff can adequately establish her wrongdoer's identity, she may well prefer doing so and thus avoid such risks and expenses.[71]

Under a collective liability regime that forces liable defendants to pay the total, rather than fractional, compensation amount, plaintiffs may, indeed, have an incentive to withhold evidence that could identify their actual wrongdoers. Under this form of liability, an increase in the number of potentially liable defendants would constitute an improvement in the plaintiff's position. Thus, if a plaintiff envisions bankruptcy on the part of her actual wrongdoer, she will prefer not to reveal his identity and instead seek redress in collective liability. The plaintiff will resort to this strategy even when she both knows her wrongdoer's identity and can adequately establish it in court. This could quickly become a pervasive problem.[72] At the very least, a collective liability regime that forces liable defendants to pay the total compensation amount would make plaintiffs indifferent with regard to proving and not proving the

[70] This argument was listed in *Smith v Eli Lilly & Co.*, 560 NE 2d 324, 339 (Ill 1990), as one of the grounds for rejecting MSL. Other American courts have, at times, conditioned application of MSL on the plaintiff successfully convincing the court that she genuinely has no means of proving the identity of the actual wrongdoer who caused her injury. Under this approach, MSL is a last recourse for a plaintiff who is unable to identify her wrongdoer. *Abel v Eli Lilly & Co.*, 343 NW 2d 164, 173 (Mich 1984).

[71] However, if this wrongdoer is particularly difficult to collect compensation from, then the plaintiff will prefer to bring suit against all the members of the wrongdoer group. Hence, the incentive described in the text does not always exist.

[72] Zitzer and Ginsberg (n. 39 above) 637.

identity of their actual wrongdoers. The fractional compensation method therefore appears to be preferable from the plaintiff-incentives perspective.

In sum, collective liability typically supplies defendants with incentive to bring evidence to reduce the extent of the wrongdoer-identification problem. Moreover, as long as this liability is imposed on a fractional rather than a total basis, it leaves plaintiffs with sufficient incentive to do the same.[73]

G. CODA

Collective liability cannot easily be reconciled with corrective justice, but it is not an impossible feat. To achieve such reconciliation, one basic condition needs to be satisfied: collective liability must provide for a mechanism for transferring compensation for damages from wrongdoers to their victims. By treating collectively wrongdoers and their victims as two parallel groups of 'givers' and 'takers', this form of liability can ensure that the 'takers' receive their due from the 'givers'. When every 'giver' wrongfully harms one of the 'takers', forcing the 'giver' to contribute to a collective compensation mechanism a sum approximating the damage that he produced would be entirely consistent with corrective justice.

In the appropriate cases, as identified in this chapter, imposition of collective liability can also be justified on grounds of deterrence. In the absence of collective liability, prospective wrongdoers would not take the precautions that are necessary for the efficient reduction of future damage. This justification, however, depends on the recurrence of the wrongdoer-identification problem within the framework of the activity in which the damage was inflicted. In cases not involving such recurrency, deterrence considerations do not carry much weight in support of imposing collective liability.

Imposition of collective liability induces prospective wrongdoers to take measures that will alleviate the wrongdoer-identification problem both before and after the infliction of the damage. Typically, members of the potential wrongdoers' group are in a better position than the victims to alleviate that problem. In the absence of collective liability, prospective wrongdoers will not take any measures for alleviating the problem. Moreover, because the problem benefits them evidentially in their future trials, some prospective wrongdoers will even seek to intensify it.

In many cases, collective liability will be justified as a vehicle for spreading the costs of the damage. Typically, members of the potential wrongdoers' group are in a better position than the victims to spread the costs of the damage, either

[73] This argument is further supported in Chris W. Sanchirico, 'Relying on the Information of Interested—and Potentially Dishonest—Parties' (2001) 3 *American Law & Economics Rev* 320 (demonstrating how deterrence can be optimally achieved by directly conditioning tort damages on the evidence that the defendants are expected and actually choose to present).

through insurance or by introducing appropriate pricing policies. In many cases, a single tort victim stands against a large number of potential wrong-doers. In such cases, imposing collective liability on all the defendants will be especially justified as a direct promotion of the loss-spreading policy.

Collective liability is, admittedly, a deviation from the traditional individual-liability principle that still governs in most areas of tort law. This form of liability is, therefore, not entirely consistent with prevalent legal doctrine. At the same time, imposing collective liability in the appropriate cases (identified in and categorized by this chapter) would promote the fundamental objectives of the law of torts.

VI

Liability for Uncertainty: Making Evidential Damage Actionable

A. THE NATURE OF EVIDENTIAL DAMAGE

MISSING evidence and the resulting uncertainty of facts are detrimental to accuracy in adjudication. Absence of information implants risk of error in the court's decision: when the facts necessary for reaching a decision are uncertain, the decision may come out wrong. Greater accuracy in fact-finding gives more space to the controlling substantive law: it implies that more wrongdoers and less faultless defendants will be held liable, and it also implies that people's rights will be vindicated in a greater number of cases. Accuracy in fact-finding is, therefore, instrumental to the deterrence and the corrective justice objectives of the law of torts; and it is also instrumental to any other chosen objective, such as distributive justice or retribution. When factual accuracy is diluted, the law's substantive objectives are frustrated.

In some cases, accuracy in fact-finding is undermined by circumstances for which no person can be blamed. In such cases, uncertainty exists simply as a given condition. In other cases, however, the existing uncertainty and the consequent inability of the court to determine the facts accurately result from a person's wrongful conduct. That person can therefore be blamed for the uncertainty of the case and the corresponding risk of error. Should such a person bear any liability for evidentially damaging the case? What should the law's criteria be for ascribing that liability? What remedies should be available to a person who has sustained evidential damage?

These are the questions we address in the present chapter. We discuss these questions by presenting a doctrine that imposes liability for wrongful infliction of evidential damage and by analysing the desirability of that doctrine. We call this doctrine the 'evidential damage doctrine'. What should the components of that doctrine be and how should they function? Can the doctrine be justified on social policy grounds? Can the law do without it?

1. Liability for Uncertainty

Under the evidential damage doctrine, the defendant would be responsible for evidential damage if his wrongful actions have impaired the plaintiff's ability or reduced his chances to establish the facts necessary for prevailing in a direct-damage lawsuit.[1] By 'direct damage' we mean any damage that is actionable in torts, which would usually be physical damage, as opposed to purely economic loss. Evidential damage must thus be perceived as an indirect or adjective damage: its existence will always depend on the actual (or sufficiently probable) occurrence of a directly actionable damage.

The evidential damage doctrine can be applied in a variety of factually uncertain cases. A paradigmatic example of such instances is provided by cases involving an unconcerted infliction of damage by two (or more) defendants, when the fraction of the damage that each defendant individually inflicted cannot be adequately established. The *Dogs Case*, which we discuss in the previous chapters, illustrates this type of case.

> *The Dogs Case.* Two dogs, each of which belongs to a different wrongdoer, simultaneously attack the plaintiff. The ensuing damage is evidentially indivisible because it is impossible to establish which dog did what.[2]

In this case, the wrongdoers caused the plaintiff evidential damage. Each wrongdoer caused this damage by wrongfully impairing the plaintiff's ability to attribute the various parts of his injury to the actual wrongdoer. Assuming the controlling legal doctrine precludes compensation for a victim who cannot attribute any specific part of his damage to the alleged wrongdoer, the wrongful evidential incapacitation will deprive the plaintiff of his ability to recover for his direct damage.[3]

In our next example, the plaintiff's direct injury is attributable to both wrongful and non-wrongful causes, and it is impossible to identify individually the effects of each cause.

> *The Appendix Case.* The plaintiff underwent a simple operation that threw him into emotional depression. Because the operation had been essential for the plaintiff's health, the ensuing emotional damage was not actionable. During the plaintiff's pre-surgical treatment, negligence had occurred, which led to further surgery that aggravated the plaintiff's

[1] We first proposed and developed the 'evidential damage doctrine' in A. Porat and A. Stein, 'Liability for Uncertainty: Making Evidential Damage Actionable' (1997) 18 *Cardozo L Rev* 1891. For critique see R. D. Friedman, 'Dealing with Evidentiary Deficiency' (1997) 18 *Cardozo L Rev* 1961; I. Gilead, ' The Evidential Damage Doctrine: Has the Burden of Proof Been Met?' (1999) 30 *Mishpatim* 317 (Hebrew). For our response see A. Porat and A. Stein, 'The Evidential Damage Doctrine: A Response to Critique' (1999) 30 *Mishpatim* 349 (Hebrew). For an indirect account of evidential damage, see J. H. King, 'Causation, Valuation, and Chance in Personal Injury Torts Involving Preexisting Conditions and Future Consequences' (1981) 90 *Yale LJ* 1353, 1390–4. On imposing liability for negligent failure to develop and disseminate data needed for risk assessment, see M. Berger, 'Eliminating General Causation: Notes towards a New Theory of Justice and Toxic Torts' (1997) 97 *Columbia L Rev* 2117.

[2] An adaptation of *Melech v Cornhauser*, 44(2) Piskey Din 89 (1990) (Hebrew).

[3] Cf. above 76–81.

depression. This actionable damage merged with the plaintiff's non-actionable damage.[4]

In this case, which we also discuss in Chapter II, the wrongful act that caused part of the plaintiff's direct damage also impaired his ability to attribute that part of the damage to the wrongdoer. Assuming that under the controlling legal doctrine, this attribution is necessary for succeeding in a direct-damage lawsuit, the wrongdoer will not only have caused the plaintiff direct injury, but also will have inflicted evidential damage on him.[5]

The evidential damage doctrine also can be applicable to cases in which the identity of the wrongdoer cannot be established. Moreover, it can apply in cases in which it cannot be established that the direct damage is a result of a wrongdoing. Take, for example, the *Hunters' Case* involving three quail hunters. One of the hunters (the plaintiff) was shot in the eye by a stray bullet negligently fired by one of the other hunters (the defendants). Since the defendants pulled their triggers simultaneously, it cannot be determined whose bullet actually injured the plaintiff.[6]

By firing at the plaintiff, either the first or the second defendant nullified the evidential significance of the injuring shot. One of them (or even both of them) thus caused the plaintiff serious evidential damage. If the non-injuring shot had not been fired, the existing evidence would have been strong enough to single out the plaintiff's injurer. But the shot was fired, and it evidentially incapacitated the plaintiff. Crystallizing in the plaintiff's inability to attribute his injury to either the first or the second defendant, the plaintiff's evidential damage equals the value of his physical damage. If the first defendant is not responsible for the latter damage, he should certainly be held responsible for the former, and the same holds true also in relation to the second defendant.

The following is another case that illustrates how infliction of evidential damage reduces the plaintiff's chances of establishing that his direct damage resulted from wrongdoing.

> *The Ringworm Case.* About fifty years ago, immigrants to Israel from North Africa underwent a series of treatments for ringworm, including radiation therapy. The radiation therapy turned out to cause various illnesses. In many cases, however, it was impossible to determine whether the illness was induced by radiation or developed independently.

In this case, the key question is whether the treatment of the plaintiffs with radiation therapy amounted to a wrongful act on the part of the state. If it did, then the plaintiffs' consequent inability to identify the cause of their injuries arguably resulted from the state's wrongful infliction of their evidential damage. Had the state not wrongfully created the uncertainty, each plaintiff

[4] An adaptation of *Nagar v Vilensky*, 43(3) Piskey Din 284 (1989) (Hebrew).

[5] Cf. above 81–3.

[6] An adaptation of *Summers v Tice*, 199 P 2d 1 (1948). See discussion below 186–93.

could have ascertained the cause of his or her illness. This implies that each plaintiff would have had a chance of attributing her illness to the radiation, which would have enabled him or her to recover compensation from the state.

The following example is adapted from a case decided by a California court. It illustrates a situation in which the defendant's wrongful omission is both a possible cause of the plaintiff's direct injury and a certain cause of her evidential damage.

> *The Swimming Pool Case.* The plaintiff sues motel operators for the wrongful deaths of her husband and son, who drowned while swimming in the motel's pool. The defendants were negligent in that they failed to provide lifeguard supervision in the pool area and failed to post a warning to bathers to this effect. No specific evidence highlighting the proximate cause of the litigated fatality is available.[7]

The defendants in the actual case were held liable by the California court in a decision that came close to explicitly recognizing the evidential damage doctrine. It ruled that the persuasion burden, in relation to the disputed issue of causation, should be shifted to the defendants and that the defendants had obviously failed to discharge this burden. The court justified its decision as follows:

> The absence of such a lifeguard in the instant case thus not only stripped decedents of a significant degree of protection to which they were entitled, but also deprived the present plaintiffs of a means of definitively establishing the facts leading to the drownings.[8]

Evidential damage can appear in two different forms, each of which is relevant to a different set of cases. In one of its manifestations, evidential damage is an outcome of the same wrongful act that inflicted the plaintiff's direct damage (or that might have inflicted it). The infliction of the plaintiff's direct damage and her evidential incapacitation thus overlap one another and effectively merge into a single wrongful action. In such cases, the direct wrongdoer (or a wrongful originator of the relevant risk of damage) and the

[7] An adaptation of *Haft v Lone Palm Hotel*, 478 P 2d 465 (Cal 1970).

[8] Ibid. at 474–5. For an analysis, see S. A. Spitz, 'From Res Ipsa Loquitur to Diethylstilbestrol: The Unidentifiable Tortfeasor in California' (1990) 65 *Indiana LJ* 591, 604–5 (explaining *Haft* and similar cases as a new rule of liability: if evidence is not available and the defendant is responsible for the non-availability of evidence, the defendant is liable). See also *Dorschell v City of Cambridge* (1980) 117 DLR (3d) 630, 635 (in an action for damage allegedly incurred through the municipality's failure to remove ice from a sidewalk or otherwise ensure the safety of its citizens from snow and ice, the onus of proof, as related to the causation issue, should be shouldered by the municipality because 'breach [of] its duty to the plaintiff to keep the sidewalk clear of ice and snow has impaired the plaintiff's opportunity of proving liability'); *Clemente v California*, 707 P 2d 818 (Cal 1985) (in an action for damages brought by the victim of a hit-and-run accident, alleging that a police officer who visited the scene of the accident negligently failed to take the name or the licence plate number of the motorcyclist who struck the plaintiff, the court exempted the plaintiff from the undischargeable burden of proving that he could have obtained a collectible judgment against the motorcyclist, an exemption justified by the defendant's actions that made the plaintiff unable to discharge this burden).

evidential wrongdoer are the same person. The examples provided thus far present this form of evidential damage.

In its other manifestation, evidential damage is a product of a distinct wrongful act. In such cases, the wrongful conduct that caused (or might have caused) the plaintiff's direct damage and the wrongful conduct that inflicted her evidential damage can easily be distinguished from each other. Therefore, the direct wrongdoer (or the wrongful originator of the relevant risk of damage) and the evidential wrongdoer may be two different people. Furthermore, the two acts need not occur concomitantly, and either can precede the other.

The following example from Israeli case law presents a typical situation in which evidential damage occurs in the latter form.

> *The Inadequate Documentation Case*. The plaintiff suffered from spinal cord problems accompanied by severe backache. He was prescribed medication and physiotherapy. Patients in this condition are prescribed spinal cord surgery only when their pain becomes unbearable, and those exhibiting neurological symptoms must undergo the surgery immediately. The plaintiff eventually had this surgery, but it could not save him from partial paralysis. The plaintiff now alleges that this outcome could have been prevented had he undergone the surgery at an earlier stage than he did, namely, when he first complained to his physician—the defendant—about his neurological problems, or shortly thereafter. According to the defendant, the plaintiff's complaints to him pointed to pain only; when a neurological problem was raised, he was immediately referred to surgery. Records monitoring the defendant's treatment of the plaintiff have been found to be fragmentary and deficient, which is in violation of the defendant's record-keeping duties.[9]

In this case, the Israeli Supreme Court accepted the plaintiff's description of the events. It justified its decision on the basis (*inter alia*) of the defendant's responsibility for the evidential damage.[10]

Below is another example of this form of evidential damage, adapted from a landmark decision of the California Court of Appeal.[11] In this case, two distinct wrongdoers inflicted the direct injury and the evidential damage that the plaintiff sustained.

[9] *Kantor v Mussayev* 39(3) Piskey Din 253 (1985) (Hebrew).

[10] For an essentially similar decision made by the Florida Supreme Court, see *Public Health Trust v Valcin*, 507 So 2d 596 (Fla 1987). See also *Welsh v United States*, 844 F 2d 1239 (6th Cir 1988); *Sweet v Sisters of Providence*, 881 P 2d 304 (Alaska 1994) (both holding the same). This position has also been endorsed in other countries; see D. Giesen, *International Medical Malpractice Law: A Comparative Law Study of Civil Liability Arising from Medical Care* (Tübingen, 1988) 521–2.

[11] *Smith v Superior Court*, 151 Cal App 3d 491 (1984). But see *Cedars-Sinai Medical Ctr. v Superior Court*, 954 P 2d 511 (1998); *Temple Community Hospital v Superior Court*, 976 P 2d 223 (1999). In these cases, the California Supreme Court repealed *Smith* and held that spoliation of evidence (both negligent and intentional) is not actionable in torts under California law. These decisions were subsequently followed in *Penn v Prestige Stations, Inc.*, 99 Cal Rptr 2d 602 (2000).

The Evidence Destruction Case. A car driven by the plaintiff was approached by a van coming from the opposite direction. Suddenly, the left rear wheel flew off the van and crashed into the windshield of the plaintiff's car, severely injuring her. The van was towed to a garage, where some of its parts, evidentially critical to the plaintiff's lawsuit against the driver of the van, were inadvertently disposed of by mechanics.[12]

In this case, the garage-owners caused the plaintiff evidential damage that is equal in magnitude to the plaintiff's physical damage.[13]

2. The Remedial Mechanism

Liability for evidential damage can be imposed in two different ways. The evidential damage doctrine can shift the burden of persuasion to the defendant whenever the latter is responsible for inflicting evidential damage on the plaintiff. Consequently, if the case is factually indeterminate, in the sense that the accounts of the parties are equally probable, the plaintiff will prevail. Alternatively, evidentially damaged plaintiffs can recover tort damages. We now discuss these two remedies and their comparative merits.

(a) The Evidential Remedy

The evidential remedy that shifts the persuasion burden to the defendant would be unsuitable in many cases. This remedy can be effective only when the plaintiff's direct damage and evidential damage are attributable to the same defendant. When the direct and the evidential wrongdoers are two different persons, as in the *Evidence Destruction Case*, shifting the burden of persuasion would not be justified: a person allegedly responsible for the plaintiff's direct damage must not bear liability for another person's wrong. Beyond this, shifting the burden would not serve as a remedy for a plaintiff whose evidential incapacitation is so severe that she cannot raise her factual scenario even up to the 50 per cent probability level. In any such case, because the defendant's case would be more probable than not, the burden-of-persuasion doctrine would be inapplicable *ab initio.* In the *Ringworm Case*, for example, it would not be unrealistic to estimate the chance that the plaintiff's illness resulted from the defendant's radiation treatment as falling below 50 per cent. Consequently, shifting the persuasion burden to the defendant would not change the finding that the plaintiff's damage did not result from the defendant's wrongdoing. Finally, shifting the persuasion burden to the defendant may, occasionally, overcompensate the plaintiff. This outcome

[12] In the actual case, the evidential damage was inflicted intentionally. The case was therefore decided analogously to the intentional tort of 'interference with prospective business advantage'. See generally Jamie S. Gorelick et al, *Destruction of Evidence* (1989) §4.3.

[13] We assume that the uncertainty created by the garage owners was foreseeable. See below 172–4.

would occur in cases in which an indeterminate fraction of the plaintiff's damage is unrelated to the defendant's wrongdoing, as in the *Appendix Case*. In such cases, the evidential remedy would place the plaintiff in a position that would be better than the one in which he would have found himself had he sustained no evidential damage. This remedy guarantees full recovery for the plaintiff's direct damage in circumstances that would have allowed for partial recovery at best had no evidential damage been inflicted. The evidential remedy therefore might result in either excessive or insufficient compensation and, correspondingly, in either excessive or insufficient deterrence.

Hence, the evidential remedy must be confined to cases in which the evidence is balanced.[14] As a matter of general principle, an evidentially balanced case should be decided in favour of the defendant. This principle and its underlying justifications are explained in Chapter I. However, the same chapter also demonstrates that this general principle is open to exceptions: on special grounds, the law may justifiably shift the persuasion burden to the defendant. The evidential damage doctrine indeed provides one such special ground. Because the defendant wrongfully inflicted the evidential damage, it is he—not the plaintiff—who should suffer from the uncertainty of the case. The law must not allow such defendants to benefit from their own wrongs.[15] Furthermore, in advancing his case in adversarial litigation, each party exposes his opponent to the risk of error. This exposure to the risk of error is acceptable because it is reciprocal. However, when a defendant inflicts evidential damage on the plaintiff, he exposes her to a non-reciprocal risk. Therefore, if the case is balanced, shifting the persuasion burden to the defendant will rectify this lack of reciprocity and the consequent inequality in the allocation of the risk of error.[16] Finally, when the case is balanced, any evidential addition to the plaintiff's case will tip the scales in her or his favour. The evidentially damaged plaintiff should therefore be entitled to recover this addition from the defendant. This outcome would be achieved by shifting the persuasion burden to the defendant.

If properly applied, the evidential remedy will promote social utility. Availability of that remedy will deter prospective wrongdoers from inflicting

[14] As explained in Chapter I, the burden of persuasion doctrine applies only in cases in which the allegations brought by the plaintiff and the defendant are equally probable.

[15] For a moral justification of this general principle, see R. Dworkin, *Law's Empire* (1986) 15–20. See also B. Coote, 'Chance and the Burden of Proof in Contract and Tort' (1988) 62 *Australian LJ* 761, 772 (parenthetically pointing to 'the merit of seeking to avoid the injustice of allowing a wrongdoer to shelter behind the uncertainty brought about by his or her own breach of duty'); *Dickerson, Inc. v Holloway*, 685 F Supp 1555, 1569 (MD Fla 1987) (in an action brought against the US government for negligent supervision of disposal of contaminated waste fluids from military bases, the plaintiffs, owners of the contaminated fuel storage tanks, were not 'held to an absolute standard of proof on the question of the chain-of-custody of the government's . . . contaminated waste fluids' because this 'would [have] permit[ted] the government to gain an advantage from the lack of proof its very actions gave rise to').

[16] Cf. G. P. Fletcher, 'Fairness and Utility in Tort Theory' (1972) 85 *Harvard L Rev* 537.

evidential damage. Moreover, this remedy will induce tort defendants to change their trial strategy in a socially desirable way. Instead of hiding in the shadows of uncertainty for which they might be held responsible, many such defendants will prefer to unfold a straightforward account of the events and to support it with unambiguous evidence. Indeed, when factual impasse does not benefit the defendant, and might even harm him, he will attempt to avoid that impasse. Committed to a tidy factual account, the defendant would bare his evidence to scrutiny. As such, it would either survive or not survive the plaintiff's falsifying attempts. The informational deficiency would consequently be rectified, partially or even entirely. Hence, proper application of the evidential remedy would induce the wrongdoers both to avoid the evidential damage and to rectify it after its occurrence.[17]

(b) The Compensatory Remedy

In numerous cases, application of the evidential remedy would generate compensation duties for the defendant that are plainly excessive. In other cases, this remedy would be altogether inapplicable. Consequently, the fundamental objectives of the law of torts—deterrence and corrective justice—would be frustrated. These cases have been identified in our discussion of the evidential remedy.

In any such case, therefore, evidential damage should be treated as a directly actionable tort. The negligence doctrine can easily accommodate liability for that damage, which would enable plaintiffs to recover compensation for their evidential incapacitation. Specifically, a plaintiff who sustained evidential damage should recover compensation for the information that the defendant took away from her by his wrongdoing. We reach this conclusion on the argument that the law should recognize that the plaintiff has a legitimate interest in ascertaining the cause of her or his direct damage whenever it is possible that this damage resulted from a wrongdoing. By inflicting evidential damage and thereby taking away from the plaintiff the information necessary for ascertaining the cause of her or his direct damage, the defendant took something of value from the plaintiff. The defendant therefore infringed the plaintiff's legitimate interest in that information.

Direct imposition of tort liability for evidential damage would raise a damage-assessment problem. This problem would not arise in every case. In cases similar to our *Hunters' Case* and *Dogs Case* examples, evidential damage can be assessed without difficulty. In such cases, both types of damage, direct and evidential, warrant the same compensatory measure. This measure is full recovery: had the evidential damage not been inflicted, the plaintiff would have obtained full recovery for her or his direct losses. In other cases,

[17] See Porat and Stein (n. 1 above) 1953–4.

however, the plaintiff's evidential incapacitation does not overlap with her or his direct damage: the information of which the plaintiff was wrongfully deprived would not have necessarily guaranteed her or him victory at trial. In such cases, the size of the evidential damage will always be smaller than that of the direct damage. Because the missing information would not have guaranteed the plaintiff a victory in her or his direct-damage litigation, the plaintiff lost only her or his *chances* of prevailing in that litigation. The plaintiff's evidential damage is, consequently, difficult to assess. This problem would arise in the *Appendix Case*, in the *Ringworm Case*, and in a variety of other cases.

We claim that in such instances the evidential wrongdoer should pay the plaintiff monetary damages. We further claim that the court should determine these damages by the expected value of the plaintiff's direct-damage lawsuit, as it was prior to the infliction of the evidential damage. This expected value should be calculated as follows: the size of the direct damage must be multiplied by the probability of the allegation that the direct wrongdoer (or the originator of the relevant risk of damage) actually inflicted that damage. This probability should be determined in a way that accounts—statistically or otherwise—for the evidential potential of the information of which the plaintiff was wrongfully deprived. This method of evaluating evidential damage may appear opaque, but we demonstrate that it is, in fact, sufficiently precise.

We also offer a solid justification for tort liability imposed under the evidential damage doctrine. This justification rests on the grounds of both corrective justice and deterrence. From the corrective justice perspective, infliction of evidential damage violates the victim's autonomy; specifically, it infringes the victim's right to ascertain the factual cause of her or his direct damage and to place valid legal demands on the direct wrongdoer when the damage is inflicted wrongfully. From the deterrence perspective, liability for evidential damage has a two-fold justification. First, it provides an incentive efficiently to minimize evidential damage, which contributes to accuracy in the allocation of liability for direct damage. Second, this liability allocates the direct damage to wrongdoers in a way that directly improves their incentives efficiently to minimize direct damage.

The evidential damage doctrine would, therefore, operate in a dual capacity. First, it would operate as a *legal technique* for attaining the corrective justice and deterrence objectives of the law of torts in relation to direct damage. The doctrine's desirability in that capacity will thus depend on its comparative necessity. Specifically, the doctrine will be justified if the substantive objectives of the law of torts are systematically frustrated in its absence and if other doctrines, already recognized by the settled law, systematically fail to protect those objectives. Indeed, this and the next chapter demonstrate that the evidential damage doctrine offers a systematic solution to the indeterminate causation problem that arises in a wide variety of tort cases. These two chapters also demonstrate that the settled tort doctrines uniformly lack this capacity.

Second, apart from creating a mechanism for imposing tort liability for direct damage *under* uncertainty, the evidential damage doctrine furnishes independent reasons that favour imposition of liability *for* uncertainty. This special feature of the evidential damage doctrine is its most interesting aspect.

In the rest of this chapter, we discuss the tort liability imposed under the evidential damage doctrine.

B. EVIDENTIAL DAMAGE, CORRECTIVE JUSTICE, AND THE LAW OF NEGLIGENCE

From the corrective justice perspective, tort liability should be imposed only for wrongful acts. Moreover, corrective justice mandates that the scope of both the wrongdoer's liability and the victim's entitlement to compensation be determined by the scope of the damage suffered by the victim. In this section, we demonstrate that the evidential damage doctrine is consistent with these demands of corrective justice.[18]

1. Wrongfulness, Omissions, Economic Losses, and Foreseeability

(a) Wrongfulness

Imposition of liability under the evidential damage doctrine will be consistent with corrective justice when the defendant wrongfully inflicts the evidential damage. Therefore, when a defendant wrongfully causes direct damage to the plaintiff and by the same action blurs the boundaries between that and other wrongfully inflicted damage (as in the *Dogs Case*), the defendant should assume liability for the plaintiff's evidential damage. Holding this defendant liable only for the direct damage that can be evidentially associated with his wrongdoing would be inadequate. The same reasoning applies to the *Hunters' Case*. In that case, each of the two defendants may or may not have caused the direct damage that the plaintiff sustained, but both certainly inflicted the plaintiff's evidential damage and wrongfully so.

In these two cases, the single wrongful action that exposed the plaintiff to the risk of sustaining his direct damage also inflicted his evidential damage. Analytically, this action can be perceived as two actions that overlap one another. In other cases, the two actions may be separate and thus easily distinguishable from each other. In such cases, the action that inflicted the evidential damage may be wrongful, while the action that exposed the plaintiff

[18] See above 106–7, 133.

to the risk of sustaining the direct damage may be innocent. Even when this second action is non-wrongful, the defendant might still be responsible for the plaintiff's evidential damage. To exemplify this point, assume that in the *Hunters' Case* only one of the defendants fired in the plaintiff's direction, while the other was merely present on the scene, and it is impossible to determine who did what. After the shooting, however, each defendant negligently (or maliciously) participated in the removal of all traces leading to the actual wrongdoer. Each defendant thus acted wrongfully towards the plaintiff. In this variation of the *Hunters' Case*, corrective justice will demand that both defendants be held liable for the plaintiff's evidential damage.

Under both corrective justice and the prevalent tort law doctrine, if the plaintiff fails to establish that the defendant acted wrongfully, the defendant will bear no liability. If in the above variation of the *Hunters' Case*, the evidential damage was caused by the mere presence of the innocent, but unidentifiable, hunter at the scene of the accident, none of the defendants can be held liable because each of them could be innocent. By his mere presence at the scene of the accident, the innocent defendant definitely inflicted evidential damage, but this damage is not actionable because it was not inflicted wrongfully. Each of the defendants was entitled to be present at the scene of the accident. Therefore, his presence was not wrongful and did not violate any recognizable entitlement of the plaintiff (such as the entitlement not to be exposed to gunfire, which was violated by both defendants in the actual case).

(b) Omissions

Both corrective justice and the prevalent tort law doctrine would justify imposition of liability for failure to prevent evidential damage, as long as that failure is wrongful.[19] As with other types of damage, a person's failure to prevent evidential damage can be considered wrongful only when he or she has violated a legal duty to prevent that damage. This duty would exist only in special cases, that is, in cases involving some special relationship between the plaintiff and the defendant. Doctors and hospitals, for example, are commonly under a duty to compile and maintain medical records documenting diagnoses and treatment of patients. Thus, evidential damage can be inflicted when a hospital violates this duty and in so doing deprives a patient of the information that could subsequently assist her in a medical malpractice lawsuit against the hospital or one of its doctors.[20]

Under corrective justice, a duty to prevent evidential damage may also derive from an imposition of the risk of injury. This duty may justifiably be

[19] A wrongful omission in this respect is an omission a reasonable person would not make.

[20] The *Inadequate Documentation Case*, above 164.

imposed on a person who exposes another person to a risk of injury—either wrongfully or non-wrongfully—and whose action correlates with other causal forces that entail similar risks (such as another wrongdoer's action that was directed at the same person). For example, this duty could justifiably be imposed on each defendant in the *Hunters' Case*. Its imposition would require the defendants to take reasonable steps to identify the source of the bullet that hit the plaintiff *even in the absence of any negligence on the part of a particular defendant in firing in the plaintiff's direction*. Admittedly, pure omissions are generally not actionable under negligence law, and corrective justice generally rejects the idea of imposing liability for such omissions. This, however, is not the case with the type of omissions that we are presently considering. In our setting, the omission is a follow-up to the defendant's previous action that—wrongfully or innocently—exposed the victim to a risk of sustaining a loss. In such circumstances, imposition of a duty to prevent evidential damage would be justified.[21] Consequently, a defendant who created a risk of injury by his non-wrongful action might find himself under the duty to take reasonable steps to eliminate the uncertainty of the case.

(c) Economic Losses

Evidential damage has the appearance of a purely economic loss. Making it actionable may therefore clash with the traditional reluctance to impose liability for purely economic losses.[22] The principles of corrective justice do not draw a distinction between a wrongdoer who inflicts physical damage on another person and a wrongdoer who damages another person's economic interest. Their central requirement for imposing liability for any type of damage is that the damaging action be wrongful: a wrongful action violates the equality among people even when the ensuing damage is economic. The prevalent tort law doctrine is generally reluctant to impose liability for economic losses for reasons unrelated to corrective justice. This reluctance originates in other concerns of the legal system. Specifically, it stems from the prediction that imposing liability for losses that are purely economic would

[21] If A non-wrongfully shoots B, thereby causing the injured B to fall into a swimming pool and start drowning, then A should be held liable according to corrective justice if he could have rescued B but did not do so (this example is taken from J. B. Ames, 'Law and Morals' (1908) 22 *Harvard L Rev* 97, 112). Similarly, if a road is blocked by C's and D's non-wrongfully broken car, they should be held liable for the damage sustained by a third person as a consequence of the blocked road if they could have easily warned him and thus prevented his damage. See *Montgomery v National C. & T.* in R. A. Epstein, 'A Theory of Strict Liability' (1973) 2 *J Legal Studies* 151, 191–2, in which the court ruled accordingly. Epstein, ibid. 191–4, asserts that in both cases, corrective justice justifies the imposition of liability on the tortfeasors.

[22] W. V. H. Rogers (ed.), *Winfield and Jolowicz On Torts* (15th edn., London, 1998) 132.

flood the courts with lawsuits and expose prospective wrongdoers to overdeterrence.[23]

However, attributing a purely economic character to evidential damage would not be entirely accurate. Evidential damage manifests itself in the plaintiff's reduced chance of recovering for her physical damage, such as injury or damage to her property. Accordingly, classifying evidential damage as falling between the 'physical' and the 'economic' categories would be far more appropriate. Evidential damage is, in fact, more physical than economic in nature. In purely analytical terms, evidential damage is economic in that it manifests in a decrease in the victim's prospects of obtaining monetary advantage at trial, as opposed to a decrease in the victim's physical well-being. However, evidential damage is always inextricably attached to the underlying physical damage. The whole essence of evidential damage is the reduction of the victim's chances of recovering compensation for his or her physical damage. Imposition of liability for evidential damage therefore contributes to the rectification of physical damage. The nominally economic character of the loss that the evidentially incapacitated victim has sustained must not obscure this pivotal feature. Moreover, recognition of this feature must actually dispel the legal system's concern of flooding the courts with lawsuits. Almost invariably, tort plaintiffs would invoke the evidential damage doctrine either within the framework of an already existing lawsuit filed in connection with the underlying direct damage or as a substitute for such a lawsuit. Rather than placing a new burden on the courts, the evidential damage doctrine would, in fact, help them to resolve the uncertainty problem that arises in tort litigation. The doctrine would thus help the courts to clear dockets and do justice. In addition, section C below demonstrates that the doctrine would actually help the legal system to raise deterrence of wrongdoers up to the optimal level. Unlike liability for losses that are purely economic in nature, liability for evidential damage would not produce overdeterrence.

(d) Foreseeability

The Anglo-American doctrine of negligence conditions liability for damage on the foreseeability of that damage.[24] If damage could not have been foreseen at the time of its infliction, the person who inflicted it will not be held liable. This foreseeability requirement squarely aligns with corrective justice.

[23] Cf. J. A. Henderson, 'Process Constraints in Tort' (1982) 67 *Cornell L Rev* 901; F. C. Zacharias, 'The Politics of Torts' (1986) 95 *Yale LJ* 698.

[24] *Winfield and Jolowicz* (n. 22 above) 209; W. P. Keeton (ed.), *Prosser and Keeton On Torts* (5th edn., St. Paul, 1984) 280.

When damage is not foreseeable, a person who inflicts it does not act wrongfully because he has no real choice between alternative courses of action.[25]

Is evidential damage typically foreseeable? We argue that it is and will now substantiate this claim. First, one must not confuse unforeseeability with the wrongdoer's antecedent belief that the law does not recognize the relevant damage as actionable in torts. In the *Ringworm Case*, for example, the defendants could argue that the evidential damage caused by the radiation was unforeseeable, even though the direct damage was foreseeable. This type of argument would, however, be misguided. If the direct damage is foreseeable, so is the evidential damage: the two types of damage are interrelated. If the defendants foresaw (or could have foreseen) that radiation treatment for ringworm was likely to cause illness, then they must also have foreseen that in some cases it would be impossible to ascertain whether the illness was caused by the radiation.[26] The defendants' (actual or imputed) awareness of the fact that their actions may or may not end up in damage entails the (actual or imputed) awareness of the ensuing causal uncertainty, that is, of the resulting evidential damage. Metaphorically, the foreseeability standard should extend to a physical damage 'with no address'. A potential wrongdoer ought to foresee the possibility that his action will inflict a traceless physical damage.

Furthermore, in cases in which the evidential damage can reasonably be perceived as unforeseeable, the unforeseeability of that damage will be at least partially attributable to its current non-recognition as actionable in torts. Evidential damage would surely become more foreseeable if the law were to recognize it as actionable, that is, as damage that individuals are occasionally required to prevent. Under this scenario, both the existence of that type of damage and its possible infliction would be mentally internalized by its potential producers.

Moreover, foreseeability of damage is not a purely factual issue. As recognized by the prevalent negligence doctrine, the core component of the foreseeability issue is normative in character. This component encompasses a variety of policy considerations that courts should consider (which, incidentally, seem to be at odds with corrective justice[27]). These policy

[25] For a view that corrective justice does not condition tort liability upon foreseeability, see Epstein (n. 21 above) 168–71.

[26] The extent of foreseeability might, however, differ between evidential and direct damage. In the *Hunters' Case*, for example, both defendants could have foreseen physical damage to the plaintiff resulting from a shot. Neither, though, is likely to have foreseen the extraordinary identification problem actually caused by their simultaneous shooting. But this case is exceptional; in most cases, the evidential damage is certainly foreseeable. A possible way to reconcile the *Hunters' Case* with the foreseeability requirement is to say that since each defendant foresaw a physical injury, each should have expected liability to the extent of the physical injury, whether we label it liability for the physical damage or for the evidential damage. See below 174.

[27] Anyone who believes that tort law should reflect corrective justice also believes that policy considerations are alien to corrective justice, since they are unrelated to the relationship

considerations must surely accommodate the need to reduce the magnitude of evidential damage and thereby make the implementation of the law of torts more accurate. They must also accommodate the efficient allocation of direct damage, an outcome that the evidential damage doctrine helps to attain. Another ground for favouring the adoption of the evidential damage doctrine is embedded in corrective justice. In numerous cases, the evidential damage doctrine would apply between wronged plaintiffs, who sustained physical damage, and wrongful defendants, who inflicted that damage. Leaving the former without any remedy and the latter with no liability would be morally unacceptable.

Finally, one of the principal objectives of the foreseeability requirement is limiting a wrongdoer's liability for damage to the extent that could reasonably be anticipated before the event. Therefore, when the evidential wrongdoer is likely to have inflicted the direct damage as well, and the direct damage is foreseeable, holding that wrongdoer liable for the evidential damage would not impose on him liability to an extent that could not reasonably be foreseen. For these reasons, the foreseeability requirement must not bar liability for evidential damage

2. The Extent of Liability

Under corrective justice, the extent of both liability and the entitlement to compensation in torts should equal the extent of the damage caused. A person who wrongfully inflicts damage should pay exactly this amount, and a person who sustains a wrongful damage should receive exactly this amount.

Liability for evidential damage that equals the amount of the entire direct damage would therefore align with corrective justice in cases in which it is clear that the plaintiff's direct damage was caused in its entirety by a wrongful act. The wrongdoer-identification problem would not disturb this alignment. Both the *Hunters' Case* and the *Dogs Case* exemplify this point. In each of those cases, compensating the plaintiff for his evidential damage would practically compensate him for his direct damage. The evidential damage doctrine can thus also be perceived as a mechanism for compensating victims for their physical injuries: under this doctrine, the victims will recover neither more nor less. Still, if we were to ignore the internal justification of the evidential damage doctrine, the defendants in such cases would appear to assume a compensation duty that exceeds the physical damage they inflicted. The justification for holding such defendants liable for the entire scope of the injuries that their respective plaintiffs sustained has two components. First, the defendants wrongfully infringed their victims' entitlement to ascertain the causes of their respective damage. Second, it is apparent that had the evidential damage not been

between the injurer and the victim; Fletcher (n. 16 above) 542–3, 569–73; E. J. Weinrib, *The Idea of Private Law* (London, 1995) 3–6.

inflicted, the victims could have recovered full compensation for their physical injuries. Only the evidential damage doctrine provides this two-fold justification. Consequently, imposition of full liability on defendants in cases similar to our *Hunters' Case* and *Dogs Case* must always satisfy this doctrine's criteria.

In a more complex category of cases, the issue of whether the plaintiff's damage, wholly or partially, resulted from the defendant's wrongful act is irreducibly uncertain. This uncertainty might create a tension between the evidential damage doctrine and the compensatory and liability principles of corrective justice. This tension will arise if the application of the doctrine is not sensitive enough to the quantification of the evidential damage. For example, this tension would arise if judges were to apply the evidential damage doctrine in a way that forces the defendant to compensate the plaintiff for his entire physical damage in circumstances in which it is uncertain whether this damage actually resulted from a wrongdoing. Any such application of the doctrine would place many plaintiffs in a position that would be better than the one in which they would have found themselves had the evidential damage not occurred. Additionally, it would result in burdening many defendants with paying monetary damages that exceed the losses that they wrongfully inflicted. This form of excessive compensation is inconsistent with corrective justice. Indeed, such an application of the evidential damage doctrine would also contradict the existing doctrinal principles of compensation.

An example analogous to the *Ringworm Case* that we discuss in previous chapters[28] can now serve to illustrate this point. This example is representative of an important category of tort cases that feature indeterminate causation and traceless damage.

> *The Radiation Case.* Glenn's factory emits carcinogenic radiation. In the area affected by the radiation, the incidence of cancer rises by 25%: while prior to the factory's operation, only 80 people out of 100,000 contracted cancer each year, 100 people now become afflicted each year. There is, however, no evidence that could preponderantly identify those people who actually contracted cancer as a result of exposure to the radiation, as opposed to those who are simply victims of misfortune. All 100 people file lawsuits against Glenn.

Each of the above hundred people claims that Glenn is responsible for her or his cancer. Alternatively, each of the claimants contends that Glenn should be held liable for her or his evidential damage, that is, for her or his inability to establish the identity of the causal factor responsible for her or his cancer. Applying the evidential damage doctrine in a way that results in Glenn's liability for the entire physical damage suffered by each claimant would be deeply problematic. Even though Glenn caused cancer to only twenty claimants, he

[28] See above 70–3, 125–8.

will be forced to pay for cancer caused to one hundred claimants. The total amount of the damage caused to the hundred claimants is about five times greater than the physical or the evidential damage wrongfully caused by Glenn. Furthermore, forcing Glenn to compensate fully each of the hundred claimants would award money damages to eighty undeserving claimants, whose affliction is unrelated to Glenn's wrong. Those eighty claimants would therefore undeservedly benefit from the uncertainty created by Glenn.

A variation of the *Dogs Case* can provide yet another paradigmatic example of indeterminate causation cases that feature a similar problem. Assume that one of the two dogs that attacked the plaintiff is a stray dog with no owner. Applying the evidential damage doctrine in a way that shifts the entire damage to the dog-owner would place the plaintiff in a better position in comparison with the no-evidential-damage scenario. Under the latter scenario, the plaintiff would have proved the exact damage inflicted by the defendant's dog and would consequently have obtained a smaller amount of compensation.[29]

In this and similar cases, a full-compensation ruling would be at odds with corrective justice. This, however, would be equally true with regard to the opposite extreme: corrective justice would be upset if claimants positioned similarly to those in the *Radiation Case* and in the variation of the *Dogs Case* were to receive no compensation. In any such case, an identified wrongdoer, who definitely caused substantial damage, would be exempted entirely from liability. This outcome is especially troubling in cases similar to our *Radiation Case* example: in such cases, the magnitude of the physical injuries wrongfully caused by the wrongdoers can easily be assessed. We therefore now consider a third solution, namely, compensating each claimant in accordance with the probability that the defendant inflicted her damage. Under this solution, each claimant in the *Radiation Case* would receive compensation that equals 20 per cent of her physical damage. Consequently, the wrongdoer would pay for the physical damage actually caused by his wrongdoing. This solution can be grounded on the 'exposure to risk' or the 'lost-chance' doctrines. However, as demonstrated in Chapter IV, these alternative approaches are problematic. The evidential damage doctrine provides us with a more solid ground for compensating each plaintiff in this way. This solution would be equally applicable to the variation of the *Dogs Case* example and similar cases.

We now justify this solution on grounds of corrective justice. This is done by presenting and substantiating our basic claim that a person sustaining any damage that might have been inflicted wrongfully is entitled to information that identifies the causal forces that produced her or his damage vis-à-vis the person who wrongfully deprived her or him of that information.

[29] See above 165–6.

This entitlement is part and parcel of a person's autonomy.[30] Wrongful infliction of evidential damage makes the victim less informed about her or his legal position. This evidential incapacitation impairs the victim's ability to exercise autonomous choice in the enforcement of her or his legal rights. Before the damage was inflicted, these choices may have included uncompromising pursuit of victory in litigation, settlement, or, admittedly, retreat from the case. These important choices and, consequently, the victim's autonomy have been altered due to the evidential damage. These choices and the corresponding autonomy are now more restricted. The fact that the lost information could potentially assist the victim in exercising her or his legal rights therefore justifies treating her or him as a person who has sustained a meaningful loss. For these reasons, measures should be taken to bring the victim as close as possible to her or his original, more autonomous, informational position. Taking these measures would implement the *restitutio ad integrum* requirement of corrective justice. The victim therefore ought to be compensated for her or his damage, and the law ought to develop a mechanism that will convert such damage into money. We argue, and explain in the next paragraphs, that the value of the lost information should be determined by its potential of assisting the plaintiff in winning her or his case against the direct wrongdoer.

In the *Radiation Case*, the victims' right to information that Glenn infringed equals the product of each victim's physical damage and the probability that it was caused by the radiation ($0.2d$, when d denotes the magnitude of the physical damage sustained by each of the 100 claimants). This amount of money equals the expected value of each claimant's lawsuit against Glenn before it became evidentially damaged. This amount therefore reflects the value of the lost information for each claimant, that is, the value of each individual damage inflicted by Glenn. Similarly, in our variation of the *Dogs Case*, the evidential damage equals the relevant fraction of the plaintiff's entire damage. This fraction must be determined in the following way. For each possible scenario, the part of the plaintiff's damage that was wrongfully

[30] According to John Stuart Mill, being less informed in making risk-related choices is tantamount to making those choices less autonomously: 'If either a public officer or any one else saw a person attempting to cross a bridge which had been ascertained to be unsafe, and there were no time to warn him of his danger, they must seize him and turn him back, without any real infringement of his liberty; for liberty consists in doing what one desires, and he does not desire to fall into the river. Nevertheless, when there is not a certainty, but only a danger of mischief, no one but the person himself can judge of the sufficiency of the motive which may prompt him to incur the risk: in this case therefore (unless he is a child, or delirious, or in some state of excitement or absorption incompatible with the full use of the reflecting faculty), he ought, I conceive, to be only warned of the danger, not forcibly prevented from exposing himself to it.' (John Stuart Mill, *On Liberty* (1859), in Mary Warnock (ed.), *John Stuart Mill: Utilitarianism; On Liberty; Essay On Bentham* (1962) 228–9.) The same would apply to a person's choices about litigation and settlement. Cf. G. Dworkin, *The Theory and Practice of Autonomy* (1988) 100–12 (a person's informed decision as to her medical treatment is justified by the intrinsic value of her autonomy).

inflicted must be multiplied by the probability of that scenario, and the resulting amounts must be aggregated into a total sum.[31]

The relevant probabilities should be determined by using all relevant information that is available to the court. In the absence of information, the court should apply the 'indifference principle', also known as the 'principle of insufficient reason', that applies in a regular probability calculus. Under this principle, the court should postulate that the unknown factual scenarios are equally probable.[32] In cases involving indeterminate causation, this approach would uphold the equality-of-causes presumption: the court would have to assume that each of the relevant causal factors could equally produce the plaintiff's direct damage.

This system of compensation relies on the causal link between the factual indeterminacy of the case and the defendant's fault. In a usual case, the defendant would have a justified complaint if the court were to find him liable upon naked statistics. He would then claim that his liability could be grounded only upon what he wrongfully did, rather than on his statistical affiliation, which cannot be wrongful.[33] However, if the indeterminacy of the case were to result from the defendant's wrongful action, the defendant's complaint against naked statistics would not be valid. The defendant could not justifiably complain against the court's use of naked statistics because this would be the only information that remains available and because it would be the defendant who had forced both the plaintiff and the court into this informational setting. Had the defendant not been wrongfully indifferent to the evidential damage, the court would not have activated the statistical principle of indifference against him.

The plaintiff's right to information and the corresponding right to autonomy (both wrongfully violated by the defendant) can be credibly converted into money by using the following locked-box metaphor. Assume that the plaintiff holds a locked box that contains evidence conclusively identifying the cause of her direct damage. The contents of this evidence are unknown. The plaintiff therefore does not know whether this evidence could bring her victory in her direct-damage lawsuit (actual or contemplated). The plaintiff also cannot unlock the box because the defendant locked it through his fault in a very special way that prevents its unlocking. This factor is, of course, the whole essence of the evidential damage for which the defendant must

[31] For a detailed explanation of this method, see below Chapter VII.

[32] See L. J. Cohen, *An Introduction to the Philosophy of Induction and Probability* (1989) 43–7.

[33] Indeed, naked statistical probabilities do not normally provide grounds for awarding recovery to plaintiffs. See D. Kaye, 'The Limits of the Preponderance of the Evidence Standard: Justifiably Naked Statistical Evidence and Multiple Causation' (1982) *American Bar Foundation Research J* 487; Brian Coote, 'Chance and the Burden of Proof in Contract and Tort' (1988) 62 *Australian LJ* 761, 762–3; A. Stein, 'An Essay on Uncertainty and Fact-Finding in Civil Litigation, With Special Reference to Contract Cases' (1998) 48 *U Toronto LJ* 299.

compensate the plaintiff. The value of the box or, more precisely, the value of the right to unlock it and reveal its contents equals the multiplication of the plaintiff's direct damage and the probability that this damage was wrongfully inflicted by an identified person. Setting the risk-aversion and transaction-cost problems aside, the plaintiff would surely be willing to pay that amount for the right to open the box; for obvious reasons, she would demand the same amount if she were to sell the box to the defendant allegedly responsible for her direct damage. This amount of money is the value of the box to the plaintiff, and it reflects the evidential damage that she sustained through the defendant's fault.

The locked box also represents the dilution in the threat-value of the plaintiff's case against her direct-damage defendant. For example, if the *Hunters' Case* were controlled by the traditional tort and evidence doctrines, the threat-value of the plaintiff's case following the infliction of the evidential damage would be zero. The locked-box metaphor helps to determine the threat-value of the plaintiff's case in the event in which no evidential damage is inflicted. This determination can be made in the following way. Assume that the box (representing the evidential damage, when locked) contains evidence unmistakably identifying one of the defendants as responsible for the plaintiff's physical injury. Assume also that the plaintiff negotiates a settlement with each of the defendants and that the negotiations are free and unaffected by any irrational constraints. There is, however, one crucial condition to these hypothetical negotiations: if the two parties fail to reach a voluntary settlement, their litigation will resume and the box will be unlocked. This hypothetical condition is crucial because its postulation will allow judges to make the precise assessment of the plaintiff's evidential damage. Under these conditions, each defendant knows that the probability that he will have to compensate the plaintiff for her entire injury equals 0.5. Since the evidential damage suffered by the plaintiff—when the box cannot be unlocked—diminished the threat-value of her case by d (as each defendant would have otherwise paid her $0.5d$ as a settlement amount), it is clear that the plaintiff was deprived of an asset that equals d. Under the corrective justice principles, each defendant should therefore make good this damage (d) as a settlement amount. The same holds true with regard to any other wrongdoer who causes a similar type of damage.

C. EVIDENTIAL DAMAGE AND DETERRENCE

The evidential damage doctrine will now be examined instrumentally by looking at the social utility that it can be expected to produce. From this angle, it will be examined as a means to a means-to-an-end. Less evidential damage entails more accurate fact-determination and, consequently, more effective execution of the controlling substantive law.[34] Individuals should therefore be deterred from causing evidential damage. As is true with other types of damage, however, evidential damage must not be prevented at any cost. When the costs of preventing damage are greater than the damage itself, taking precautions will be sub-optimal. Tort liability for evidential damage will therefore be efficient only when it cost-effectively minimizes this damage, that is, when the total sum representing both the damage and the costs of its prevention is kept at its lowest. This outcome can be attained by allocating responsibility for the damage to a person situated in the comparatively best position to minimize the above sum. This person will thus be singled out as the 'cheapest cost-avoider'.[35]

The evidential damage doctrine does not seek only to minimize evidential damage efficiently; it is also aimed at efficiently allocating the direct damage, given the evidential damage and the uncertainty that it produces.

In cases featuring evidential damage inflicted by direct-damage defendants, lack of liability for evidential damage will preclude the efficient allocation of direct damages. This inefficiency will occur because cheapest cost-avoiders of direct damage will be allowed to pay less, or even nothing, for the direct damage that they are likely to have inflicted. Allocation of liability for evidential damage to its cheapest cost-avoider may, accordingly, achieve two utilitarian goals simultaneously. It may optimize deterrence not only in relation to the evidential damage, but also in connection with the direct damage itself. This, once again, will happen in cases where the cheapest cost-avoider of the evidential damage is also likely to have inflicted the direct damage. In such cases, deterrence will be optimally furthered by charging each defendant the expected value that would attach to the plaintiff's lawsuit against the direct wrongdoer in the scenario in which no evidential damage is inflicted. Were there no evidential damage, deterrence could be optimized more accurately by charging the defendant for the actual losses that he inflicted. But here the case is evidentially damaged, which precludes accurate deterrence. Approximate deterrence with regard to the direct damage, an objective that the evidential damage doctrine promotes, is therefore the best that can be attained.

[34] The controlling substantive law will be presumed to be efficient because, otherwise, judicial fact-finding would have no economic value. We thus examine the utility of the evidential damage doctrine similarly to the utility of the law of evidence and procedure. This follows Jeremy Bentham's approach, as formulated by Gerald Postema: 'We are to judge the adequacy of a system of judicial procedure not directly in terms of the Principle of Utility [*sic*] but rather in terms of the system's success (or likely success) in properly executing the substantive law, and only indirectly in terms of the system's utility.' G. J. Postema, 'The Principle of Utility and the Law of Procedure: Bentham's Theory of Adjudication' (1977) 11 *Georgia L Rev* 1393, 1396–7.

[35] For discussions of the cheapest cost-avoider status, see G. Calabresi, *The Costs of Accidents* (1970) 68–94, 135–73, 244–65; G. Calabresi and J. T. Hirschoff, 'Toward a Test for Strict Liability in Torts' (1972) 81 *Yale LJ* 1055; R. A. Posner, 'A Theory of Negligence' (1972) 1 *J Legal Studies* 29.

The cheapest cost-avoider status will not, however, always attach to the same person with regard to both the direct and the evidential damage. These two kinds of damage may have two separate cheapest avoiders. Any such case will exhibit tension between deterrence as related to the evidential damage, and deterrence in connection with the direct damage. In such cases, optimizing both kinds of deterrence will be impossible, which entails that one of these objectives can be promoted to its full extent only at the full expense of the other. Alternatively, some compromise can be struck between these two objectives, which would produce insufficient deterrence with regard to both evidential and direct damage.

1. Convergence Between the Two Objectives Exemplified

Let us take our hypothetical *DES Case* with its insoluble defendant-identification problem and consider how it could be resolved under the evidential damage doctrine.[36] In this case, each of the manufacturers was clearly the cheapest avoider of both the direct and the evidential damage. Each manufacturer was best positioned to consider the means for substantially reducing the extent of—if not altogether eliminating—the identification problem (for example, by marketing the drug under its brand rather than generic name or by maintaining records documenting the purchasers of the drug).[37] Arguably, the plaintiffs' mothers could have eliminated the problem even more efficiently by recording their drug purchases. This argument is, however, unconvincing. The mothers' inadequate information about the drug and its producers, accompanied in some cases by psychological barriers, will make any attempt to assign them the 'cheapest cost-avoider' status implausible. It must also not be forgotten that the drugs purchased by the plaintiffs' mothers were advertised as both *chemically identical* and safe. The plaintiffs' mothers were perfectly entitled to rely on this warranty, explicitly or implicitly given by each manufacturer. This warranty sent out the unequivocal message that it would be a waste of time for consumers to differentiate between different DES producers across the country. Because the plaintiffs' mothers purchased not only the drugs but also their accompanying warranties, they cannot be blamed for the evidential damage. Consequently, each manufacturer will have to compensate each plaintiff by paying her the expected value that would attach to her lawsuit in the absence of the evidential damage. This amount equals the product of the plaintiff's direct injury multiplied by the

[36] The application of the evidential damage doctrine in the *DES Case* will result in the imposition of liability on each manufacturer, the extent of which is generally the same as under Market Share Liability. See below 186–7, 191–3.

[37] Such monitoring could be arranged with drugstore retailers. See, e.g., G. O. Robinson, 'Multiple Causation in Tort Law: Reflections on the DES Cases' (1982) 68 *Virginia L Rev* 713, 729, 734–5; R. P. Murray, 'Note, *Sindell v Abbott Laboratories*: A Market Share Approach to DES Causation' (1981) 69 *California L Rev* 1179, 1202.

probability of the allegation that the manufacturer actually inflicted that injury.[38]

This approach, however, would not necessarily optimize deterrence with regard to both direct and evidential damage. As demonstrated in Chapter V, free-riding and collective action problems may sometimes prevent manufacturers from efficiently reducing direct damages. Such a reduction of damages, however, would always be the best economic alternative, so the evidential damage doctrine must facilitate it. The doctrine furthers this objective by inducing each defendant to take measures that disassociate him from the evidential damage. In the *DES Case*, for example, the defendants would be induced to monitor purchases of their drugs through their drugstore retailers. The ensuing records would eliminate the evidential damage that could otherwise be inflicted by the defendant. The defendant may consequently find it profitable to eliminate or to reduce the risk of injury associated with his drugs by making an appropriate investment in research and technology. He may find it profitable because other manufacturers would no longer be able to take a free-ride on his investment and thereby reduce their liability in torts at his expense. Other manufacturers might then follow the same strategy, which would contribute to social welfare. Arguably, as long as the evidential damage doctrine is not accompanied by punitive damages, some manufacturers might still benefit from the uncertainty, so they will try to retain and even intensify it. This argument is essentially correct. However, those manufacturers would have even stronger incentives to retain and intensify the uncertainty if they were altogether exempt from liability in torts.[39]

The same economic reasoning will apply to indeterminate-victim cases, such as our *Radiation Case* example. In such cases, the defendant will be the cheapest cost-avoider of both the evidential damage and the direct damage. None of the plaintiffs that he unilaterally exposed to the risk of contracting cancer was in a position to know about this exposure, let alone prevent it. Holding the defendant responsible for each plaintiff's evidential damage will put in motion the proposed remedial mechanism. Operation of this mechanism will force the defendant to fully internalize the costs of his actions. This application of the evidential damage doctrine would thus produce optimal deterrence with regard to both the direct damage and the evidential damage.

2. Tension Between the Two Objectives Exemplified

Take a tort action brought by a person who sustained two discrete injuries in two car accidents, separated from each other by one year, and hypothesize that those injuries have inseparably merged into one. Prior to the second accident, the plaintiff's physical condition could be inexpensively determined by

[38] For a more detailed explanation, see discussion below 186–7. [39] See above 150–8.

doctors. He none the less decided not to seek that determination because he thought he had more exciting things to do.[40] In this and similar cases, the costs of the plaintiff's decision should be internalized by the plaintiff, because neither the first nor the second defendant could have prevented the evidential damage more cheaply than the plaintiff could. The plaintiff's decision not to seek medical information therefore amounted to a mismanagement of the risk: he was uniquely well-positioned to prevent the evidential damage, but failed to do so. The deterrence objective, as related to the evidential damage, will therefore allocate this damage to the plaintiff.[41]

At the same time, absolving the defendants from liability would undermine deterrence in relation to the direct damage. A conflict between the two utilitarian objectives thus becomes transparent. This conflict is difficult to resolve because neither of the conflicting objectives can easily be sacrificed for the sake of the other. A compromise between the two objectives, that is, the adoption of some comparative fault mechanism, will consequently be in order.

3. The Victim's Burden

Evidential damage will be regarded as self-inflicted and consequently non-compensable if its victim was also its cheapest cost-avoider. Mentioned in our preceding discussion, this point needs to be supplemented by another point concerning the victim's burden. In some cases, the victim will be in the best position to rectify the evidential damage *ex post* by providing substitute evidence that can fill in the informational gap. He will, however, refrain from doing that, if the substitute evidence does not promote his compensatory objective and if liability for the evidential damage falls upon his opponent. This problem is one of the manifestations of the more general difficulty that arises in legal systems that attempt to attain socially optimal deterrence through private litigation. This difficulty represents a fundamental divergence between the private and the social incentives to use the adjudication facility.[42] For example, one of our DES plaintiffs could actually have evidence identifying the manufacturer of the drug taken by her mother. Fearful of the manufacturer's possible bankruptcy, she may, none the less, decide to withhold this evidence. Consequently, application of the evidential damage doctrine may end up in a social disutility.

[40] Cf. *Ryan v Mackolin*, 237 NE 2d 377, 382–3 (Ohio 1968) (a similar factual setting, in regard to which the court reached a conclusion different from ours).

[41] This allocation of the damage will impel insurers of physical injuries to condition their coverage on timely medical examination of the insured. Absence of this condition would jeopardize the insurer's subrogation claim against the tortfeasor.

[42] See S. Shavell, 'The Fundamental Divergence Between the Private and the Social Motive to Use the Legal System' (1997) 26 *J Legal Studies* 575. For a further discussion of this difficulty, see A. Stein, 'Of Two Wrongs that Make a Right: Two Paradoxes of the Evidence Law and Their Combined Economic Justification' (2001) 79 *Texas L Rev* 1199 1226–31.

In Chapter V, we discuss this argument at length. In the context of our present discussion, this argument simply means that evidential damage will not always be real. In litigation, an issue of this kind would therefore have to be resolved through discovery proceedings and by examining witnesses and other evidence. If there is no evidence pointing to the plaintiff's attempted misuse of the evidential damage doctrine, the plaintiff would obviously prevail. If she prevails undeservedly, her case would simply be categorized as one of the unfortunate, but unavoidable, instances of injustice. This injustice should certainly count as a social disutility. It is clear, however, that such occasional disutilities ought to be tolerated in order to prevent the distortions and, indeed, the systematic injustice that are likely to occur in the absence of the evidential damage doctrine. Unaided by this doctrine, the law of torts may too easily be defeated by wrongdoers.

VII

The Evidential Damage Doctrine: Applications and Evaluation

THIS chapter concludes our discussion of the factual uncertainty problem in the implementation of the law of torts. In what follows, we return to the paradigmatic cases featuring this problem and apply to them the evidential damage doctrine, as developed in Chapter VI. Throughout this discussion, we evaluate the advantages of the evidential damage doctrine.

Evaluation of that doctrine can be conducted on two different levels. First, one can evaluate the doctrine's effect on the allocation of direct damages *under* uncertainty. This approach represents the instrumental evaluation of the doctrine. Second, one can evaluate the internal justification for the doctrine as imposing liability *for* uncertainty. This internal evaluation was already conducted in Chapter VI. In the present chapter, our primary concern is the instrumental evaluation of the doctrine. This evaluation assumes the form of a comparison between the evidential damage doctrine, on the one hand, and other solutions to the uncertainty problem, on the other hand. The framework of our subsequent discussion can thus be reformulated as the following basic question:

> Which of the two available approaches to the uncertainty problem—liability *under* uncertainty or liability *for* uncertainty—is normatively superior?

We answer this question by revisiting each basic category of factually uncertain cases that Chapter II identified as paradigmatic and that cannot be adequately resolved by the general burden-of-proof principles. To recap, there are five such categories, namely:

(1) cases of wrongful damage where the wrongdoer is unidentifiable;
(2) cases of wrongful damage where the injured party is unidentifiable;
(3) cases of wrongful conduct that may or may not have resulted in damage;
(4) cases of damage wrongfully inflicted by separate wrongdoers;
(5) cases of damage originating both from a wrongdoer and a non-wrongful cause.

The normative criteria that we use in this comparison are similar to those employed throughout the book. Our frame of reference is that of deterrence and corrective justice. We do not employ other normative criteria, such as retribution and distributive justice. Throughout this book, we have alluded to those criteria only peripherally, treating them as supplementary, rather than determinative, factors in imposing liability in torts.

A. CASES OF WRONGFUL DAMAGE WHERE THE WRONGDOER IS UNIDENTIFIABLE

1. Application of the Evidential Damage Doctrine

The evidential damage doctrine accommodates and adequately resolves many of the cases that fall into the present category. In many such cases, the person who is likely to be the direct wrongdoer is also the person who wrongfully inflicted the evidential damage. The *Hunters' Case*, to which we have referred throughout the book,[1] clearly substantiates this point. In this and similar cases, the plaintiff's evidential damage is equal to his physical damage. As explained in Chapter VI, one of the defendants in the *Hunters' Case* caused both the direct and evidential damage to the plaintiff, while the other defendant inflicted only evidential damage. The evidential damage created the uncertainty that prevented the plaintiff from successfully suing the actual wrongdoer for his direct injury.[2]

In the *DES Case*,[3] the evidential damage doctrine would hold each of the manufacturers liable for a fraction of each plaintiff's damage. This fraction would have to be proportional to the degree of the risk of injury to which the manufacturer exposed the plaintiff. The degree of that risk would be determined by the manufacturer's share in the DES market. The *DES Case* differs from the *Hunters' Case* in that in the former, the evidential damage that each manufacturer inflicted on the plaintiff does not overlap with the direct injury she sustained, whereas in the latter case, the two types of damage are of equal magnitude. Presumably, each DES manufacturer could argue that the plaintiff would have probably been unable to identify her wrongdoer and recover from him the appropriate compensation for her direct injury, even if he—the manufacturer allegedly responsible for the plaintiff's evidential incapacitation—did not inflict any evidential damage. This seems to be a powerful argument, which, if correct, would absolve the manufacturer from any liability. The appeal of this argument, however, is superficial at best. This argument collapses for the reason that the evidentially incapacitated plaintiff is entitled to say to *each* manufacturer: 'Had you not wrongfully exposed me to the risk of injury, I would not have found myself short of the information

[1] See above 58, 134, 162, 167, 174–5.

[2] If in the *Hunters' Case*, there were three defendants who had fired in the plaintiff's direction, each would be liable in an amount equal to one third of the direct damage. In the next paragraphs, we explain this solution as applied to the *DES Case*.

[3] See above 58.

concerning *your part* in my injury: it is because of your wrongful action that I am now lacking this information.' None of the manufacturers can adequately respond to this claim. Therefore, each manufacturer should compensate the plaintiff for her evidential damage. The amount of compensation should reflect the value of the plaintiff's entitlement to information,[4] violated by each manufacturer. This value would equal the amount of money that the plaintiff would be willing to pay to each manufacturer to ascertain whether it is the one which actually inflicted her injury. This amount of money would therefore be derived from the magnitude of the risk of injury to which each manufacturer exposed the plaintiff. More precisely, this amount would be determined by the multiplication of the statistical probability that each specific manufacturer actually inflicted the plaintiff's injury and the value of that injury in terms of monetary damages. The statistical probability that each manufacturer actually inflicted the plaintiff's injury would be represented by each manufacturer's respective share in the DES market. The solutions provided by the evidential damage doctrine and the market-share-liability doctrine (in its most common version) would therefore be similar in *DES*-types of cases.[5]

In both the *DES Case* and the *Hunters' Case*, each defendant was established to have acted wrongfully. This, however, might not always be the case, as occureed in the *Injured Shoulder Case*[6] and similar cases falling under the present category. At first glance, such cases present no real problem: if the plaintiff was not wronged by the defendant—so that neither her direct injury nor her evidential damage can be linked to the defendant's wrongful action—the defendant should assume no liability whatsoever. At the same time, the proposition that the plaintiff was not wronged by the defendant must always be carefully examined. The defendant may not have acted wrongfully, but he may have inflicted evidential damage by omission if, for instance, he negligently failed to keep appropriate records or other documentation. In the *Injured Shoulder Case*, for example, liability for the plaintiff's evidential damage could be imposed on the defendants' employer, the hospital, even if it is not vicariously liable for the direct damage.[7] This liability can be justified by the hospital's negligent failure to keep full medical records: if those records had been properly compiled and maintained by the hospital, the plaintiff

[4] Arguments supporting recognition of this entitlement are discussed in Chapter VI above.

[5] Another view, which we consider problematic, deems each manufacturer the legal cause of the entire evidential damage that the plaintiff sustained. This view replaces the *sine qua non* standard for causation with the sufficient-cause standard. The sufficient-cause standard attributes liability for damage to a wrongdoer whose action was sufficient to inflict the damage. See R. W. Wright, 'Causation, Responsibility, Risk, Probability, Naked Statistics, and Proof: Pruning the Bramble Bush by Clarifying the Concepts' (1988) 73 *Iowa L Rev* 1001. See also H. L. A. Hart and T. Honoré, *Causation in the Law* (2nd edn., Oxford, 1985) 122–9.

[6] See above.

[7] See above 69.

would have been able to identify the wrongdoer responsible for his injury.[8] In such a case, the hospital should be held liable in an amount that is equal to the entire direct damage that the plaintiff sustained. Similarly, each of the defendants in the *Cargo Case*[9] (or at least one of them) should have kept accurate documentation, which would have resolved the plaintiff's evidential uncertainty problem. If this were the case, each defendant would have to bear liability toward the plaintiff to the extent that equals the plaintiff's direct damage. In any such case, the key issue is the origin of the duty to compile and maintain the relevant records. In medical malpractice cases, this duty can and, indeed, should be derived from the patient's general right to receive full information concerning her or his diagnosis and treatment.[10] In cases similar to our *Cargo Case* example, the duty to compile and maintain the appropriate documentation should be recognized as part of the general duty of care that both cargo carriers and port authorities owe to the owners of shipped goods. Arguably, each defendant should have anticipated the significance of keeping records when there is a substantial risk that one of the defendants will wrongfully cause a traceless damage to a plaintiff's goods. This factor justifies imposing a duty to maintain adequate documentation on both defendants.

2. Does the Evidential Damage Doctrine Attain Desirable Results?

In many cases falling under the present category, both deterrence and corrective justice justify the outcomes that the evidential damage doctrine would attain. Both theories justify these outcomes independently of the doctrine's internal justification.

From the deterrence perspective, application of the evidential damage doctrine in the present category of cases would be socially desirable. This doctrine would induce prospective wrongdoers to base their actions on a socially advantageous cost-benefit analysis. This analysis would be socially advantageous because it aligns with the analysis that prospective wrongdoers would conduct in the absence of the wrongdoer-identification problem. Prospective wrongdoers would have to base their actions on this analysis due to the liability framework set by the evidential damage doctrine. This framework would deprive wrongdoers of their ability to externalize damages from the twilight zone of indeterminate causation. Under this framework, each wrongdoer would have to detract the full amount of expected damage associated with his wrongdoing from the benefit that he expects to derive from his

[8] See above 164. [9] See above 59.

[10] R. Nelson-Jones and F. Butron, *Medical Negligence Case Law* (2nd edn., London, 1995) 102–14.

contemplated action. The resulting regime would thus maintain optimal deterrence.[11]

For obvious reasons, holding such wrongdoers not liable would produce insufficient deterrence. The alternative approach, holding the defendant liable for the entire direct damage that the plaintiff sustained,[12] would not be without merit. However, when the evidential damage is less than the amount of the direct damage, application of this approach would produce excessive deterrence. This would happen, for example, in the *DES Case*, if each manufacturer were to compensate the plaintiff for her entire injury and if contribution suits among the manufacturers were impractical (due to insolvency or for other reasons).[13] In addition, one should bear in mind that it is not only the efficient allocation of the direct damage, given uncertainty, that is at stake. Elimination of the uncertainty is yet another goal that the evidential damage doctrine strives to achieve. As demonstrated in Chapters V and VI, deterrence would be substantially improved if uncertainty were to be substantially reduced or eliminated.[14] This observation has general applicability. Indeed, it would hold true even in legal regimes that recognize both the evidential damage doctrine and collective liability in torts. Therefore, in applying the evidential damage doctrine, one should consider the promotion of both goals. Hence, the legal regime should identify the cheapest cost-avoiders of both direct and evidential damage as suitable candidates for liability in torts.[15]

From the corrective justice perspective, cases covered by the present category require more delicate treatment because corrective justice is generally opposed to liability for bare risk.[16] However, this limitation only emphasizes the internal justification of the evidential damage doctrine. In cases similar to our *Hunters' Case* example, making evidential damage actionable is the only way to align the principles of corrective justice with the strong moral intuition that the defendants should pay for the plaintiff's damage. As explained in Chapter VI, the plaintiff's right not to be evidentially damaged derives from his or her general right to autonomy that the principles of corrective justice protect.[17]

The solutions offered above to the *DES* type of cases are more readily reconcilable with corrective justice. This reconciliation is possible even if we evaluate the evidential damage doctrine in strictly instrumental terms. In such cases, each defendant both acted wrongfully and inflicted direct damage (on

[11] Both here and throughout our other discussions, we assume that there are no serious drawbacks in law enforcement. When such drawbacks are present, they can be inexpensively rectified by imposing punitive damages. See Chapter I above.

[12] See above 138, 148.

[13] Other considerations, such as compensating victims, may still justify this outcome.

[14] See above 150–8, 160–9.

[15] See above 179–84.

[16] See above 103–10.

[17] See above 167, 177.

unidentifiable victims). As demonstrated in Chapter V, holding the defendants collectively liable—for example, by applying the market-share liability doctrine—is justified by corrective justice. The evidential damage doctrine produces the same result and therefore can be justified on the same grounds underlying the market-share liability doctrine. Moreover, the principles of corrective justice also support holding the DES manufacturers liable for the evidential damage suffered by each plaintiff, for the same reasons underlying the internal justification of the doctrine.

The *Injured Shoulder* and *Cargo* types of cases are, admittedly, more problematic. In these and similar cases, none of the defendants has been established as having acted wrongfully. Arguably, none of these defendants should therefore be held responsible for the plaintiff's damage.

Our examination of these cases will begin with deterrence. On the one hand, wrongfulness on the part of the defendant is still a probable scenario, even though it has not been preponderantly established. Therefore, one must consider the possibility of holding each defendant liable to the extent that his wrongfulness is probable. This is an attractive possibility because it would force all potential wrongdoers—including the low-probability wrongdoers—to act in light of the expected damage that would originate from their actions. On the other hand, this possibility could intensify overuse of the adjudication facility, and Chapter I demonstrates that this outcome would be socially deleterious. For reasons outlined in the previous chapters,[18] one should therefore separate cases that involve a recurrent infliction of damage (such as the *Cargo Case*) from cases in which the infliction of damage is not recurrent. In the former group of cases, savings in the form of prevented damages would offset the costs that would be incurred by an excessive resort to adjudication. This would not necessarily be so in the latter group of cases, where the damaging events are not recurrent. There is also an intermediate group of cases, with a recurrent damaging event but rotating wrongdoers. The *Two Cars Case*[19] is representative of this intermediate group. In Chapter V, we demonstrated how the collective liability doctrine advances the deterrence objectives that we have just described.

Application of the evidential damage doctrine in such cases would serve as an instrument for allocating the direct damage in a way that induces potential wrongdoers to act in light of the expected amount of that damage. As already explained, both in the *Cargo Case* and the *Injured Shoulder Case*, the defendants might have been negligent in causing the evidential damage. Finding the *Cargo Case* defendants liable for the evidential damage would induce them (and similarly situated corporations and agencies) to internalize the entire risk associated with their wrongdoings. Optimal deterrence would thus be achieved. In contrast, finding the hospital liable for the evidential

[18] See Chapters I and V above.

[19] See above 59.

damage in the *Injured Shoulder Case* would not directly resolve the underdeterrence problem vis-à-vis medical staff. However, this liability would augment the hospital's incentive to act in a way that reduces uncertainty and consequently increases the chances of identifying the actual wrongdoers.[20] Ultimately, because fewer wrongdoers would escape identification, the level of deterrence would rise with respect to direct damage as well.

Does the evidential damage doctrine, when applied in the *Cargo Case* and *Injured Shoulder Case*, allocate direct damage in a way that aligns with corrective justice? Under corrective justice, absence of an identifiable wrongdoer thwarts any attempt to impose liability in torts. In Chapter V, we argued that the corrective justice principles would still justify liability in cases involving recurrent damaging events, if the unidentified wrongdoer belongs to a well-defined group of potential wrongdoers. This liability is justified on the theory that each potential wrongdoer must have wrongfully caused damage on some unidentified occasion. If so, each defendant should then be held liable to the extent that his actions caused unidentified losses in the long run of cases. More specifically, this liability should be determined by the probability that each defendant actually caused the litigated damage. This formula would transfer the appropriate amount of monetary damages from defendants, who wrongfully caused damage to plaintiffs, given that these plaintiffs were exposed to the risks of damage that the defendants created and ultimately suffered damage. The fact that wrongdoers do not make direct payment to their specific victims is immaterial.[21] This solution, however, is inapplicable to cases in which incidents of unaffiliated damage are not recurrent within a group of potential wrongdoers (such as the *Injured Shoulder Case*). In such cases, imposing liability on all the defendants would force some of them to pay for damage that they definitely did not inflict. This outcome would be manifestly inconsistent with corrective justice.

The internal justification of the evidential damage doctrine may, none the less, support the imposition of liability on the hospital in the *Injured Shoulder Case*. Under corrective justice, if the hospital inflicted evidential damage on the plaintiff, the plaintiff is entitled to compensation for that damage. Under such a scenario, the amount of compensation that the plaintiff would receive from the hospital would equal the value of his physical injury.

3. The Evidential Damage Doctrine versus Market-Share Liability

We now compare the evidential damage doctrine with the doctrine of market-share liability ('MSL'). Both doctrines aim at resolving the same problem, namely, causal indeterminacy. Do these doctrines overlap one another when

[20] We assume no vicarious liability on the part of the hospital. See above 69.

[21] See above 132–8.

applied in the context of the present category of cases? If so, to what extent? And which of the two doctrines is normatively preferable to the other?

First, many opponents of MSL argue that this doctrine deviates from the principles of corrective justice and individual responsibility that underlie the traditional law of torts. They argue that it is better not to impose liability on defendants in the *DES*-type of cases than violate these foundational principles.[22] They also argue that if these principles are violated, the essentially private nature of the law of torts—as a system of rules that apply between individual wrongdoers and their individual victims—would be destroyed. This system would be replaced by the public law of torts, an entirely different system governed by distributive justice and other societal goals. These goals would be promoted through imposition of compensatory duties on individuals, which would be no different from imposing taxes (but, arguably, less efficient and less fair than taxation). The law of torts would thus cease to be law of 'torts'.[23]

The arguments raised by these opponents of MSL would be inapplicable with regard to the evidential damage doctrine. As we have demonstrated, the latter doctrine is commensurate with the principles of corrective justice and individual responsibility. The evidential damage doctrine holds a wrongdoer liable for damage inflicted by him towards the specific plaintiff who suffered that damage. Therefore, these opponents of MSL would probably not resist the evidential damage doctrine.

Second, the evidential damage doctrine would apply to a much broader spectrum of cases than MSL. Thus far, MSL has been applied primarily in the DES cases adjudicated by the American courts.[24] Indeed, American courts have emphasized that MSL is particularly suitable for DES cases because all DES drugs are identically composed: it was this feature of the drugs (coupled with their marketing under a generic, rather than brand, name) that allowed the courts to allocate liability on a market-share basis. Absent that factor, apportionment of liability on a market-share basis would not have been sufficiently accurate.[25]

The evidential damage doctrine does not raise such a strict barrier for imposing liability. This doctrine applies whenever evidential damage is wrongfully inflicted. Indeed, the whole point of this doctrine is to avoid the problems that arise in imposing liability *under* uncertainty by imposing liability *for* uncertainty. Moreover, unlike MSL, the evidential damage doctrine is not restricted to cases that feature recurrent damaging events. Indeed, even if

[22] See I. Englard, *The Philosophy of Tort Law* (Dartmouth, 1993) 219–23. For a different opinion, see D. Rosenberg, 'The Causal Connection in Mass Exposure Cases: A "Public Law" Vision of the Tort System' (1984) 97 *Harvard L Rev* 849, 881–5.

[23] Englard (n. 22 above).

[24] For some other cases in which MSL was applied, see above 66–7.

[25] For further details, see above 61–7.

MSL were to be expanded in the future, the evidential damage doctrine would still be supported by a broader platform.

B. CASES OF WRONGFUL DAMAGE WHERE THE INJURED PARTY IS UNIDENTIFIABLE

1. Application of the Evidential Damage Doctrine

The discussion of this category of cases focuses on the *Radiation Case* example.[26] To recap, this case involves the emission of radioactive rays from a factory, which has raised the incidence of cancer in the vicinity by 25 per cent. One hundred residents of the area, all of whom contracted cancer, are suing the factory owner for their personal injuries. Consequently, it is statistically evident that the defendant exposed each of the plaintiffs to a 20 per cent risk of contracting cancer (because the number of afflicted individuals raised from 80 to 100). This risk materialized in twenty out of a hundred cases and did not materialize in the remaining eighty cases. Hence, twenty out of the hundred plaintiffs have become afflicted through the fault of the defendant; the remaining eighty plaintiffs cannot blame their affliction upon the defendant. There is, however, no evidence that can single out the twenty plaintiffs who actually sustained an injustice from the eighty plaintiffs who are simply the victims of misfortune. Accordingly, none of the plaintiffs can establish that his or her direct injury resulted from the defendant's wrongful act.

Under the evidential damage doctrine, the plaintiffs would not be denied recovery. Because the defendant's wrongful activity evidentially incapacitated each plaintiff, each would have a valid claim against the defendant. In Chapter VI, we explained at length the application of the doctrine in this example. Briefly, because the defendant's wrongful activity deprived each plaintiff of his or her ability to identify the cause of his or her injury, the defendant should compensate each plaintiff for this evidential damage.

At first glance, the evidential damage doctrine would not be of assistance to these plaintiffs because the defendant could still argue that it is more probable than not that each plaintiff could not benefit from knowing the cause of his or her injury. If this is the case, the evidential damage that each plaintiff sustained did not tangibly weaken his or her direct-damage lawsuit. Arguably, none of the plaintiffs should, therefore, be entitled to compensation.

This argument, however, is based on an antecedent refusal to recognize the plaintiff's right to information. Specifically, it represents a refusal to recognize the individual's entitlement to any valuable information that affects his or her legal position. The evidential damage doctrine is premised on this entitlement: by refusing to recognize that entitlement, we are refusing to recognize the

[26] See above 70.

doctrine itself. The value of the information that the defendant wrongfully took away from each plaintiff equals 20 per cent of the plaintiff's injury. This is so because each plaintiff would be willing to pay this amount in order to obtain this information (assuming the plaintiff is risk-neutral). Therefore, the defendant should pay each plaintiff 20 per cent of his or her injury.

2. Does the Evidential Damage Doctrine Attain Desirable Results?

From the deterrence perspective, holding the defendant liable for 20 per cent of the plaintiffs' injuries would align the incentives of similarly situated wrongdoers with the risks generated by their activities. Note that the defendant in the *Radiation Case* is the cheapest cost-avoider with respect to both the increment in the incidence of cancer and the evidential damage.[27] The plaintiffs' ability to minimize both types of damage is manifestly limited in comparison with that of the defendant. This asymmetry justifies imposing liability on the factory's owner, provided that the extent of that liability does not exceed the magnitude of his externalized risk (20 per cent). The evidential damage doctrine facilitates the attainment of this outcome. As such, it induces potential wrongdoers to optimally minimize direct damage.

Because the factory's owner wrongfully imposed the risk of cancer on others and because this risk has materialized in twenty cases, holding him liable also would be justified by corrective justice, even if we were to ignore the internal justification of the evidential damage doctrine. Forcing the factory's owner to pay for 20 per cent of the plaintiffs' injuries would exact from him monetary damages that would cover the amount of the damage he inflicted. Admittedly, under this compensation system, none of the plaintiffs would be appropriately compensated for his or her injury. In fact, eighty plaintiffs who deserve no compensation at all, would be overcompensated by 20 per cent, while the remaining twenty plaintiffs, who deserve full compensation, would be undercompensated by 80 per cent. This outcome would not be commensurate with corrective justice. However, because the damaging event dealt with in the *Radiation Case* can recur time and time again—theoretically, *ad infinitum*—corrective justice would be undermined even more severely if all the plaintiffs were to be denied recovery. Therefore, holding the factory's owner liable for 20 per cent of the plaintiffs' injuries would be justified by corrective justice as a second-best solution for the problem at hand.

From the perspective of its internal justification, the evidential damage doctrine achieves a first-best solution to the problem. The value of the information of which the factory's owner wrongfully deprived each plaintiff equals

[27] Avoidance of evidential damage in this and similar cases can be achieved by avoiding the wrongful radiation. The fact that it may be impossible to avoid the evidential damage alone while the wrongful risk remains intact is immaterial. Actually, it is a rather common phenomenon for one wrongful act to produce more than one type of damage simultaneously.

20 per cent of the plaintiff's damage. This valuation reflects the damage to the plaintiff's autonomy. More specifically, it determines the value of the plaintiff's infringed entitlement to making informed choices concerning his or her legal rights. As our preceding discussion reveals, none of the existing legal doctrines offers such a solution.[28]

C. CASES OF WRONGFUL CONDUCT THAT MAY OR MAY NOT HAVE RESULTED IN DAMAGE

1. Application of the Evidential Damage Doctrine

In cases belonging to this category, the plaintiff cannot determine the cause of his or her damage and, consequently, cannot sue for it. This inability constitutes evidential damage, as exemplified by the following modification of the *Radiation Case*. Assume that a factory's owner wrongfully exposed the plaintiff to radiation; that the risk of contracting cancer attendant upon this exposure amounts to 20 per cent; and that the plaintiff is the only person who contracted cancer following this exposure. Another paradigmatic example is provided by *Hotson v East Berkshire Area Health Authority*,[29] identified here as the *Thigh Case*. To recap, the plaintiff was admitted to hospital with a thigh injury, where his doctors negligently failed to detect the gravity of his condition until it was too late, and the plaintiff was permanently disabled. This disability would have had a 25 per cent chance of being prevented had the plaintiff's dangerous condition been properly diagnosed.[30]

In both of these examples, the evidential damage doctrine would render the defendants liable: in the modified *Radiation Case*, the defendant would have to compensate the plaintiff for 20 per cent of his injury; in the *Thigh Case*, for 25 per cent. In both cases, even if the defendant's wrongful conduct did not actually cause the injury that the plaintiff sustained, it did prevent the plaintiff from identifying the cause of that injury. Specifically, it prevented the plaintiff from both verifying and eliminating the possibility that his injury had resulted from the defendant's wrongful conduct. This deprivation constitutes evidential damage. As in other cases, the extent of the evidential damage—that is, the value of the missing information—is a function of the probability that this information would have identified the defendant's wrongful conduct as the cause of the plaintiff's injury. The full amount of monetary damages due for the plaintiff's injury must be multiplied by that probability (20 per cent in the modified *Radiation Case* and 25 per cent in the *Thigh Case*).

Note that in the *Thigh Case* and its like, calculation of the relevant probability would be different had the wrongdoer not eliminated completely the

[28] See above 71–3. [29] [1987] 2 All ER 909 (HL). [30] See above 74.

victim's initial chances of recovery. Thus, if the defendant's malpractice brought the plaintiff's 50 per cent chances of recovery down to 25 per cent and the plaintiff ultimately did not recover, the probability that the malpractice is the cause of the plaintiff's entire injury would equal 33 per cent rather than 25 per cent. This scenario puts the plaintiff in a group of, say, a hundred similarly situated patients. This group contains seventy-five patients, including the plaintiff, who did not recover. These seventy-five patients include fifty patients who were doomed not to recover and twenty-five patients who would have recovered had they not been subjected to their doctors' malpractice. The probability that the plaintiff is one of those twenty-five patients therefore equals 25/75, that is, 1/3.[31]

As articulated by Prosser and Keeton, the American doctrine that awards compensation for lost chances commonly holds that the plaintiff should recover only 25 per cent of his or her damage (50 per cent–25 per cent).[32] Chronologically, this amount represents only position 1 into which the defendant's malpractice forced the plaintiff and in which the plaintiff still had a hope of recovery. However, the baseline set by Prosser and Keeton is anomalous, since we know that the plaintiff is now in position 2, where, regrettably, that hope no longer exists. The evidential damage doctrine eliminates this anomaly.[33]

2. Does the Evidential Damage Doctrine Attain Desirable Results?

In the *Thigh Case* and similar instances involving medical malpractice, the patient's initial chances of recovery are typically lower than 50 per cent. Therefore, in such cases, absolving medical professionals from tort liability would dilute their incentive for optimally reducing damage to patients. This dilution would produce sub-optimal deterrence. Thus, medical professionals should bear liability for malpractice even when their patients' initial chances of recovery are slim. These professionals, however, would be excessively deterred if the law were to ignore the patient's initial chances of recovery—especially when these chances are slim—and to force the careless professional to compensate the afflicted patient for her entire damage. Therefore, as in many other instances, a negligent professional should compensate his afflicted patient for an appropriate fraction of the patient's loss. This fraction equals the patient's damage multiplied by the probability of the allegation that causally links that damage with the malpractice. For the present category of cases, this would be the optimal amount of compensation.

[31] See above 120–4.

[32] W. P. Keeton (ed.), *Prosser and Keeton On Torts* (5th edn., St. Paul, 1984) 272.

[33] Cf. above 123–4. See A. Porat and A. Stein, 'Liability for Uncertainty: Making Evidential Damage Actionable' (1997) 18 *Cardozo L Rev* 1891, 1902–5.

The evidential damage doctrine would secure this socially desirable outcome. Admittedly, this outcome would also be attained under the doctrine that allows victims of medical malpractice to obtain compensation for their lost chances of recovery. As indicated in Chapters II and IV, this approach was adopted by a number of American and Israeli courts.[34] Although justified in purely instrumental terms of deterrence, this approach must contend with the conceptual objections discussed in Chapter IV. More specifically, we claim that liability for lost chances in past injury cases (as opposed to future injury cases) cannot be reconciled with corrective justice.[35] Indeed, the evidential damage doctrine offers a more principled and conceptually tidier solution to both future and past injury cases that feature indeterminate causation. Moreover, this solution is consistent with corrective justice.

Before further developing this argument, we should first address an important concern that arises in connection with our proposal. Arguably, the compensatory remedy that the evidential damage doctrine would afford to plaintiffs in the present category of cases might undermine their truth-seeking incentives.[36] If an injured person can recover compensation from any probable wrongdoer, she will reduce her efforts to uncover the real cause of her damage. The extent of the reduction in her truth-seeking efforts would depend directly on the probability of the argument causally attributing her injury to a particular wrongdoer: the higher the probability, the lesser the effort. The truth-seeking efforts, of course, also would depend on the further particularities of the case. For example, a self-interested plaintiff would prefer to sue a probable wrongdoer rather than the actual wrongdoer, if the former happens to be a wealthy corporation and the latter a pauper. A plaintiff can be expected to pursue the same strategy when she suspects her injury to have resulted from natural causes, from her own actions, or from some other causal factors for which no person can be blamed. In these and similar circumstances, victims of torts would prefer to leave the identification problem unresolved. This distortion in the victim's truth-seeking incentive is particularly disturbing when the victim is the cheapest cost-avoider of the evidential damage, a status that may attach to the victim both before the infliction of that damage and after.

Indeed, this factor may justify a distinction between past injuries and future ones. Under such a distinction, a plaintiff can recover compensation for her worsened prospects for well-being only when the prospects are still prospects—that is, when the event in relation to which the compensation is being claimed is a future or hypothetical, rather than accomplished, occurrence.[37] This concern also justifies a distinction between the different origins of the indeterminate causation problem. This problem may arise for an entirely objective reason:

[34] See above 74–6, 122. [35] See above 122–3.

[36] In Chapter V, we discuss this point in relation to collective liability. See above 155–8.

[37] Cf. above 120–5. See also *Lawson v Laferriere*, 78 DLR (4th) 609 (1991).

it may originate from some general epistemic limitation, such as the failure of scientists to identify the cause of the relevant damage. However, the problem may also arise for a reason that is either entirely or partially subjective: the plaintiff may have simply failed to prove her specific allegations because of her poor litigation effort.

These concerns are well-founded. However, they are valid only with regard to the lost-chance doctrine, as adopted by some courts in Israel and the United States. The evidential damage doctrine, which this book proposes to adopt, provides an adequate response to these concerns. The objective existence of evidential damage as a factor that the plaintiff must positively establish is the whole essence of the evidential damage doctrine. Thus, if there is good reason to believe that the plaintiff can properly identify the actual cause of her damage, the evidential damage doctrine will be inapplicable. To summon this doctrine in support of her case, the plaintiff therefore would have to positively eliminate any such reason. Furthermore, the plaintiff would be unable to discharge this burden if the circumstances of the case single her out as the cheapest cost-avoider of the evidential damage either before the occurrence of her physical injury or after. By contrast, under the American and Israeli versions of the lost-chance doctrine, it is the defendant who must deactivate the doctrine; and in order to succeed in that endeavour, the defendant must establish that the plaintiff intentionally suppressed some potentially probative evidence, so that the court can draw the appropriate adverse inference against the plaintiff.[38] This crucial difference between the two doctrines speaks loudly in favour of the evidential damage doctrine. Moreover, this difference clearly shows that the evidential damage doctrine might distort the truth-seeking incentive of the victims of torts only to a limited extent. Indeed, it is doubtful that this doctrine could ever intensify the already existing incentives to distort the truth.[39]

We now turn to the relationship between the principles of corrective justice and the application of the evidential damage doctrine in the present category of cases. We focus on past injury cases because the evidential damage doctrine is especially important in this type of cases. In any such case, the evidential damage doctrine would constitute the only solid basis for imposing liability in torts. Thus, as has just been indicated, forcing the wrongdoer in a past injury case to compensate his alleged victim for her lost chances to remain undamaged would be at odds with corrective justice.[40] The evidential damage doctrine does not suffer from this predicament. This doctrine rectifies a

[38] On circumstances in which such inferences will be appropriate, see D. A. Nance, 'Evidential Completeness and the Burden of Proof' (1998) 49 *Hastings LJ* 621.

[39] For a brief analysis of those incentives, see A. Stein, 'Allocating the Burden of Proof in Sales Litigation: The Law, Its Rationale, a New Theory, and Its Failure' (1996) 50 *U Miami L Rev* 335, 337–8; A. Stein, 'An Essay on Uncertainty and Fact-Finding in Civil Litigation, With Special Reference to Contract Cases' (1998) 48 *U Toronto LJ* 299, 327–8.

[40] See above 122–3.

person's infringed entitlement to information, not a statistical dilution of a good prospect. These two different objects of rectification have a common, albeit not necessarily identical, valuation criterion. Arguably, the value of a person's good prospect depends on the prospect's probability of being fulfilled. The value of information capable of substantiating one's legal right depends on the probability of that information substantiating that right. Take a person whose wrongful action reduces another person's probability *not* to sustain damage D from p to q. Further assume that the latter person subsequently sustains damage D and that the actual cause of that damage is unidentifiable. This, of course, is the basic structure of most past injury cases that fall under the present category. In such circumstances, the lost-chance doctrine—as authoritatively interpreted by Prosser and Keeton—would require the wrongdoer to pay the victim $(p–q)$D in monetary damages. The evidential damage doctrine would require the judge to embark on a substantively different valuation. Under this doctrine, the judge would have to determine the value of the information of which the wrongdoer wrongfully deprived the victim. The judge would thus have to evaluate the potential of the missing information to identify the causal forces that produced the victim's damage. This potential would be valuable to the extent that it could transform into a valuable asset, that is, to the extent that it could yield the victim the right to recover compensation from the wrongdoer responsible for her damage. This extent equals the probability of its underlying factual scenario, as opposed to that of *damnum sine injuria*—the competing scenario that attributes the victim's damage to a non-actionable causal factor. Hence, prior to the wrongdoing, the victim's probability of sustaining the damage equalled $1–p$, which is parallel to the probability of her remaining undamaged (p). After the wrongdoing, the victim's probability of sustaining the damage became $1–q$, which is parallel to her probability of escaping the damage (q). Because the victim actually sustained the damage, her case falls into the $1–q$ category. This statistical category comprises two scenarios that describe the victim's initial position in a jointly exhaustive and mutually exclusive way. Under the first scenario, the victim sustains the damage irrespective of the wrongdoing. As already indicated, the probability of that scenario equals $1–p$. Under the second scenario, the victim sustains the damage through wrongdoing. The probability of this scenario equals $(1–q)–(1–p)$, i.e., $p–q$. This probability overlaps the reduction in the victim's chances of remaining undamaged, as effected by the wrongdoing.

We now inquire into the probability of the scenario that the wrongdoing was the actual cause of the victim's damage. This probability is represented by the fraction of scenarios featuring a victim who could not sustain her or his damage without being subjected to a wrongdoing in the more general cluster of cases that feature a damaged victim, a wrongdoing, and the exhaustive variety of causal factors that could inflict the same damage on the victim. The above fraction of scenarios equals p–q. The spectrum of cases covering all possible scenarios equals 1–q. The probability that the victim's damage was caused by the wrongdoing and is, therefore, actionable in torts thus equals (p–q)/(1–q). The probability of this damage having been inflicted by a non-actionable causal factor amounts to 1–p. The value of the information of which the wrongdoer wrongfully deprived the victim therefore equals [(p–q)/(1–q)]D+(1–p)D*. Since we know that D*=0 (because in all cases represented by (1–p) the damage is non-actionable), the informational loss sustained by the victim equals [(p–q)/(1–q)]D. As already explained, this compensatory mechanism satisfies the demands of corrective justice. Take for example, the *Medical Malpractice (Past Injury) Case*, discussed in Chapter IV. In that case, the patient did not recover after suffering malpractice that reduced her chances of recovery from 25 to 10 per cent. Under our compensatory mechanism, this patient would recover from the wrongdoer (approximately) 17 per cent of her direct loss, while the Prosser-Keeton formula would yield her only 15 per cent. In other past-injury cases, this difference might be even more substantial.

The amounts of monetary damages payable under the evidential damage doctrine, on the one hand, and under the lost-chance doctrine, as interpreted by Prosser and Keeton, on the other hand, would be equal only in cases in which the defendant's wrongful action eliminated the victim's chances of remaining undamaged. Formally, these compensation amounts would be equal only when q=0; consequently, the defendant would have to pay the plaintiff pD under both doctrines. The two doctrines would thus overlap one another only occasionally, which, once again, emphasizes the important differences between the doctrines. As indicated by the doctrines' compensation formulae, these differences are not merely conceptual, but also operational. Admittedly, the operational difference between the two doctrines could be eliminated if the lost-chance doctrine were to align its compensation formula with that of the evidential damage doctrine.

The lost-chance doctrine, as understood by Prosser and Keeton, is based on the following idea. Since the plaintiff is unable evidentially to attribute her damage to the defendant's wrongful action and since the defendant is also unable evidentially to disassociate his action from the plaintiff's damage, the plaintiff should be allowed to realize her legal rights as they existed at any point in time after her exposure to the wrongful action and before the occurrence of the damage. During that period—regardless of how short it may have been—the plaintiff was evidently worse off in comparison with her previous position: the increase in her chances of sustaining damage impaired her well-being. Although 'chance' is still a purely epistemic notion, this kind of damage is real: it is both meaningful and empirically verifiable.[41] Therefore,

[41] This point is fully explained in Chapter IV above.

forcing the defendant to pay the plaintiff for this damage is the least that the law should do, however artificial it may appear. The appropriate compensation amount should, accordingly, equal $(p-q)$D. Therefore, by clinging to its interpretation by Prosser and Keeton, the lost-chance doctrine would retain its independent identity.

By adopting $[(p-q)/(1-q)]$D as an improved compensation formula, this doctrine would shift to an entirely new idea, namely, to the idea of compensating plaintiffs for their lost chances of recovering from defendants for damage that those defendants might have wrongfully inflicted. This idea, however, can be attacked with the following objection: Why should those defendants have to pay the plaintiffs for their lost chances? What singles out those defendants, as opposed to the plaintiffs, as peculiarly responsible for those lost chances? What marks the causal uncertainty problem—from which those chances originate—as a factor that should work against the defendant and not the plaintiff? Indeed, why not treat similarly all other types of uncertainty that pertain to issues other than causation?

One persuasive response to this objection is that the defendant should be held liable because he is responsible for the uncertainty of the case.[42] Had the defendant not committed his wrongful act, the indeterminate causation problem would not have arisen. This response is, indeed, compelling. As such, it unveils the true nature of the lost-chance doctrine. In effect, this doctrine provides an implicit and consequently underdeveloped variant of the evidential damage doctrine.

D. CASES OF DAMAGE WRONGFULLY INFLICTED BY SEPARATE WRONGDOERS

1. Application of the Evidential Damage Doctrine

In cases falling under this category, paradigmatically represented by our *Dogs Case* example, two or more wrongdoers separately damage the plaintiff in a way that merges the different incidents of inflicted damage into one. Any such wrongdoer thus becomes responsible for the plaintiff's inability to isolate the damage caused by each wrongdoer from the rest of the damage that he suffered. This inability constitutes the evidential damage for which each of the wrongdoers should be held responsible.

Application of the evidential damage doctrine to the *Dogs Case* is a straightforward matter: had the wrongdoers inflicted no evidential damage, then the plaintiff could have recovered from each wrongdoer the right amount of compensation for his injury. The total amount of monetary damages that the

[42] For other responses, see above 120–5.

plaintiff could have then recovered would have compensated him for his entire injury. Therefore, each of the wrongdoers should bear liability for the plaintiff's entire injury. The wrongdoers should then divide amongst themselves the compensation burden in accordance with the risk to which each of them exposed the plaintiff. Our implicit assumption here is that in the presence of evidential damage, the plaintiff would not succeed in court absent the evidential damage doctrine, because he would not be able to satisfy the burden of proving his damage.

An interesting complication would arise if we were to add an additional owned dog to our *Dogs Case* example. In such a case, the evidential damage individually inflicted by Dog-owner 1 would not causally prevent the plaintiff from recovering the right amount of compensation for his injury from Dog-owners 2 and 3. Thus, even if the plaintiff were not to suffer any evidential damage from Dog-owner 1, he would still be unable to prove the extent of the injury inflicted by Dog-owners 2 and 3. For obvious reasons, the same claim can be made by Dog-owners 2 and 3, respectively. However, similarly to the solution offered to the *DES Case*, each dog-owner should still be held liable for the information that relates to *his* part in the plaintiff's injury. This information is missing due to fault on the dog-owner's part, so he is *certainly* responsible for its absence.[43]

In the absence of any special information about the dogs, the risks of injury to which the wrongdoers exposed the plaintiff (r_1, r_2, and r_3) should be deemed equal.[44] When such information—say, information about the dogs' relative strength and ferocity—is available, it should affect the values to be ascribed to r_1, r_2, and r_3. The evidential damage inflicted, respectively, by Dog-owners 1, 2, and 3 would consequently equal $r_1D/(r_1+r_2+r_3)$, $r_2D/(r_1+r_2+r_3)$, and $r_3D/(r_1+r_2+r_3)$ (when D represents the entire physical damage that the plaintiff sustained). Indeed, none of these wrongdoers should pay monetary damages for the plaintiff's inability to prove his case against the others.[45]

2. Does the Evidential Damage Doctrine Attain Desirable Results?

From the deterrence perspective, the above application of the evidential damage doctrine is desirable. Under this doctrine, each wrongdoer would assume liability for the average direct damage associated with his wrongdoing.[46]

[43] See above 186–7.

[44] As explained in Chapter VI above, this assumption derives from the principle of indifference or the principle of insufficient reason, both of which underlie statistical reasoning.

[45] Arguably, each of the three dog-owners should still be held liable for the plaintiff's entire evidential damage as a sufficient cause of that damage. See above 187 n.5. However, as the number of wrongdoers increases, this solution becomes more and more complicated.

[46] When the number of wrongdoers is only two, each will bear liability for the entire direct damage, as explained in the previous section. The indemnification claims between the two

Consequently, prospective wrongdoers would contemplate their actions by taking their future liability amounts as their actions' expected damage. Holding defendants not liable is not a viable alternative for the present category of cases. This would create insufficient deterrence, a repercussion that would be especially harmful in cases involving recurrent wrongs. Cases falling under the present category encompass a large variety of frequent activities that often inflict traceless damage. For example, car accident victims frequently sustain their injuries from more than one vehicle. Society, therefore, can hardly afford itself insufficient deterrence in relation to such activities.[47]

As for corrective justice, its principles do not introduce into the present category of cases any issue that has not been discussed previously. The relationship between these principles and the proposed applications of the evidential damage doctrine is, therefore, encapsulated here in one general proposition. In cases falling into the present category, corrective justice would justify the outcomes reached under the evidential damage doctrine to the extent that it justifies the doctrine itself (both instrumentally and internally).

3. The Evidential Damage Doctrine versus the Alternatives

As in many other settings discussed in this book, some of the problems that arise in the present category of cases have doctrinal solutions in the settled law. Some of these solutions produce results similar to those of the evidential damage doctrine. Other solutions produce different results but they are still close to our basic proposals. Thus, when adjudicating cases that belong to the present category, some courts have adopted a risk-based liability approach. Under this approach, the amount of monetary damages that the wrongdoer must pay his or her victim is determined in proportion to the risk to which the wrongdoer exposed the victim.[48]

Shifting the persuasion burden to the wrongdoers is yet another approach that courts have adopted. Under this approach, when the products of separate wrongful actions irreducibly merge into a single damage, each of the wrongdoers assumes liability for the entire damage; and it is incumbent on each wrongdoer—if he or she desires to do so—to provide evidence that preponderantly disassociates him or her from any fraction of the damage that the plaintiff sustained. Failure to provide such evidence will result in the imposition of full liability on the wrongdoer. Consequently, the wrongdoers would be held liable for the plaintiff's entire damage, similar to joint-tortfeasor situations.[49]

wrongdoers will set their final compensation burden equal to the average direct damage attributable to their respective wrongdoings. This discussion assumes that the wrongdoer is the cheapest cost-avoider of both his share in the plaintiff's direct injury and the evidential damage.

[47] As in other cases, however, the victim himself may turn out to be the cheapest cost-avoider of the evidential damage. This factor should obviously affect the allocation of liability for that damage and, consequently, for the victim's direct injury. Ultimately, such victims should receive less compensation.

[48] See above 78–9.

[49] See above 79–81.

As developed in Chapter VI, the evidential damage doctrine would shift the persuasion burden to the defendant only in balanced cases, that is, only in those cases in which the probabilities of the allegations respectively levelled by the plaintiff and the defendant are equal. Both deterrence and corrective justice justify such a shifting of the burden. If the probability of the plaintiff's case falls below 50 per cent, the remedy that would become available to the plaintiff under the doctrine is that of proportionate recovery. Any such plaintiff would recover from the defendant only a fraction of her or his direct damage. Because the persuasion burden—under its own internal conditions—provides a rule of decision for balanced cases alone, placing this burden on the defendant would not help such a plaintiff, unless it were supplemented by a legal presumption that ascribes the entire damage sustained by the plaintiff to the defendant's wrongful action. This presumption was, indeed, at work, implicitly or explicitly, in the court decisions that resolved the problem at hand by shifting the persuasion burden to defendants. This artificial presumption is no more than a fiction: in cases falling into the present category, it is positively known that none of the defendants actually inflicted the entire damage that the plaintiff sustained.[50] This presumption is, therefore, at odds with both deterrence and corrective justice. The evidential damage doctrine does not present any of these failings: as long as the number of wrongdoers is higher than two, each wrongdoer will assume liability equal to the average direct damage associated with his wrongdoing.[51]

The evidential damage doctrine has an additional feature that its competitors lack. This doctrine would require judges to identify the person responsible for the evidential damage, and this responsibility—in part or in its entirety—may well fall on the plaintiff. For example, judges deciding a case under the deterrence-based approach may find the plaintiff to be the cheapest cost-avoider of the evidential damage. In such a case, one possible solution that the evidential damage doctrine offers is to absolve the defendant from any liability for the evidential damage. Consequently, if the plaintiff fails to establish the defendant's liability for her direct damage, the defendant will bear no liability at all. However, in cases falling under the present category, defendants would typically bear at least *some* liability because the indivisibility of their plaintiffs' injuries—which constitutes evidential damage—is a product of their wrongful actions. Therefore, if the plaintiff wrongfully contributed to this indivisibility, his share in the evidential damage would have to be deducted from the full compensation for that damage. None of the existing legal solutions takes this important factor into account.

[50] However, when the damage is bodily injury, it can (somehow) be argued that each wrongdoer is the cause of the entire damage. See above 79–80.

[51] For the case of two wrongdoers, see above 202, note 46.

E. CASES OF DAMAGE ORIGINATING BOTH FROM A WRONGDOER AND A NON-WRONGFUL CAUSE

1. Application of the Evidential Damage Doctrine

In this category of cases, part of the plaintiff's direct damage was inflicted by the defendant's wrongful action and the remaining part by a non-wrongful causal factor; the two parts irreducibly merge into a single damage, so it is impossible to determine which part was inflicted by the wrongdoer. As in cases belonging to the previous category, the indivisibility of the plaintiff's direct damage constitutes evidential damage; and because the defendant's wrongful action generated this indivisibility, the defendant should be held responsible for the plaintiff's evidential incapacitation. In other words, because the indivisibility of the plaintiff's damage originates from the defendant's wrongful action, the defendant should not be allowed to benefit from the causal indeterminacy. This indeterminacy thus cannot be treated as a reason for holding the plaintiff's lawsuit against the defendant unsubstantiated.[52]

The compensation principles set forth in our preceding discussion would consequently require the defendant to pay the plaintiff monetary damages. The amount of these damages would equal the direct damage that the plaintiff sustained (D) multiplied by the relevant probability. This probability equals $r_w/(r_w+r_{nw})$, with r_w and r_{nw} denoting, respectively, the relevant risks of damage to which the plaintiff was exposed. One of those risks (r_w) is wrongful, and the defendant is responsible for it. The other risk (r_{nw}) is non-wrongful. The defendant must thus pay the plaintiff $r_wD/(r_{w}+r_{nw})$. This amount reflects the value of the information of which the defendant wrongfully deprived the plaintiff. Under the same principles, if there is no information that could determine the relevant risks, the risks should be deemed equal. If this is indeed the case, the defendant should pay the plaintiff half of the plaintiff's direct damage.

2. Does the Evidential Damage Doctrine Attain Desirable Results?

Imposition of this compensation duty on the defendant allocates direct damages in a way that optimizes deterrence. Therefore, the evidential damage doctrine is instrumentally justified in this category of cases. The reasons supporting this conclusion are similar to those we provided with respect to the previous category of cases. There is, however, one important difference

[52] Here again we assume that the lawsuit can only succeed under the evidential damage doctrine because the plaintiff is unable to link the defendant to any part of her damage by a preponderance of the evidence.

between the two categories. In the two-wrongdoers cases that fall into the previous category (such as the *Dogs Case*[53]), the evidential damage doctrine may impose full liability on each of the two wrongdoers. The two wrongdoers would consequently be responsible, both jointly and severally, for the entire injury that the plaintiff sustained. This possibility is predicated on the indemnification right that each wrongdoer could exercise against the other, thus securing the other's participation in the payment of damages to the plaintiff. Because in the present category of cases, indemnification is not an option, $r_wD/(r_w+r_{nw})$ (the compensation formula offered by the evidential damage doctrine) is the only formula that allocates direct damage in a way that satisfies the optimal deterrence criterion. Imposition of full liability would fail to satisfy this criterion. This liability would produce excessive deterrence with regard to direct damage because it exceeds the amount of damage that the wrongdoers actually inflicted.

The doctrinal solutions that different courts have applied in the present category of cases are essentially similar to those applied in the previous category. However, shifting the persuasion burden to the defendant seems to be the preferred approach.[54] As has just been indicated, this approach generates excessive deterrence, a social disutility that the evidential damage doctrine avoids.

[53] See above 77.

[54] See above 82–3. This approach, indeed, can trace its ancestry to common law: *Armory v Delamirie* (1772) 93 Eng Rep 664 (KB). In this famous case, the defendant, a goldsmith, converted a jewel from the plaintiff's ring. Hence, the jury was instructed to 'presume the strongest' against the goldsmith and appraise the missing jewel at the highest conceivable value.

Index